T0235413

CORE SOFTWARE SECURITY

SECURITY AT THE SOURCE

CORE SOFTWARE SECURITY

SECURITY AT THE SOURCE

JAMES RANSOME
ANMOL MISRA

CONTRIBUTING AUTHOR (CHAPTER 9): BROOK SCHOENFIELD

FOREWORD BY
HOWARD SCHMIDT

CRC Press
Taylor & Francis Group
Boca Raton London New York

CRC Press is an imprint of the
Taylor & Francis Group, an **Informa** business
AN AUERBACH BOOK

CRC Press
Taylor & Francis Group
6000 Broken Sound Parkway NW, Suite 300
Boca Raton, FL 33487-2742

© 2014 by Taylor & Francis Group, LLC
CRC Press is an imprint of Taylor & Francis Group, an Informa business

First issued in paperback 2021

No claim to original U.S. Government works

Version Date: 20131031

ISBN 13: 978-1-03-202741-8 (pbk)
ISBN 13: 978-1-4665-6095-6 (hbk)

Library of Congress Cataloging-in-Publication Data

Ransome, James F.
    Core software security : security at the source / James Ransome and Anmol Misra.
      pages cm
    Includes bibliographical references and index.
    ISBN 978-1-4665-6095-6 (hardback)
    1. Computer security. I. Title.

QA76.9.A25R356 2013
005.8--dc23   2013042460

Visit the Taylor & Francis Web site at
http://www.taylorandfrancis.com

and the CRC Press Web site at
http://www.crcpress.com

Publisher's Note
The publisher has gone to great lengths to ensure the quality of this reprint but points out that some imperfections in the original copies may be apparent.

Dedication

To Dr. Tony (Vern) Dubendorf, who passed away earlier this year. He was a true friend, co-worker, collaborator, confidant, co-researcher, co-author, and co-architect of the Getronics Wireless Integrated Security, Design, Operations & Management (WISDOM) solution.

—James Ransome

To Dad, Mom, Esu, Anu, Mausi, and Prince.

—Anmol Misra

Contents

Foreword

The global cyber security threat is increasing on a regular basis, if not daily. The recurring question is how we address the current threat of global cyber security. The authors have aptly named their book in response to this question, in that the answer is to create software that has as minimal vulnerabilities as possible. In other words, focus on securing at the source first, instead of taking shortcuts by only trying to secure network infrastructure. Perimeter security and defense-in-depth have their place in security, but software security is the first line of defense and should come first. If you have fewer vulnerabilities at the source, it also takes out the financial benefit of nation states or organized crime stockpiling cyber weapons based on current vulnerabilities. Not only must we get better at it, we must make the solutions cost-effective, operationally relevant, and feasible, based on real-world experience, and worth the investment. Securing at the source requires securing the software, which is at the heart of cyber infrastructure. One of the things we have been constantly facing over the last 20 years is that software has become a critical component of every part of our critical infrastructure and everyday lives. We are already seeing software embedded within a vast variety of things we use in our daily lives—from smart meters in our home to cars we drive. Unfortunately, software security has not evolved at the same pace, and many software products are still developed in an environment with the intent that they fix the problem after release rather than doing it right the first time around. There are two major issues with this:

1. There are no shortages of threats out there today; therefore, people who are looking to exploit software vulnerabilities have a pretty

fertile field in which to work. As a consequence, we have to make sure we are doing better vulnerability management. We also have to look toward the future and ask ourselves, "How can we avoid having these types of vulnerabilities in future generations of software that we are increasingly dependent on?" The answer to this question is particularly important because it is very beneficial to companies to reduce these vulnerabilities and to stop them during the software development process. It is significantly less expensive to build security in through the use of a SDL than to come back and fix it post-release.

2. The second issue is that we need to start looking at a whole generation of what is referred to as "zero-day vulnerabilities." If we can eliminate the likelihood of finding a zero day by not allowing the vulnerabilities to take place from the very beginning by adhering to the best practices of a solid SDL, it will save companies money, make the software and its users more secure, the critical infrastructure more resilient, and overall, more beneficial to us all.

As the Executive Director of the Software Assurance Forum for Excellence in Code (SAFECode), a nonprofit organization dedicated exclusively to increasing trust in information and communications technology products and services through the advancement of effective software assurance methods, I currently have a major focus on security training for developers. The lack of security awareness and education among the software engineering workforce can be a significant obstacle to organizations working to implement software security programs. However, better training for software developers so they have the skills needed to write secure code is just one of the variables in the software security equation. Software projects are under the constraints of costs and tight timelines. In those situations, it is inevitable that security is sacrificed somewhere because of shortcuts taken. Cost, time, and resources are typically the triad of software development supporting security, and if you sacrifice one of the three, security and quality suffer. A software development environment is built around a programmer who is pressured on every side to work faster, to cut corners, and to produce more code at the expense of security and quality.

It is impossible to have 100 percent security, but the developers and their management should always strive to maximize the mitigation of risk. It is about making it so difficult to access in an unauthorized manner that adversaries:

- Have to utilize traceable and obvious means to gain access, so they are noticed right away
- Spend so much time trying to gain access that they eventually are noticed
- Give up and move on to easier targets

Ensuring that everyone touching the product development lifecycle has the knowledge they need to support an organization's software security process is a fundamental challenge for any organization committed to software security success. The goal is to remove the pain that organizations face in developing a custom program of their own resource constraints and knowledge vacuums.

Developers are often under intense pressure to deliver more features on time and under budget. Few developers get the time to review their code for potential security vulnerabilities. When they do get the time, they often don't have secure-code training and lack the automated tools, embedded processes and procedures, and resources to prevent hackers from using hundreds of common exploit techniques to trigger malicious attacks. Like it or not, the hard work of developers often takes the brunt of malicious hacker attacks. So what can software vendors do? A big part of the answer is relatively old-fashioned: The developers need to be provided with incentives, better tools, and proper training.

Unfortunately, it currently makes more business sense not to produce secure software products than it does to produce secure software products. Any solution needs to address this as a fundamental market failure instead of simply wishing it were not true. If security is to be a business goal, then it needs to make business sense. In the end, security requirements are in fact the same as any business goals and should be addressed as equally important. Employers should expect their employees to take pride in and own a certain level of responsibility for their work. And employees should expect their employers to provide the tools and training they need to get the job done. With these expectations established and goals agreed on, perhaps the software industry can do a better job of strengthening the security of its products by reducing software vulnerabilities.

This book discusses a process and methodology to develop software in such a way that security considerations play a key role in its development. It speaks to executives, to managers at all levels, and to technical leaders, and in that way it is unique. It also speaks to students and developers so they can understand the process of developing software with security in mind and find resources to help them do so. The information in this book provides a foundation for executives, project managers, and technical leaders to improve the software they create and to improve the security, quality, and privacy of the software we all use.

Software developers know how to write software in a way that provides a high level of security and robustness. So why don't software developers practice these techniques? This book looks to answer this question in two parts:

1. Software is determined to be secure as a result of an analysis of how the program is to be used, under what conditions, and the security requirements it must meet in the environment in which it is to be deployed. The SDL must also extend beyond the release of the product in that if the assumptions underlying the software in an unplanned operational environment and their previously implied requirements do not hold, the software may no longer be secure and the SDL process may start over in part or as a whole if a complete product redesign is required. In this sense, the authors establish the need for accurate and meaningful security requirements and the metrics to govern them as well as examples of how to develop them. It also assumes that the security requirements are not all known prior to the development process and describes the process by which they are derived, analyzed, and validated.

2. Software executives, leaders, and managers must support the robust coding practices and required security enhancements as required by a business-relevant SDL as well supporting the staffing requirements, scheduling, budgeting, and resource allocations required for this type of work. The authors do an excellent job of describing the process, requirements, and management of metrics for people in these roles so they can accurately assess the impact and resources required for a SDL that is relevant to and work best in their organization and environment. Given that this is an approached designed from real-life, on-the-ground challenges and experiences, the authors describe how to think about issues in order to develop effective approaches and manage them as a business process.

I particularly like the addition of Brook Schoenfield to the book as the author of Chapter 9, bringing a seasoned principal enterprise and software security architect with "in the trenches" experience to explain how security architecture fits into the SDL process in the "real world." In particular, he provides a unique and valuable approach to addressing the aspects of SDL and security architecture that has been field-tested and really works in the agile software development process.

I have known Dr. James Ransome for many years, and I am very pleased that he has chosen this topic for his 10th book on information security. Having recently served as the Special Assistant to the President and the Cyber Security Coordinator for the federal government, in addition to many senior leadership roles in the cyber security government and enterprise space, I can confidently say that this is currently the most critical area of information and global cyber security to fix. This has been and continues to be more of a business and process issue than it is technical. *Core Software Security: Security at the Source* adds great value to the typical training resources currently available in that it takes the elements of the best publically known SDLs and provides operational, business-relevant, cost-effective metrics. I believe that what James Ransome and Anmol Misra have written has hit the mark on this topic and will serve the community for many years to come as both a practical guide for professionals and as an academic textbook.

Hon. Howard A. Schmidt
Partner, Ridge Schmidt Cyber
Executive Director, The Software Assurance Forum for Excellence in
Code (SAFECode)

About Hon. Howard A. Schmidt

Hon. Howard Schmidt serves as a partner in the strategic advisory firm Ridge Schmidt Cyber, an executive services firm that helps leaders in business and government navigate the increasing demands of cyber security. He serves in this position with Tom Ridge, the first Secretary of the U.S. Department of Homeland Security. Prof. Schmidt also serves as executive director of The Software Assurance Forum for Excellence in Code (SAFECode).

Prof. Schmidt brings together talents in business, defense, intelligence, law enforcement, privacy, academia, and international relations, gained from a distinguished career spanning 40 years. He recently served as Special Assistant to the President and the Cyber Security Coordinator for the federal government. In this role, Mr. Schmidt was responsible for coordinating interagency cyber security policy development and implementation, and for coordinating engagement with federal, state, local, international, and private-sector cyber security partners.

Previously, Prof. Schmidt was the President and CEO of the Information Security Forum (ISF). Before serving on the ISF, he was Vice President and Chief Information Security Officer and Chief Security Strategist for eBay Inc., and formerly served as the Chief Security Officer for Microsoft Corp. He also served as Chief Security Strategist for the US-CERT Partners Program for the Department of Homeland Security. Mr. Schmidt also brings to bear over 26 years of military service. Beginning active duty with the Air Force, he later joined the Arizona Air National Guard. With the Air Force he served in a number of military and civilian roles, culminating as Supervisory Special Agent with the Office of Special Investigations (AFOSI). He finished his last 12 years as an Army Reserve Special Agent with the Criminal Investigation Division's Computer Crime Unit, all while serving for over a decade as a police officer with the Chandler, Arizona, Police Department.

Prof. Schmidt holds a bachelor's degree in business administration (BSBA) and a master's degree in organizational management (MAOM) from the University of Phoenix. He also holds an Honorary Doctorate degree in Humane Letters. Howard is a Professor of Research at Idaho State University, Adjunct Distinguished Fellow with Carnegie Mellon's CyLab, and a Distinguished Fellow of the Ponemon Privacy Institute.

Howard is also a ham radio operator (W7HAS), private pilot, outdoorsman, and avid Harley-Davidson rider. He is married to Raemarie J. Schmidt, a retired forensic scientist and researcher, and instructor in the field of computer forensics. Together, they are proud parents, and happy grandparents.

Preface

The age of the software-driven machine has taken significant leaps over the last few years. Human tasks such as those of fighter pilots, stock-exchange floor traders, surgeons, industrial production and power-plant operators that are critical to the operation of weapons systems, medical systems, and key elements of our national infrastructure, have been, or are rapidly being taken over by software. This is a revolutionary step in the machine whose brain and nervous system is now controlled by software-driven programs taking the place of complex nonrepetitive tasks that formerly required the use of the human mind. This has resulted in a paradigm shift in the way the state, military, criminals, activists, and other adversaries can attempt to destroy, modify, or influence countries, infrastructures, societies, and cultures. This is true even for corporations, as we have seen increasing cases of cyber corporate espionage over the years. The previous use of large armies, expensive and devastating weapons systems and platforms, armed robberies, the physical stealing of information, violent protests, and armed insurrection are quickly being replaced by what is called cyber warfare, crime, and activism.

In the end, the cyber approach may have just as profound affects as the techniques used before in that the potential exploit of software vulnerabilities could result in:

- Entire or partial infrastructures taken down, including power grids, nuclear power plants, communication media, and emergency response systems
- Chemical plants modified to create large-yield explosions and/or highly toxic clouds

- Remote control, modification, or disablement of critical weapon systems or platforms
- Disablement or modification of surveillance systems
- Criminal financial exploitation and blackmail
- Manipulation of financial markets and investments
- Murder or harm to humans through the modification of medical support systems or devices, surgery schedules, or pharmaceutical prescriptions
- Political insurrection and special-interest influence through the modification of voting software, blackmail, or brand degradation though website defacement or underlying Web application takedown or destruction

A side effect of the cyber approach is that it has given us the ability to do the above at a scale, distance, and degree of anonymity previously unthought of from jurisdictionally protected locations through remote exploitation and attacks. This gives government, criminal groups, and activists abilities to proxy prime perpetuators to avoid responsibility, detection, and political fallout.

Although there is much publicity regarding network security, the real Achilles heel is the (insecure) software which provides the potential ability for total control and/or modification of a target as described above. The criticality of software security as we move quickly toward this new age of tasks previously relegated to the human mind being replaced by software-driven machines cannot be underestimated. It is for this reason that we have written this book. In contrast, and for the foreseeable future, software programs are and will be written by humans. This also means that new software will keep building on legacy code or software that was written prior to security being taken seriously, or before sophisticated attacks became prevalent. As long as humans write the programs, the key to successful security for these programs is in making the software development program process more efficient and effective. Although the approach of this book includes people, process, and technology approaches to software security, we believe the people element of software security is still the most important part to manage as long as software is developed, managed, and exploited by humans. What follows is a step-by-step process for software security that is relevant to today's technical, operational, business, and development environments, with a focus on what humans can do to control and manage the process in the form of best practices and metrics. We will always have security issues, but this book should help in minimizing them when software is finally released or deployed. We hope you enjoy our book as much as we have enjoyed writing it.

About the Book

This book outlines a step-by-step process for software security that is relevant to today's technical, operational, business, and development environments. The authors focus on what humans can do to control and manage a secure software development process in the form of best practices and metrics. Although security issues will always exist, this book will teach you how to maximize your organization's ability to minimize vulnerabilities in your software products before they are released or deployed, by building security into the development process. The authors have worked with Fortune 500 companies and have often seen examples of the breakdown of security development lifecycle (SDL) practices. In this book, we take an experience-based approach to applying components of the best available SDL models in dealing with the problems described above, in the form of a SDL software security best practices model and framework. *Core Software Security: Security at the Source* starts with an overview of the SDL and then outlines a model for mapping SDL best practices to the software development lifecycle, explaining how you can use this model to build and manage a mature SDL program.   Although security is not a natural component of the way industry has been building software in recent years, the authors believe that security improvements to development processes are possible, practical, and essential. They trust that the software security best practices and model presented in this book will make this clear to all who read the book, including executives, managers, and practitioners.

Audience

This book is targeted toward anyone who is interested in learning about software security in an enterprise environment, including product security and quality executives, software security architects, security consultants, software development engineers, enterprise SDLC program managers, chief information security officers, chief technology officers, and chief privacy officers whose companies develop software. If you want to learn about how software security should be implemented in developing enterprise software, this is a book you don't want to skip.

Support

Errata and support for this book are available on the CRC Press book website.

Structure

This book is divided into three different sections and 10 chapters. Chapter 1 provides an introduction to the topic of software security and why it is important that we get it right the first time. Chapter 2 introduces challenges of making software secure and the SDL framework. Chapters 3 through 8 provide mapping of our SDL with its associated best practices to a generic SDLC framework. Chapter 9 provides a seasoned software security architect's view on the successful application of the solutions proposed in Chapters 3 through 8. Chapter 9 also explains real-world approaches to the typical challenges that are presented when making secure software. We conclude, in Chapter 10, by describing real-world security threats that a properly architected, implemented, and managed SDL program will mitigate against.

Assumptions

This book assumes that a reader is familiar with basics of software development (and methodologies) and basic security concepts. Knowledge of the SDL, different types of security testing, and security architecture is recommended but not required. For most topics, we gently introduce readers to the topic before diving deep into that particular topic.

Acknowledgments

Writing a book is a journey, and without support from mentors, friends, colleagues, and family, it can be a difficult one. Many people have been instrumental in helping us write this book. First, we would like to thank our editor, John Wyzalek, at CRC Press, for his patience, support, and commitment to the project. We would also like to thank the production team at DerryField Publishing: Theron Shreve, Lynne Lackenbach, and Marje Pollack.

Both authors would like to thank the Hon. Howard A. Schmidt [Partner, Ridge Schmidt Cyber; Executive Director, The Software Assurance Forum for Excellence in Code (SAFECode); and former Special Assistant to the President and the Cyber Security Coordinator for the federal government], and Dena Haritos Tsamitis (Director, Information Networking Institute; Director of Education, Training, and Outreach, CyLab Carnegie Mellon University) for their support with this project. We would also like to thank Brook Schoenfield, who has joined us in this journey to prove there is another way to architect, implement, and manage software security than what is the current status quo, and for his contribution in writing a chapter of this book as a contributing author. We would like to thank the security community to which we both belong and are proud of. Finally, we would like to thank the people with whom we have worked and interacted over the years.

—James Ransome and Anmol Misra

I would like to take this opportunity to give thanks to my wife, Gail, for her patience and understanding and for serving as my preliminary proof-reader. A special thanks to my co-author, Anmol Misra, who has joined me as a partner in developing this critical message over the last three years that has resulted in the book you are about to read. A special thanks to Howard Schmidt for writing the foreword for this book on a subject and message for which we both share a passion, and that we both want to get out to practitioners and decision makers alike. And finally, I leave you with the following quote by Walter Bagehot: "The greatest pleasure in life is doing that which people say we cannot do."

—James Ransome

Over the years, many people have mentored and helped me. I would like to thank them all, but space is limited. You know who you are, and I would like to thank you for your patience, encouragement, and support. I would like to thank my co-author, James Ransome. He has been a mentor and a partner over the years and has helped me in more ways than I can mention. Finally, I would like to take this opportunity to thank my family—Mom, Dad, Sekhar, Anupam, and Mausi. Nothing would be possible without their unquestioning support and love. You have been asking me if I am going to take a break from my writing and if I will finally have a "normal" schedule. Yes, I will now—hopefully.

—Anmol Misra

About the Authors

James Ransome, Ph.D., CISSP, CISM

Dr. James Ransome is the Senior Director of Product Security and responsible for all aspects of McAfee's Product Security Program, a corporate-wide initiative that supports McAfee's business units in delivering best-in-class, secure software products to customers. In this role, James sets program strategy, manages security engagements with McAfee business units, maintains key relationships with McAfee product engineers, and works with other leaders to help define and build product security capabilities.

His career has been marked by leadership positions in private and public industries, including three chief information security officer (CISO) and four chief security officer (CSO) roles. Prior to entering the corporate world, James had 23 years of government service in various roles supporting the U.S. intelligence community, federal law enforcement, and the Department of Defense.

James holds a Ph.D. in Information Systems. He developed/tested a security model, architecture, and provided leading practices for converged wired/wireless network security for his doctoral dissertation as part of a NSA/DHS Center of Academic Excellence in Information Assurance Education program. He is the author of several books on information security, and *Core Software Security: Security at the Source* is his 10th. James is a member of Upsilon Pi Epsilon, the International Honor Society for the Computing and Information Disciplines, and he is a Certified Information Security Manager (CISM), a Certified Information Systems Security Professional (CISSP), and a Ponemon Institute Distinguished Fellow.

Anmol Misra

Anmol Misra is an author and a security professional with a wide range of experience in the field of information security. His expertise includes mobile and application security, vulnerability management, application and infrastructure security assessments, and security code reviews. He is a Program Manager in Cisco's Information Security group. In this role, he is responsible for developing and implementing security strategy and programs to drive security best practices into all aspects of Cisco's hosted products. Prior to joining Cisco, Anmol was a Senior Consultant with Ernst & Young LLP. In this role, he advised Fortune 500 clients on defining and improving information security programs and practices. He helped corporations to reduce IT security risk and achieve regulatory compliance by improving their security posture.

Anmol is co-author of *Android Security: Attacks and Defenses,* and is a contributing author of *Defending the Cloud: Waging War in Cyberspace.* He holds a master's degree in Information Networking from Carnegie Mellon University and a Bachelor of Engineering degree in Computer Engineering. He is based out of San Francisco, California.

Chapter 1

Introduction

Welcome to our book about what we believe to be the most important topic in information security for the foreseeable future: software security. In the following sections, we will cover five major topics that highlight the need, value, and challenges of software security. This will set the stage for the remainder of the book, where we describe our model for software security: building security into your software using an operationally relevant and manageable security development lifecycle (SDL) that is applicable to all software development lifecycles (SDLCs). The topics and reasons for including them in this introductory chapter are listed below.

1. **The importance and relevance of software security**. Software is critical to everything we do in the modern world and is behind our most critical systems. As such, it is imperative that it be secure by design. Most information technology (IT)-related security solutions have been developed to mitigate the risk caused by insecure software. To justify a software security program, the importance and relevance of the monetary costs and other risks for not building security into your software must be known, as well as the importance, relevance,

and costs for building security in. At the end of the day, software security is as much a business decision as it is about avoiding security risks.

2. **Software security and the software development lifecycle**. It is important to know the difference between what are generally known in software development as *software security* and *application security*. Although these terms are often used interchangeably, we differentiate between them because we believe there is a distinct difference in managing programs for these two purposes. In our model, *software security* is about building security into the software through a SDL in an SDLC, whereas *application security* is about protecting the software and the systems on which it runs after release.

3. **Quality versus secure code**. Although secure code is not necessarily quality code, and quality code is not necessarily secure code, the development process for producing software is based on the principles of both quality and secure code. You cannot have quality code without security or security without quality, and their attributes complement each other. At a minimum, quality and software security programs should be collaborating closely during the development process; ideally, they should be part of the same organization and both part of the software development engineering department. We will discuss this organizational and operational perspective later in the book.

4. **The three most important SDL security goals**. At the core of all software security analysis and implementation are three core elements of security: *confidentiality, integrity,* and *availability,* also known as the C.I.A. model. To ensure high confidence that the software being developed is secure, these three attributes must be adhered to as key components throughout the SDL.

5. **Threat modeling and attack surface validation**. The most time-consuming and misunderstood part of the SDL is threat modeling and attack surface validation. In today's world of Agile development, you must get this right or you will likely fail to make your software secure. Threat modeling and attack surface validation throughout the SDL will maximize your potential to alleviate post-release discovery of security vulnerabilities in your software product. We believe this function to be so important that we have dedicated a SDL section and a separate chapter to this topic.

1.1 The Importance and Relevance of Software Security

The 2005 U.S. President's Information Technology Advisory Committee (PITAC) report stated: "Commonly used software engineering practices permit dangerous errors, such as improper handling of buffer overflows, which enable hundreds of attack programs to compromise millions of computers every year."[1] This happens mainly because "commercial software engineering today lacks the scientific underpinnings and rigorous controls needed to produce high-quality, secure products at acceptable cost."[2]

The Gartner Group reports that more than 70 percent of current business security vulnerabilities are found within software applications rather than the network boundaries.[3] A focus on application security has thus emerged to reduce the risk of poor software development, integration, and deployment. As a result, software assurance quickly became an information assurance (IA) focus area in the financial, government, and manufacturing sectors to reduce the risk of unsecure code: Security built into the software development lifecycle makes good business sense.

A U.S. Department of Homeland Security 2006 Draft, "Security in the Software Lifecycle," states the following:

> The most critical difference between secure software and insecure software lies in the nature of the processes and practices used to specify, design, and develop the software . . . correcting potential vulnerabilities as early as possible in the software development lifecycle, mainly through the adoption of security-enhanced process and practices, is far more cost-effective than the currently pervasive approach of developing and releasing frequent patches to operational software.[4]

At the RSA 2011 USA conference, cloud security issues were highlighted but very little discussion was devoted to addressing the problem; however, at the 2012 conference, it was all about addressing the security issues in the cloud that had been so aptly identified the year before. The same thing happened in 2012, starting with a few key conferences, and continued with a major focus on discussing solutions for software security in 2013. For example, in early 2012, *Information Week* identified "Code gets externally reviewed" as one of the ten security trends to watch in

2012,[5] and stated that "this business mandate is clear: Developers must take the time to code cleanly, and eradicate every possible security flaw before the code goes into production." There was also a popular security article published on March 1, 2012, titled "To Get Help with Secure Software Development Issues, Find Your Own Flaws," that highlighted panel discussions at RSA 2012 in San Francisco.[6] This panel did a great job of identifying some of the critical issues but did not address solving the software security challenges that it identified. However, things started to change mid-year 2012: The agenda for Microsoft's inaugural Security Development Conference, held in May 2012,[7] was less about Microsoft and more about bringing secure software development thought leadership together and in three separate tracks to include "security engineering," "security development lifecycle (SDL) & business," and "managing the process" to discuss solutions to the most important security issue in industry, secure software development. This trend continued with the Black Hat USA 2012 Conference,[8] the RSA 2013 Conference,[9] and the 2013 Microsoft Security Development Conference.[10]

Think about it: What really causes a majority of the information security problems we have today? What is the primary target of hackers, cyber-criminals, and nation-state cyber warriors? It is insecure code. What has quickly become the highest unnecessary cost to software development? It is flaws arising from insecure code in software products that have already been released to the market. When these flaws are discovered and/or exploited, they cause interruptions in current product development cycles to fix something that should have been fixed during the development of the product that has the flaw; they cause delays in product release dates because individuals or teams working on current products are pulled off cycle to fix issues in a previously released product; and they result in vulnerability scope creep because vulnerabilities discovered in one product may affect the security of others in Web, software-as-a-service (SaaS), and cloud applications. They also create legal issues, reputation degradation, and public relations nightmares such as those experienced by Sony, Symantec, and RSA over the last couple of years. They can also result in significant liability to the company. In an age of extensive regulations governing privacy and exposure of data, this quickly adds up even for big corporations. The point here is that even as the high-tech world, its consumers, customers, regulators, and the media have started to realize that not only is it imperative to fix software security problems, there is, in fact, a way to solve these issues in the form of a structured security software development lifecycle or framework, such that all eyes will be on those who develop software code, particularly code that is used in critical and sensitive applications to see if the developers are adhering to this practice within their own environment whether it be traditional/Waterfall, Scrum/Agile, or a blended development methodology.

Every sector of the global economy, from energy to transportation, finance, and banking, telecommunications, public health, emergency services, water, chemical, defense, industrial, food, agriculture, right down to the postal and shipping sectors, relies on software. Anything that threatens that software, in effect, poses a threat to our life. Because of all the potential harm that could occur from exploitation of coding defects, the product not only has to work right (*quality*), it also has to be secure (*security*). Hence, we believe the title and content of this book addresses perhaps the most critical challenge we face in information and cyber security over the next few years.

Many believe that you can just fix software vulnerabilities after the product has been developed and be done with it. This is not that easy, however, because the cost to fix vulnerabilities increases over the SDLC, as shown in Figure 1.1, and most security activities happen post-release, including code audits, remediation, bug fixes, required patches, and also hacking. In a cloud environment, there may be multiple versions of an application running and it is often a challenge to fix security vulnerabilities across all of them. Exposure in one version of an application in a cloud environment can result in exploitation of all of them unless there are stringent network segmentation controls in place. Even these might prove to be insufficient in the event of sophisticated attacks.

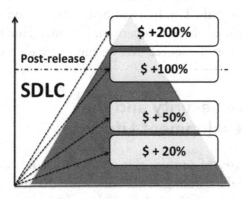

Figure 1.1 Cost to address software problems mapped to SDLC phases.

The cost associated with addressing software problems increases as the lifecycle of a project matures (see Figure 1.1). In 1988 Barry Boehm stated that defects found in the field cost 50–200 times as much to correct as those corrected earlier.[11] Years later, Boehm stated that this ratio was 5:1 for small noncritical systems.[12] Data presented by Fortify in 2008 indicate that the cost of correcting security flaws at the requirements level is up to 100 times less than the cost of correcting security flaws in fielded software.[13] No matter what numbers are used, it is clear from the references above and others used in industry that there are substantial cost savings to fixing security flaws early in the development process rather than fixing them after software is fielded. For vendors, the cost is magnified by the expense of developing and patching vulnerable software after release and can be a costly way of securing applications. Furthermore, patches are not always applied by owners/users of the vulnerable software; and patches can contain yet more vulnerabilities.[14] We have seen patches that fix one security problem but open (or re-open) other security issues. Companies are not always able to give each patch (fix) the attention it deserves, or it may not go through the regular software development cycle, resulting in more security problems than the patch/fix is designed to mitigate.

For a number of years, the information security industry has focused on network and application security, assuming that software is secure and their security controls are all that is needed instead of actually protecting organizations against software security failures. As we review the security development lifecycle and its associated best practices in this book, it should be clear that the network and application should come later in a comprehensive and layered defense-in-depth security program, and that software security should be considered the first step in the information security lifecycle, not the last. In a nutshell, network and application security programs are more about compensating controls, but it is only through addressing security at the source that we can really address problems.

1.2 Software Security and the Software Development Lifecycle

One significant area of confusion in the security industry over the years has been a misunderstanding of the difference between software security and application security. Gary McGraw has provided an excellent description of the difference between the two:

On one hand, **software** security is about building secure software: designing software to be secure; making sure that software is secure; and educating software developers, architects, and users about how to build security in. On the other hand, **application** security is about protecting software and the systems that software runs in a post facto, only after development is complete.[15]

Software security has come a long way since first attacks on a reasonably large scale started to materialize toward the end of the 1980s. Software back then was written without much thought for security (e.g., UNIX code, TCP/IP stack). After the advent of Microsoft Windows and then the Web, attacks started increasing in sophistication and frequency and thus it became necessary to look at software security. Industry started to look for short-term fixes through various "add-ons." These resulted in anti-virus, firewalls, anti-spyware, and so on. However, the real issue—how code was being developed and written—was not addressed. This started to change only in the last decade when SDL practices started to be taken seriously. Many enterprises impacted by software security defects (e.g., Microsoft) started to look seriously at how to build security in software code by improving software development practices. This resulted in recommended SDL practices from academia and software giants such as Microsoft. We now had the theory and guidelines on how to build security into the code from the start and thus lessen the possibility of software loopholes that could be exploited by attackers.

Confidentiality, integrity, and availability are the three primary goals that the industry considers to be of the utmost importance in any secure software development process. What the developers do to protect, enforce, and ensure these primary goals will equate to the "justifiably high confidence" part of the secure code definition. A developer can write very efficient code that is easy to maintain and reusable; however, if that code allows an unauthorized user to access the application's assets, then that code is either exposed or it is not, and there is no second chance for getting it right.

SDLs should not be confused with the standard software development lifecycle. SDL methodology, as the name suggests, is really aimed at developing *secure* software, not necessarily *quality* software. As defined in the IT Law Wiki, the "Security Development Lifecycle is a software development process used to reduce software maintenance costs and increase reliability of software concerning software security related bugs."[16] In January 2002, many Microsoft software development groups prompted "security pushes" to find ways to improve existing security code. Under this directive, the Trustworthy Computing (TwC) team formed the concepts that led to the Microsoft Security Development Lifecycle. Established as a mandatory policy in 2004, the Microsoft SDL was designed as an integral part of the software development process at Microsoft.[17] The term SDL has been used by others since then both for representing the Microsoft process and as a generic term for the process defined in the IT Law Wiki link above. Our use of the term SDL throughout this book will be to represent a secure development process composed of software security best practices based on comparative research on Microsoft's SDL and alternative models developed since 2004, the authors' experience and research into what does and does not work in most current development organizations, and the business realities of today's development austerity requirements coupled with the increasing demands for securing code at the source with relevant, cost-effective, and realistic software security practices.

The goals of SDL are twofold: The first goal is to reduce the number of security vulnerabilities and privacy problems; the second goal is to reduce the severity of the vulnerabilities that remain. There are industry standards that define what needs to be done in software development, such as ISO/IEEE which define the primary phases of a traditional software development approach to software engineering. The elements of an SDL are typically very adaptive and are incorporated into the standard development lifecycle for an organization.

Static analysis and threat modeling are among the tools used to develop secure code. Static analysis tools look for a fixed set of patterns or rules in the code in a manner similar to virus-checking programs. While some of the more advanced tools allow new rules to be added to the rule base, the tool will never find a problem if a rule has not been written for it. The greatest promise of static analysis tools derives from their ability to automatically identify many common coding problems. Unfortunately, implementation bugs created by developer errors are often only part of the problem. Static analysis tools cannot evaluate design and architectural flaws. They cannot identify poorly designed cryptographic libraries or improperly selected algorithms, and they cannot point out design problems that might cause confusion between authentication and authorization. They also cannot identify passwords or magic numbers embedded in code. Static analysis tools can, however, peer into more of a program's dark corners with less fuss than dynamic analysis, which requires actually running the code. Static analysis also has the potential to be applied before a program reaches a level of completion at which testing can be meaningfully performed. The earlier security risks are identified and managed in the software development lifecycle, the better.

While these SDL practices have been good in theory, when applied to enterprises, results have been mixed. There are multiple reasons for this. Legacy code still forms a large codebase of our software industry, so going back in time and applying these practices is very difficult. Software outsourcing or off-shoring is another area where these practices are difficult to implement efficiently. Software developers and companies often work under tight deadlines to put a product out before competition, and thus software security has typically taken a back seat. There is a lack of management commitment to effectively implement SDL practices in such a fast-moving environment where software security is often done as an afterthought.

Even though some security practices are common to both software and application security, such as penetration testing, source code scanning, security-oriented testing, and security education, there is no substitute for integrating security into the software development lifecycle. The human element of the process is key to the success of any security development process and requires very seasoned software security architects and engineers to be successful. Threat modeling, applying principles such as *least privilege* and *defense in depth,* is perhaps the most understood, important, and needed element of the software development lifecycle and requires human expertise and not tools to accomplish. One must also gather the real security requirements for a system and consider compliance, safety issues, contractual requirements, what data the application will process, and business risk.

Training is another critical element of the SDL that requires the human element. Training helps to reduce the cost of security, and an effective training program will motivate your development team to produce more secure software with fewer problems with more efficiency and cost effectiveness. It should be emphasized that no point solutions will provide a single solution for software security; rather, a holistic defense-in-depth approach is required, including a blend of people, process, and technology with a heavy emphasis on people. Although tools can parse through large quantities of code rapidly, faster than a human could, they are no replacement for humans. For the foreseeable future, software security will still be considered an art, but the art can be augmented through process and technology and, contrary to myths perpetrated by some practitioners, the art can be taught through proper mentorship by seasoned software security architects and engineers. These are the team members who have the experience, can think like an adversary, and do it throughout the development process, which is a key element for the success of any SDL. Some authors differentiate between secure-coding best practices and secure-design principles; we will address both in the software security best practices presented in this book and leverage the experience of the seasoned architects and engineers identified above to accomplish this.

Software security requires a focused effort to be successful and is not a natural outcome of conventional software development processes, even from development groups that have good traditional "quality" practices. Software security, however, should be a key of a mature quality program. As we will explain in this book, secure code does not necessarily mean quality code, and quality code does not necessarily mean secure code, but the foundation of software applications and the development processes that produce them should be based on common best practices of both quality code and secure code.

1.3 Quality Versus Secure Code

The foundation of software applications, and the development processes that produce them, is based on the common best principles of quality code and secure code. These principles are the driving force behind the concepts and design of industry best practices. To produce secure code that will stand the test of time, you must learn how to incorporate these principles into the development process. Remember that secure code is not necessarily quality code, and quality code is not necessarily secure code.[18]

Secure code does not mean quality code: You must know how to write quality code before you can write secure code. A developer can write very secure code that authorizes and authenticates every user transaction, logs the transaction, and denies all unauthorized requests; however, if the code does not return expected results, then even this very secure code may never see the light of day. Software quality characteristics are not the same as security. Quality is not measured in terms of confidentiality, integrity, and availability, but rather in terms of ease of use and whether it is reusable and maintainable.[19]

Quality code does not mean secure code: A developer can write efficient code that is easy to maintain and reusable, but if that code allows an unauthorized user to access the application's assets, then the code is of no use. Unlike software quality, software security is not subjective. Sensitive information is either exposed or it is not, and there is no second chance to get it right. Ultimately, quality, security, and maintainability are the three primary goals the industry considers to be of the upmost importance in any secure software development process.[20]

You cannot have quality without security or security without quality. These two attributes complement each other, and both enhance overall software product integrity and market value. Good developers should be able to identify what quality factors are in software and how to code them. Likewise, good developers should know how the software they develop can be attacked and what the weakest areas are in the software; if the code allows an unauthorized user to access the application's assets, then that code is either exposed or it's not, and there is no second chance to get it right.[21]

1.4 The Three Most Important SDL Security Goals

Any competent developer can write very efficient code that is maintainable and easy to reuse; however, if the code allows an unauthorized user to access the application's assets, then that code is not secure. Unfortunately, security is still an area that is often either overlooked or minimally applied during the software development lifecycle. There are three minimum goals that that the information security industry considers of primary importance for a SDL:

1. Confidentiality
2. Integrity
3. Availability

These three goals are generally referred to collectively by the acronym C.I.A. It is generally accepted that if the developers ensure, enforce, and protect C.I.A. throughout the software development lifecycle through generally accepted practices, this will justify high confidence that the code is secure.

Information security, confidentiality, integrity, and availability are defined as follows in *44 U.S.C., Sec. 3542:*

> **Information security:** The protection of information and information systems from unauthorized access, use, disclosure, disruption, modification, or destruction in order to provide confidentiality, integrity, and availability.
>
> **Confidentiality:** Preserving authorized restrictions on information access and disclosure, including means for protecting personal privacy and proprietary information.
>
> **Integrity:** Guarding against improper information modification or destruction, and includes ensuring information non-repudiation and authenticity.
>
> **Availability:** Ensuring timely and reliable access to and use of information.[22]

Confidentiality, availability and integrity combined provide information security.

Confidentiality is achieved by keeping unauthorized users (human or software) from accessing confidential information. By maintaining confidentiality, the software will be considered trustworthy. Authorization and authentication are the two properties that support confidentiality in that *authorization* ensures that the user has the appropriate role and privilege to view data, and *authentication* ensures that the user is who he or she claims to be and that the data come from the appropriate place. The integrity of the application is defined by the way in which the application accepts, transmits, and stores data. The data must remain unchanged by unauthorized users and remain very reliable from the data entry point all the way to the database and back. Data encryption, digital signatures, and public keys are just some examples of how to maintain integrity and confidentiality. Excluding any scheduled downtimes, availability refers to the percentage of time a system or software is available during its normally scheduled hours of operations. As key components of software security, the lack of confidentiality, availability, and integrity will degrade the reputation of the product, resulting in both loss of reputation and loss of sales. In the end, software security is as much about a good business process as it is about quality.

1.5 Threat Modeling and Attack Surface Validation

Threat modeling and attack surface validation are perhaps the most time-consuming, misunderstood, and difficult parts of the SDL. They require the attention of the most seasoned and experienced person of the software security team: the software security architect. The idea behind threat modeling is simply to understand the potential security threats to the system, determine risk, and establish appropriate mitigations (What? How bad is it? How can it be fixed?). When it is performed correctly, threat modeling occurs early in the project lifecycle and can be used to find security design issues before code is committed. This can lead to significant cost savings because issues are resolved early in the development lifecycle. Threat modeling also helps businesses manage software risk, creates awareness of security dependencies and assumptions, and provides the ability to translate technical risk into business impact. The bottom line is that the earlier security risks are identified and managed in the software lifecycle, the better.

The correct way of doing threat modeling requires getting into the mind of the hacker, and this takes a special breed of software security professional: one who can think like a hacker and imagine all the ways that an adversary could attack or exploit the software. It is thus a slightly different way to test applications. While quality assurance professionals can do security testing and can typically discover some vulnerabilities, they usually have the customers' thoughts in mind rather than those of the hacker. In many cases, companies do not have this talent internally and have to hire third-party contractors to do this work.

A U.S. Data and Analysis Center for Software (DACS) October 2008 report, "Enhancing the Development Lifecycle to Produce Secure Software: A Reference Guidebook on Software Assurance," defines a threat to a software-intensive system as "any actor, agent, circumstance, or event that has the potential to cause harm to that system or to the data or resources to which the system has or enables access."[23] A threat can be categorized based on its intentionality. For example, a threat can be unintentional,

intentional but nonmalicious, or malicious; a malicious threat is assumed to be intentional. Although threats in all three categories have the potential to compromise the security of software, only malicious threats are realized by attacks. The DACS report also states:

> The majority of attacks against software take advantage of, or exploit, some vulnerability or weakness in that software; for this reason, "attack" is often used interchangeably with "exploit," though the BuildSecurityIn Attack Pattern Glossary makes a clear distinction between the two terms, with attack referring to the action against the targeted software and exploit referring to the mechanism (e.g., a technique or malicious code) by which that action is carried out.

Modeling software is a way to envision the interactions of the proposed software within its intended environment. The better the model reflects the intended environment, the more useful the modeling approach becomes. Therefore, secure software design and development benefits from modeling that explicitly incorporates security threats. As described in the DACS 2007 Software Security Assurance State-of-the-Art Report (SOAR), "the primary issues in modeling are doing it well; doing it thoroughly enough; and knowing what to do with the results (e.g., how to transform the analysis into a metric and/or otherwise usable decision point." Combining the concepts of threats and modeling, the report defines threat modeling as ". . . a methodical approach for assessing and documenting the weaknesses of security risks associated with an application. It allows a development team to identify the highest risk components by approaching security from the perspective of an adversary who has specific goals in attacking an application."[24]

Given the normal constraints of time and resources, it is not possible to test all code in an application However, at a minimum, testing should cover the entry points and exit points of an application that may be accessible to an attacker, commonly referred to as the application's *attack surface*. Accessibility increases the attack surface. For example, code that is restricted to local access by an administrator has a smaller attack surface than code exposed to remote access by an anonymous user.

The attack surface should be fully tested by exercising all the code paths in an application that are part of the attack surface. The elements of the attack surface can be identified with the use of scanning tools, such as port scanning tools for open ports, and code analysis tools to locate the portions of the code that receive input and send output. It may even be necessary to develop custom tools, for example, to locate entry point's specific to a custom application. The minimum attack surface is typically defined early in the software development lifecycle and measured again through the later phases. It is often helpful to formally define and measure the attack surface before testing. As we will discuss later in the book, although tools will be useful at this stage of analysis, a human element is still required, and it will take the expertise of the seasoned software security architect described above.

1.6 Chapter Summary—What to Expect from This Book

Software is only as secure as the quality and relevance of the best practices that the software development team uses. Software security must be built in from the very beginning. It must be a critical part of the design from the very beginning and included in every subsequent development phase all the way through fielding a complete system. Correcting vulnerabilities as early as possible in the SDLC through the adoption of security-enhanced processes and practices is far more cost-effective than attempting to diagnose and correct such problems after the system goes into production. This will greatly reduce the need to patch the software to fix security holes discovered by others after release of the product, which will degrade the reputation and credibility of the vendor and adversely impact it financially. Today, we are seeing an increased need for security in software development in that security requirements, design, and defensive principles have to be worked into the traditional SDLC and, most important, in choosing security development practices that embrace this need throughout all the activities of the SDLC.

We have worked with Fortune 500 companies and have often seen examples of breakdown of SDL practices. In this book, we take an experience-based approach to applying components of the best available SDLs models in dealing with the problems described above in the form of a SDL software security best practices model and framework. We shall begin by giving an overview of the secure development lifecycle and then outline a model for mapping SDL best practices to the software development lifecycle and how you can use this to build a mature SDL program. Although security is not a natural component of the way industry has been building software in recent years, we believe that security improvements to development processes are possible, practical, and essential, and we trust that the software security best practices and model presented in this book will make this clear to all who read this book, whether you are an executive, manager, or practitioner.

References

1. President's Information Technology Advisory Committee (2005), *Cybersecurity: A Crisis of Prioritization*, Executive Office of the President, National Coordination Office for Information Technology Research and Development, 2005, p. 39. Retrieved from http://www.nitrd.gov/Pitac/reports/20050301_cybersecurity/cybersecurity.pdf.
2. Ibid.
3. Aras, O., Ciaramitaro, B., and Livermore, J. (2008), "Secure Software Development—The Role of IT Audit," *ISACA Journal,* vol. 4, 2008. Retrieved from http://www.isaca.org/Journal/Past-Issues/2008/Volume-4/Pages/Secure-Software-Development-The-Role-of-IT-Audit1.aspx.
4. U.S. Department of Homeland Security (2006), *Security in the Software Lifecycle: Making Software Development Processes—and Software Produced by Them—More Secure*, DRAFT Version 1.2, p. 13. Retrieved from http://www.cert.org/books/secureswe/SecuritySL.pdf.
5. Schwartz, M. (2012), "10 Security Trends to Watch in 2012." Retrieved from http://www.informationweek.com/security/vulnerabilities/10-security-trends-to-watch-in-2012/232400392.
6. Parizo, E. (2012), "To Get Help with Secure Software Development Issues, Find Your Own Flaws." Retrieved from http://searchsecurity.techtarget.com/news/2240129160/To-get-help-with-secure-software-development-issues-find-your-own-flaw.
7. Microsoft Corporation (2012), Security Development Conference 2012 webpage, May 15–16, 2012, Washington, DC. Retrieved from https://www.securitydevelopmentconference.com/main.aspx.
8. blackhat.com (2013), Black Hat USA 2012 Conference webpage, July 21–26, 2012, Las Vegas, NV. Retrieved from http://www.blackhat.com/html/bh-us-12.
9. rsaconference.com (2013), RSA 2013 Conference USA webpage, February 25–March 1, 2013, San Francisco, CA. Retrieved from http://www.rsaconference.com/events/2013/usa.
10. securitydevelopmentconference.com (2013), Security Development Conference

2013, May 14–15, 2013, San Francisco, CA. Retrieved from http://www.securitydevelopmentconference.com.

11. Boehm, B., and Papaccio, P. (1998), "Understanding and Controlling Software Costs," *IEEE Transactions on Software Engineering,* vol. 14, no. 10, October 1988, pp. 1462–1477.

12. Beohm, B., and Basili, V. (2001), "Software Defect Reduction Top 10 List," *Computer,* vol. 34, no. 1, January 2001, pp. 135–137.

13. Meftah, B. (2008), "Business Software Assurance: Identifying and Reducing Software Risk in the Enterprise," 9th Semi-Annual Software Assurance Forum, Gaithersburg, MD, October 2008. https://buildsecurityin.us-cert.gov/swa/downloads/Meftah.pdf.

14. Viega, J., and McGraw, G. (2006), *Building Secure Software: How to Avoid Security Problems the Right Way,* Boston: Addison-Wesley.

15. McGraw, G. (2006), *Software Security: Building Security In,* Boston: Addison-Wesley, p. 20.

16. IT Law Wiki (2012), "Security Development Lifecycle Definition." Retrieved from http://itlaw.wikia.com/wiki/Security_Development_Lifecycle.

17. Microsoft Corporation (2012), "Evolution of the Microsoft SDL." Retrieved from http://www.microsoft.com/security/sdl/resources/evolution.aspx.

18. Grembi, J. (2008), *Secure Software Development: A Security Programmer's Guide,* Boston: Course Technology.

19. Ibid.

20. Ibid.

21. Ibid.

22. United States Government (2006), *44 U.S.C., SEC. 3542: United States Code, 2006 Edition,* Supplement 5, Title 44; CHAPTER 35 – COORDINATION OF FEDERAL INFORMATION POLICY, SUBCHAPTER III – INFORMATION SECURITY, Sec. 3542 – Definitions. Retrieved from http://www.gpo.gov/fdsys/pkg/USCODE-2011-title44/pdf/USCODE-2011-title44-chap35-subchapIII-sec3542.pdf.

23. Goertzel, K., et al., for Department of Homeland Security and Department of Defense Data and Analysis Center for Software (2008), *Enhancing the Development Life Cycle to Produce Secure Software: A Reference Guidebook on Software Assurance,*" Version 2, October 2008. Retrieved from https://www.thedacs.com/techs/enhanced_life_cycles.

24. Goertzel, K., et al. (2008), *Software Security Assurance: State-of-the-Art Report (SOAR),* July 31, 2008. Retrieved from http://iac.dtic.mil/iatac/download/security.pdf.

Chapter 2

The Secure Development Lifecycle

We start this chapter by introducing the concept of overcoming the challenges of making software secure through the use of a secure development lifecycle (SDL). There will be further discussions of the models, methodologies, tools, human talent, and metrics for managing and overcoming the challenges to make software secure. We will close with a discussion of the mapping of our SDL with its associated best practices to a generic software development lifecycle (SDLC), which will be the subject of the next six chapters, followed by a chapter mapping our SDL best practices to several of the most popular software development methodologies.

There is still a need for better static and dynamic testing tools and a formalized security methodology integrated into SDLCs that is within the reach of a majority of software development organizations. In the past decade or so, the predominant SDL models have been out of reach for all but the most resource-rich companies. Our goal in this book is to create a SDL based on leveraged minimal resources and best practices rather than requiring resources that are out of reach for a majority of software security teams.

2.1 Overcoming Challenges in Making Software Secure

As mentioned in Chapter 1, SDLs are the key step in the evolution of software security and have helped to bring attention to the need to build security into the software development lifecycle. In the past, software product stakeholders did not view software security as a high priority. It was believed that a secure network infrastructure would provide the level of protection needed against malicious attacks. In recent history, however, network security alone has proved inadequate against such attacks. Users have been successful in penetrating valid channels of authentication through techniques such as Cross-Site Scripting (XSS), Structured Query Language (SQL) injection, and buffer overflow exploitation. In such cases system assets were compromised and both data and organizational integrity were damaged. The security industry has tried to solve software security problems through stopgap measures. First came platform security (OS security), then came network/perimeter security, and now application security. We do need defense-in-depth to protect our assets, but fundamentally it is a software security flaw and needs to be remediated through a SDL approach.

The SDL has as its base components all of the activities and security controls needed to develop industry and government-compliant and best practices–hardened software. A knowledgeable staff as well as secure software policies and controls is required in order to truly prevent, identify, and mitigate exploitable vulnerabilities within developed systems.

Not meeting the least of the activities found within the SDL provides an opportunity for misuse of system assets from both insider and outsider threats. Security is not simply a network requirement, it is now an information technology (IT) requirement, which includes the development of all software for the intent to distribute, store, and manipulate information. Organizations must implement the highest standards of development in order to insure the highest quality of products for its customers and the lives which they protect.

Implementation of a SDL program ensures that security is inherent in good enterprise software design and development, not an afterthought included later in production. Taking an SDL approach yields tangible benefits such as ensuring that all software releases meet minimum security criteria, and that all stakeholders support and enforce security guidelines.

The elimination of software risk early in the development cycle, when vulnerabilities are easier and less expensive to fix, provides a systematic approach for information security teams to collaborate with during the development process.

The most well known SDL model is the Trustworthy Computing Security Development Lifecycle (or SDL), a process that Microsoft has adopted for the development of software that needs to withstand malicious attack. Microsoft's SDL[1] has been evolving for over a decade and is considered the most mature of the top three models. Other popular SDL models are the Cigital Software Security Touchpoints model,[2] the OWASP SDL,[3] and the Cisco Secure Development Lifecycle (CSDL).[4]

The Microsoft SDL also has a Security Development Lifecycle (SDL) Optimization Model[5] designed to facilitate gradual, consistent, and cost-effective implementation of the SDL by development organizations outside of Microsoft. The model helps those responsible for integrating security and privacy in their organization's software development lifecycle to assess their current state and to gradually move their organizations toward adoption of the proven Microsoft program for producing more secure software.

The SDL Optimization Model enables development managers and IT policy makers to assess the state of the security in development. They can then create a vision and roadmap for reducing customer risk by creating more secure and reliable software in a cost-effective, consistent, and gradual manner. As it moves through the maturity levels of the SDL Optimization Model, your organization's executive commitment to the goals and results of SDL will increase from tentative acceptance to a strong mandate.[6]

2.2 Software Security Maturity Models

In recent years, two very popular software security maturity models have been developed and continue to mature at a rapid rate. One is the Cigital BSIMM,[7] and the other is the OWASP Open SAMM.[8] BSIMM is short for Building Security In Maturity Model. The BSIMM is a study of real-world software security initiatives organized so that you can determine where you stand with your software security initiative and how to evolve your efforts over time. It is a set of best practices that Cigital developed by analyzing real-world data from nine leading software security initiatives and creating a framework based on common areas of success. There are 12 practices organized into four domains. These practices are used to organize the 109 BSIMM activities (BSIMM 4 has a total of 111 activities).

By studying what the nine initiatives were doing, BSIMM's creators were able to build a best practices model that is broken into 12 categories that software makers can follow:

1. Strategy and Metrics
2. Compliance and Policy
3. Training
4. Attack Models
5. Security Features and Design
6. Standards and Requirements
7. Architecture Analysis
8. Code Review
9. Security Testing
10. Penetration Testing
11. Software Environment
12. Configuration and Vulnerability Management[9]

The fourth release of BSSIM was announced on September 18, 2012; some of its highlights follow.

- For the first time in the BSIMM project, new activities were observed in addition to the original 109, resulting in the addition of two new activities to the model going forward. The activities are Simulate Software Crisis and Automate Malicious Code Detection.
- BSIMM4 includes 51 firms from 12 industry verticals.
- BSIMM4 has grown 20 percent since BSIMM3 and is ten times bigger than the original 2009 edition.
- The BSIMM4 data set has 95 distinct measurements (some firms measured multiple times, some firms with multiple divisions measured separately and rolled into one firm score).
- BSIMM4 continues to show that leading firms on average employ two full-time software security specialists for every 100 developers.
- BSIMM4 describes the work of 974 software security professionals working with a development-based satellite of 2039 people to secure the software developed by 218,286 developers.[10]

The OWASP Software Assurance Maturity Model (SAMM) is a flexible and prescriptive framework for building security into a software development organization. Covering more than typical SDLC-based models for security, SAMM enables organizations to self-assess their security assurance program and then use recommended roadmaps to improve in a way that is aligned to the specific risks facing the organization. Beyond that, SAMM enables creation of scorecards for an organization's effectiveness at secure software development throughout the typical governance, development, and deployment business functions. Scorecards also enable management within an organization to demonstrate quantitative improvements through iterations of building a security assurance program.[11]

2.3 ISO/IEC 27034—Information Technology—Security Techniques—Application Security

In 2011, the International Standards Organization (ISO)/International Electrotechnical Commission (IEC) published Part 1 of 6 of the ISO/IEC 27034-1:2011 standard for Application Security.[12] The standard offers a concise, internationally recognized way to get transparency into a vendor/supplier's software security management process. It was designed to be flexible enough to align with diverse engineering organizations but specific enough to address real-world risk. Although it is not complete yet, it is coming and will likely be similar to the ISO/IEC 27001 for IT Security in that both customers and partners will expect compliance and their engineering groups will be expected by both customers and partners. As a standard for software security from an international body and not a vendor, it is also not tied to specific technology. As of this writing, Parts 2-6 are still in working Draft and composed of the following: Part 2, Organization Normative Framework; Part 3, Application Security Management Process; Part 4, Application Security Validation; Part 5, Protocols and Application Security Control Data Structure; and Part 6, Security Guidance for Specific Applications.[13] Over the years, as organizations (and their customers) started paying attention to information security, the security and compliance industry came up with a plethora of attestations, certifications, and methodologies. These standards/attestations all claimed to be unique in the way they would measure the security posture of an organization. Competition and marketing hype drove confusion, with different organizations standardizing on different attestations. The authors have seen organizations pushing their customers (in most cases, other companies) to adopt their recommended attestation. For Fortune 500 companies this meant getting multiple attestations/certifications as a proof of security posture. It didn't help that most of these attestations/certifications focused on "compliance controls" or "policy based security." The situation became worse with regulations such as SOX, GLBA, Safe Harbor, and HIPAA adding to the confusion. Companies often went for a set of certifications, one each for compliance, security, privacy, credit card, physical security, and so on.

The ISO)/IEC developed the ISO/IEC 27001 (incorporating ISO/IEC 17799, which had been the previous *de facto* ISO standard for information security). It is an information security management system (ISMS) standard that specifies a management system intended to bring information security under formal management control. It mandates specific requirements that need to be met when an organization adopts the standard. The standard addresses information security holistically and encompasses everything from physical security to compliance. Industry has enthusiastically adopted the practices, and ISO/IEC 27001 is the leading standard for an information security management system (ISMS) today. Most of the controls from other standards can be mapped back to ISO/IEC 27001. This has enabled organizations to consolidate multiple security efforts under one standard, pursue a single framework with holistic security in mind, and collect metrics in a consistent manner to measure and govern security in an organization.

The authors see the landscape for software security (and SDL) similar to what it was for information security as a whole a few years ago before ISO/IEC 27001 came along. There are multiple SDL methodologies (open and proprietary), each claiming to be better than the next. Confusion prevails over the best way to accomplish software security in an organization. Applying any one framework to an organization either requires the organization to adopt different processes or to customize an SDL framework that will work in their environment. With the coming of ISO/IEC 27034, the authors see consolidation on software security standards/framework as the ISO/IEC 27001 has done for information security. Even in its infancy, there is awareness of the importance of ISO/IEC 27034. Microsoft has declared its SDL methodology to be in conformance with ISO/IEC 27034-1.[14] We expect to see similar results for other frameworks in the near future.

The ISO/IEC 27034 standard provides guidance to help organizations embed security within their processes that help secure applications running in the environment, including application lifecycle processes. It is a risk-based framework to continuously improve security through process integrating/improvements in managing applications. It takes a process approach by design.

The authors' recommended SDL framework can be mapped to ISO/IEC 27034 frameworks. We will lay out relevant mapping with ISO/IEC 27034 in Appendix A.

2.4 Other Resources for SDL Best Practices

There are other sources for SDL best practices, and some of the most popular are described below.

2.4.1 SAFECode

The Software Assurance Forum for Excellence in Code (SAFECode) is a nonprofit organization dedicated to increasing trust in information and communications technology products and services through the advancement of effective software assurance methods. SAFECode is a global, industry-led effort to identify and promote best practices for developing and delivering more secure and reliable software, hardware, and services. It is meant to provide a foundational set of secure development practices that have been effective in improving software security in real-world implementations by SAFECode members across their diverse development environments. These are the "practiced practices" employed by SAFECode members, which we identified through an ongoing analysis of members' individual software security efforts. By bringing these methods together and sharing them with the larger community, SAFECode hopes to move the industry beyond defining theoretical best practices to describing sets of software engineering practices that have been shown to improve the security of software and are currently in use at leading software companies.[15,16]

2.4.2 U.S. Department of Homeland Security Software Assurance Program

Since 2004, the U.S. Department of Homeland Security (DHS) Software Assurance Program has sponsored development of the Build Security In (BSI) website.[17] BSI content is based on the principle that software security is fundamentally a software engineering problem and must be managed in a systematic way throughout the SDLC.

The Department of Homeland Security National Cyber Security Division's (NCSD) Software Assurance (SwA) Program seeks to reduce software vulnerabilities, minimize exploitation, and address ways to improve the routine development and deployment of trustworthy software products. Consistent with the Open Government Directive, the program enables public–private collaboration in developing, publishing, and promoting the use of practical guidance and tools, fostering investment in more secure and reliable software. The DHS Software Assurance Program collaborates with the private sector, academia, and other federal departments and agencies to enhance the security of software lifecycle processes and technologies through activities such as the Software Assurance Forum that it co-sponsors with the Department of Defense (DoD) and the National Institute of Standards and Technology (NIST). A key initiative funded by the DHS NCSD and the National Security Agency (NSA) is the Common Weakness Enumeration (CWE). CWE is a joint effort of DHS with NSA and the software community, including government, the private sector, and academia, with the MITRE Corporationproviding technical leadership and project coordination. Over 800 software weaknesses have been identified and cataloged. More than 47 products and services already use CWE in a compatible manner. With the aim of reducing the most significant exploitable programming errors, the SANS Institute, an active participant of the Software Assurance Forum, has promoted the Top 25 CWEs. SANS came up with the idea of focusing on the Top 25 CWEs, and this effort represents a community collaboration to prioritize the most exploitable constructs that make software vulnerable to attack or failure. This promotes the DHS co-sponsored CWE efforts and plays off the "Top XXX" brand that SANS has built since 2001, starting with their Top 10—the first prioritized list of security problems that organizations should address.[18]

The CWE is an important component of the NCSD's Software Assurance Program. This list of errors brings CWE to a practical, actionable, and measurable focus that will enable people to make and demonstrate real progress. Public–private collaboration forms the foundation of NCSD's SwA Program. CWE is a good example of the type of public–private collaboration the department has been advocating. Consistent with the Open Government Directive, the SwA Program's sponsorship of CWE enables community participation, collaboration, and transparency. CWE provides the requisite characterization of exploitable software constructs; thus it better enables the needed education and training of programmers on how to eliminate all-too-common errors before software is delivered and put into operation. This aligns with the Build Security In approach to software assurance so that software is developed more securely on the front end, thereby avoiding security issues in the longer term. The CWE provides a standard means for understanding residual risks and thus enables more informed decision making by suppliers and consumers concerning the security of software.[19]

2.4.3 National Institute of Standards and Technology

The National Institute of Standards and Technology (NIST) continues to be of great value in providing research, information, and tools for both the government and corporate information security community. The following are some of the key areas in which NIST contributes to the software security community.

The NIST SAMATE (Software Assurance Metrics And Tool Evaluation) project is dedicated to improving software assurance by developing methods to enable software tool evaluations, measuring the effectiveness of tools and techniques, and identifying gaps in tools and methods. This project supports the Department of Homeland Security's Software Assurance Tools and R&D Requirements Identification Program—in particular, Part 3, Technology (Tools and Requirements), the identification, enhancement, and development of software assurance tools. The scope of the SAMATE project is broad, ranging from operating systems to firewalls, SCADA to web applications, source code security analyzers to correct-by-construction methods.[20]

NIST Special Publication (SP) 800-64, *Security Considerations in the System Development Life Cycle,* has been developed to assist federal government agencies in integrating essential information technology security steps into their established IT system development lifecycle. This guideline applies to all federal IT systems other than national security systems. The document is intended as a reference resource rather than as a tutorial and should be used in conjunction with other NIST publications as needed throughout the development of the system.[21]

The National Vulnerability Database (NVD) is the U.S. government repository of standards-based vulnerability management data represented using the Security Content Automation Protocol (SCAP). These data enable automation of vulnerability management, security measurement, and compliance. The NVD includes databases of security checklists, security-related software flaws, misconfigurations, product names, and impact metrics.[22] The NVD Common Vulnerability Scoring System (CVSS) provides an open framework for communicating the characteristics and impacts of IT vulnerabilities. Its quantitative model ensures repeatable accurate measurement while enabling users to see the underlying vulnerability characteristics that were used to generate the scores. Thus, the CVSS is well suited as a standard measurement system for industries, organizations, and governments that need accurate and consistent vulnerability impact scores. Two common uses of the CVSS are in prioritizing vulnerability remediation activities and in calculating the severity of vulnerabilities discovered on one's systems. The NVD provides CVSS scores for almost all known vulnerabilities. In particular, the NVD supports the CVSS Version 2 standard for all CVE vulnerabilities. The NVD provides CVSS "base scores" which represent the innate characteristics of every vulnerability. It does not currently provide "temporal scores" (scores that change over time due to events external to the vulnerability). However, the NVD does provide a CVSS score calculator to allow you to add temporal data and even to calculate environmental scores (scores customized to reflect the impact of the vulnerability on your organization). This calculator contains support for U.S. government agencies to customize vulnerability impact scores based on FIPS 199 System ratings. We will discuss the use of CVSS scores for managing software security later in the book.[23]

2.4.4 MITRE Corporation Common Computer Vulnerabilities and Exposures

The MITRE Corporation Common Computer Vulnerabilities and Exposures (CVE) is a list of information security vulnerabilities and exposures that aims to provide common names for publicly known problems.

The goal of CVE is to make it easier to share data across separate vulnerability capabilities (tools, repositories, and services) with this "common enumeration." Information security *vulnerability* is a mistake in software that can be used directly by a hacker to gain access to a system or network. See the Terminology page of the CVE website for a complete explanation of how this term is used in the CVE. An information security *exposure* is a mistake in software that allows access to information or capabilities that can be used by a hacker as a stepping-stone into a system or network. Using a common identifier makes it easier to share data across separate databases, tools, and services, which, until the creation of CVE in 1999, were not easily integrated. If a report from a security capability incorporates CVE Identifiers, you may then quickly and accurately access fix information in one or more separate CVE-compatible tools, services, and repositories to remediate the problem. With CVE, your tools and services can "speak" (i.e., exchange data) with each other. You will know exactly what each covers, because CVE provides you with a baseline for evaluating the coverage of your tools. This means that you can determine which tools are most effective and appropriate for your organization's needs. In short, CVE-compatible tools, services, and databases will give you better coverage, easier interoperability, and enhanced security.

Bugtraq IDs are identifiers for a commercially operated vulnerability database that are used in security advisories and alerts, as well as for discussions on the Bugtraq mailing list. CVE Identifiers are from an international information security effort that is publicly available and free to use. CVE Identifiers are for the sole purpose of providing a common name. For this reason, CVE Identifiers are frequently used by researchers and the makers of security tools, websites, databases, and services as a standard method for identifying vulnerabilities and for cross-linking with other repositories that also use CVE Identifiers. A CVE Identifier will give you a standardized identifier for any given vulnerability or exposure. Knowing this identifier will allow you to quickly and accurately access information about the problem across multiple information sources that are CVE-compatible. For example, if you own a security tool whose reports contain references to CVE Identifiers, you may then access fix information in a separate CVE-compatible database. CVE also provides you with a baseline for evaluating the coverage of your tools.

The CVE List feeds the U.S. National Vulnerability Database (NVD), which then builds upon the information included in CVE entries to provide enhanced information for each CVE Identifier such as fix information, severity scores, and impact ratings. NVD also provides advanced searching features such as by individual CVE-ID; by OS; by vendor name, product name, and/or version number; and by vulnerability type, severity, related exploit range, and impact.

CVE is sponsored by the National Cyber Security Division (NCSD) at the U.S. Department of Homeland Security. US-CERT is the operational arm of the NCSD. US-CERT incorporates CVE Identifiers into its security advisories whenever possible and advocates the use of CVE and CVE-compatible products and services to the U.S. government and all members of the information security community. The MITRE Corporation maintains CVE and this public website, manages the compatibility program, and provides impartial technical guidance to the CVE Editorial Board throughout the process to ensure that CVE serves the public interest.[24,25]

2.4.5 SANS Institute Top Cyber Security Risks

The SANS Top Cyber Security Risks, formerly the SANS Twenty Most Critical Internet Security Vulnerabilities, is a consensus list of the most critical problem areas in Internet security that require immediate remediation if present on your systems. Step-by-step instructions and pointers to additional information useful for correcting these security flaws are included as part of the list. The SANS list includes CVE Identifiers to uniquely identify the vulnerabilities it describes. This helps system administrators use CVE-compatible products and services to make their networks more secure.[26,27,28]

2.4.6 U.S. Department of Defense Cyber Security and Information Systems Information Analysis Center (CSIAC)

In September 2012, the Data & Analysis Center for Software (DACS), Information Assurance Technology Analysis Center (IATAC), and Modeling and Simulation Information Analysis Center (MSIAC) were merged to create the Cyber Security and Information Systems Information Analysis Center (CSIAC). The CSIAC, one of eight Information Analysis Centers (IACs) sponsored by DTIC, performs the Basic Center of Operations (BCO) functions necessary to fulfill the mission and objectives applicable to the Department of Defense Research Development Test and Evaluation (RDT&E) and Acquisition communities' needs for cyber security, information assurance, knowledge management and information sharing, software-intensive systems engineering, and modeling and simulation.29 In the past, the DACS has produced some great documents on software security and the SDL for the community, most notably, *Enhancing the Development Lifecycle to Produce Secure Software: A Reference Guidebook on Software Assurance* (2008)[30] and the joint IATAC/DACS report *Software Security Assurance: State-of-the-Art Report (SOAR)* (2008),[31] and we expect them to continue to do so under the umbrella of the CSIAC.

2.4.7 CERT, Bugtraq, and SecurityFocus

In addition to the sources we have discussed so far, the Carnegie Mellon Computer Emergency Readiness Team (CERT),[32] Bugtraq,[33] and SecurityFocus[34] are three other sources to be aware of.

CERT provides timely alerts on security vulnerabilities as well as a weekly summarized bulletin on vulnerabilities (*CERT Cyber Security Bulletin*). Information in the bulletin includes CVSS scores as well as CVE IDs to uniquely identify vulnerabilities. The compilation is based on vulnerabilities recorded in the NIST NVD[35] over the previous week. We will be discussing the CVSS scoring process in more detail later in the book.

Bugtraq is an electronic security mailing list that provides information on security vulnerabilities as well as security bulletins and announcements from vendors. The list often contains additional information such as examples of exploitations as well as fixes for the issues identified. Bugtraq is part of the SecurityFocus security portal which is currently owned by Symantec. Bugtraq is one of the many security mailing lists available through SecurityFocus. There are other useful mailing lists as well, such as those dedicated to Microsoft, Linux, IDS, and incidents.

2.5 Critical Tools and Talent

As with all security tasks, whether they are offensive or defensive in their approach, there is always a blend of process, technology, and people that are required to make it successful. So far, the processes and models that are available for software security have been discussed in this section. There are two elements of the technology (tool) side of the triad that will make or break you in terms of software security, and another on the people (talent) side.

2.5.1 The Tools

Three primary tools are basic to the SDL, which are categorized as fuzzing, static, and dynamic analysis tools. Although we will go over the details of the best practices for their use in the SDL later in the book, a high-level overview follows.

2.5.1.1 Fuzzing

Fuzz testing or fuzzing is a black-box software testing technique which can be automated or semiautomated, which provides invalid, unexpected, or random data to the inputs of a computer software program. In other words, it finds implementation bugs or security flaws by using malformed/semimalformed data injection in an automated fashion. Inputs to the software program are then monitored for exception returns such as crashes, failing built-in code assertions, and potential memory leaks. Fuzzing has become a key element in the testing for software or computer system security problems. Fuzz testing has a distinct advantage over other tools in that the test design is extremely simple and free of preconceptions about system behavior

Fuzzing is a key element of software security and must be embedded in the SDL. There are many vendors to choose from in this space, and some developers even develop their own tools. Two popular fuzzing tools are Codenomicon,[36] which is one of the most mature fuzzing tools available commercially, and the Peach Fuzzing Tool,[37] which is one of the more popular open-source tools. As you will see later on in the book, the timing at which the fuzzing tools are used in the SDL is critical. It should also be noted that fuzzing is used for both security and quality assurance testing.

Fuzzing has recently been recognized as both a key element and a major deficiency in many software development programs, so much so that it is now a Department of Defense Information Assurance Certification and Accreditation Process (DIACAP) requirement.

2.5.1.2 Static Analysis

Static program analysis is the analysis of computer software that is performed without actually executing programs. It is predominantly used to perform analysis on a version of the source code; however, this kind of analysis may also be done on some form of the object code. In contrast, dynamic analysis is performed by actually executing software programs. Static analysis is performed by an automated software tool and should not be confused with human analysis or software security architectural reviews, which involve manual human code reviews, program understanding, and comprehension. When used properly, static analysis tools have a distinct advantage over human static analysis in that analysis can be performed much more frequently and with security knowledge generally superior to that of the standard software developer. It also frees up the time of seasoned software security architects or engineers so that they only need be brought in when absolutely necessary.

Static analysis, also known as static application security testing (SAST), identifies vulnerabilities during the development or quality assurance phase of a project. It provides line-of-code level detection that enables development teams to remediate vulnerabilities quickly.

The use of static analysis tools and your choice of the appropriate vendor for your environment is another technology factor key to your success. Any technology that beneficially automates any portion of the software development process should be welcome, but this software has become "shelf-ware" in many organizations because the right people and right process was not used in selecting the tool or tools. Not all tools in this space are created equal, and some are better at some languages than others while others have great governance/risk/compliance (GRC) and metric analysis front ends. In some cases you may have to use up to three different tools to be effective. In the end, you need to choose tools which support your language, are scalable, can be embedded with your development processes, and have minimum false positives.

Software development is a complex business, and anything you can do to make the process more repeatable, predictable, and reduce "friction" is a big win for most organizations. There are many benefits to using static analysis tools. The most important reasons include the following.

- Static analysis tools can scale. They can review a great deal of code very quickly, something humans cannot do very well.

- Static analysis tools don't get tired. A static analysis tool running for four straight hours at 2:00 a.m. is just as effective as if it runs during business hours. You can't say the same thing about human reviewers.
- Static analysis tools help developers learn about security vulnerabilities. In many cases you can use these tools and educational resources from the vendor to educate your development teams about software security.

2.5.1.3 Dynamic Analysis

Dynamic program analysis is the analysis of computer software that is performed by executing programs on a real or virtual processor in real time. The objective is to find security errors in a program while it is running, rather than by repeatedly examining the code offline. By debugging a program in all the scenarios for which it is designed, dynamic analysis eliminates the need to artificially create situations likely to produce errors. It has a distinct advantage of having the ability to identify vulnerabilities that might have been false negatives and to validate findings in the static code analysis.

Dynamic analysis, also known as dynamic application security testing (DAST), identifies vulnerabilities within a production application. These tools are used to quickly assess a system's overall security and are used within both the SDL and SDLC. The same advantages and cautions about using static analysis tools apply to dynamic analysis tools. Some of the popular SAST vendor products are Coverity,[38] HP Fortify Static Code Analyzer,[39] IBM Security AppScan Source,[40] klocwork,[41] Parasoft,[42] and Veracode,[43] while the more popular DAST vendor products include HP Webinspect[44] and QAinspect,[45] IBM Security AppScan Enterprise,[46] Veracode,[47] and Whitehat Sentinel Source.[48]

The timing of the use of SAST and DAST tools in the SDL is critical, and takes place primarily in the design and development phase of the SDL we will be presenting later in this book, as shown in Figure 2.1.

2.5.2 The Talent

2.5.2.1 Software Security Architects

As mentioned in Chapter 1, qualified senior software security architects will make or break your software security program. On the people front,

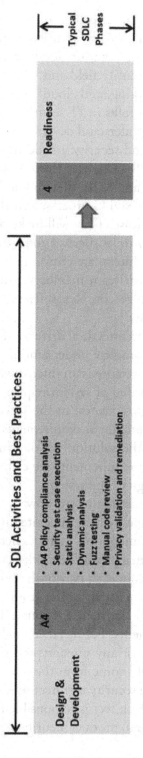

Figure 2.1 Design and development (A4) stage of the SDL activities and best practices.

the most critical element of an effective software security program is a cadre of senior level 3 and 4 software security architects. These are individuals who have five to ten years of development/coding experience before they come into the security field and who are also experienced in the areas of software, networking, and cloud/SaaS architectural design.

These are not the typical folks in IT security who run tools; they are experienced architects who understand development and system architecture as well as they understand security. In addition, they must also have great political and people skills. These are the folks who are going to touch every element of the SDLC and SDL; they should be part of the sign-off process at each stage of the SDLC process, and they must be involved from pre-commit to post-release. They will make or break your software security practice and are key to its survival and success. Your senior software/application security architects are critical to handle product security escalations, train development team members, provide internal/external customer responses, and solve complex software/applications issues in SaaS and cloud environments.

Distinguishing between architectural drivers and other requirements is not simple, as it requires a complete understanding of the solution objectives. Software security architecture is an interactive process that involves assessment of the business value of system requirements and identifying the requirements that are most critical to the success of a system. These requirements include the functional requirements, the constraints, and the behavior properties of the solution, all of which must be classified and specified. These critical requirements are called *architectural drivers,* because they shape the design of the system.

The security architect must figure out how, at the architectural level, necessary security technologies will be integrated into the overall system. In the cloud or SaaS environment, this includes network security requirements, such as firewalls, virtual private networks, etc. Architects explicitly document trust assumptions in each part of the system, usually by drawing trust boundaries (e.g., network traffic from outside the firewall is untrusted, but local traffic is trusted). Of course, these boundaries must be reflect business requirements. For instance, high-security applications should not be willing to trust any unencrypted shared network media. Security requirements should come from the user. A typical job description for a seasoned software security architect might be as follows.

The Software Security Architect is responsible for providing architectural and technical guidance to product security across all of Company X.

The Architect will design, plan, and implement secure coding practices and security testing methodology; ensure that practices meet software certification processes; drive the security testing of the products; test and evaluate security-related tools; and manage third-party vendors to meet those responsibilities above. Specific roles and responsibilities include:

- Drive overall software security architecture.
- Provide technical leadership in the comprehensive planning, development, and execution of Company X software security efforts.
- Work closely with product and engineering development teams to ensure that products meet or exceed customer security and certification requirements. This includes ensuring that the security architecture is well documented and communicated.
- Provide planning and input into the software engineering and product development process, related to security, sensitive to the constraints and needs of the business.
- Monitor security technology trends and requirements, such as emerging standards, for new technology opportunities.
- Develop and execute security plans. This may include managing joint development with third-party vendors, and providing guidance (with other departments) to the engineering and testing practices.
- Ensure, and create as needed, security policies, processes, practices, and operations to ensure reproducible development and high quality, while keeping costs under control.
- Engage in hands-on, in-depth analysis, review, and design of the software, including technical review and analysis of source code with a security perspective. Will include reviews of in-house developed code, as well as review of technologies provided by third-party vendors.
- Provide primary technical role in the security certifications process, including preparing extensive documentation and working with third-party evaluations.
- Provide training to staff, contractors, development, and quality assurance teams, and product/software security champions related to product security.
- Guide Company X software development teams through the Company X Security Development Lifecycle (SDL) for its SDLC by participating in design reviews, threat modeling, and in-depth security penetration testing of code and systems. These responsibilities

extend to providing input on application design, secure coding practices, log forensics, log design, and application code security.

The software security architects are the cadre who will be critical in overseeing and training the efforts of software security champions that should be identified through a cross–business unit/software security education and awareness program. The architects will also spot and assess candidates for software security champions, as they are involved in various software products SDLs from concept commit to post-release.

2.5.2.2 Software Security Champions

Funding for corporate security departments, whether IT, physical, or software, is not likely to get any better in the foreseeable future, which means that you will have to be very judicious with your resources if you plan to be successful. As we implied earlier, seasoned software security architects are far and few between, and at best you will not likely be able to find and afford more than a handful in today's market. As you look at the SDL model used in this book or others referenced earlier in this chapter, you may be asking yourself how you can ever scale to this task given the resources that security software and the development teams working with them will have. The answer is that if you manage the software security team or have that function working for you, you will use the recruitment and leverage of software security champions (SSCs) to manage this daunting task. Candidates for this role should typically have a minimum of three to five years of software development experience; a passion for or background in software security; time to be trained in software security and on the centralized software security teams tools, plans, and processes; and, most important, must not only know how to develop (build) software but also how to deconstruct (take it apart) while "thinking like a hacker" regarding all possible paths or exploits (attack planes) that an adversary could take to exploit the software. Each product development organization should have at least one individual who has the technical capability to be trained as a software security champion and eventually as a junior software security architect to assist the centralized software security team in architecture security analysis/threat modeling. It is also important that SSCs be volunteers and not assignees who may lack the passion to succeed at this very challenging but rewarding role. Each business unit for software development within a company should have at least one SSC; for larger development organizations, it is preferable to have one for each tier product per business unit. A typical job description for a software security champion is as follows.

- SSCs must have a minimum of three to five years of software development experience; a passion for or background in software security; time to be trained in software security and on the centralized and business unit–specific software security tools, plans, and processes; and, most important, must not only know how to develop (build) software but also how to deconstruct it (take it apart) while "thinking like a hacker" regarding all possible paths or exploits (attack planes) that an adversary could take to exploit the software.
- Each product development organization will have one individual that has the technical capability to be trained as a software security architect to assist the centralized software security group in architecture security analysis/threat modeling. Ideally, each team should have an additional product security champion whose role is to assist as a change agent (more project/program oriented individual) in addition to the technically oriented product security champion if deemed necessary.
- Specific roles and responsibilities include:
  - Enforce the SDL: Assist the centralized software security group in assuring the security tenants of confidentiality, integrity, availability, and privacy are adhered to in the SDL as part of the Company X SDLC.
  - Review: Assist the centralized software security team software security architects in conducting architecture security analysis, reviews, and threat modeling.
  - Tools Expert: Be the representative centralized software security team software security tool expert (e.g., static and dynamic, including fuzzing) within each development team, product group, and/or business unit.
  - Collocate: Be the eyes, ears, and advocate of the centralized software security team within each development team, product group, and business unit.
  - Attend Meetings: Participate in monthly phone meetings and, as budgets permit, twice-a-year face-to-face meetings, as members of a global Company X team of software security champions.

2.6 Principles of Least Privilege

In information security, computer science, and other fields, the principle of *least privilege* (also known as the principle of minimal privilege or the principle of least authority) requires that in a particular abstraction layer of a computing environment, every module (such as a process, a user, or a program, depending on the subject) must be able to access only the information and resources that are necessary for its legitimate purpose.[49,50]

Limiting the elevation of privilege is a significant part of threat modeling as a core component of the Architecture (A2) phase of our SDL, which we will discuss in Chapter 4. The concept of *elevation of privilege* is considered so important that it is the theme of a Microsoft Security Development Lifecycle card game designed to train developers and security professionals to quickly and easily find threats to software or computer systems.[51] An unauthorized privilege escalation attack takes advantage of programming errors or design flaws to grant the attacker elevated access to the network and its associated data and applications. These attacks can be either *vertical,* where the attacker grants himself privileges, or *horizontal,* where the attacker uses the same level of privileges he has already been granted, but assumes the identity of another user with similar privileges.

Ensuring least privilege prevents the disclosure of sensitive data, and prevents unauthorized users from gaining access to programs or areas they were never meant to have. Software design should follow the principle of least privilege, and this is a critical element in software development. Limiting the level of privilege is critically important because the elevation of privilege can result in an attacker gaining authorizations beyond those granted to a normal user. For example, an attacker with general user privileges that are set for "read only" permissions may be able to hack the software to elevate his access to include "read and write." Facilitating least privilege requires that a user be given no more privilege than is necessary to perform a given task. During the design phase of the SDL/SDLC, you will need to determine the minimum set of privileges required to perform that job, and restrict the user to a domain with those privileges and nothing more. Ensuring least privilege includes limiting not only user rights but also resource permissions such as CPU limits, memory, network, and file system permissions. This requires that multiple conditions have been met before granting permissions to an object, because checking access to only one condition may not be adequate for strong security. For example, an attacker may be restricted from conducting a successful attack if he is able to obtain one privilege but not a second. Compartmenting software into separate components that require multiple checks for access can inhibit an attack or potentially prevent an attacker from taking over an entire system. Careful delegation of access rights can restrict attackers from successfully attacking software or a system. The minimum rights and access to the resource should be limited to the shortest duration necessary to do the task.

2.7 Privacy

Protecting users' privacy is another important component of the SDL process and should be considered a system design principle of significant importance in all phases of the SDLC. Just as with a failure in security, a failure to protect the customer's privacy will lead to an erosion of trust. As more and more cases of unauthorized access to customers' personal information are disclosed in the press, the trust in software and systems to protect customers' data is deteriorating. In addition, many new privacy laws and regulations have placed an increased importance on including privacy in the design and development of both software and systems. As with security, software that has already progressed through the development life cycle can be very expensive to change; it is much less expensive to integrate privacy preservation methodologies and techniques into the appropriate phases of the SDLC to preserve the privacy of individuals and to protect personally identifiable information (PII) data. Some key privacy design principles included in Microsoft's SDL include the ability to provide appropriate notice about data that is collected, stored, or shared so that users can make informed decisions about their personal information; enable user policy and control; minimize data collection and sensitivity; and the protection of the storage and transfer of data.[52]

It is imperative that privacy protections be built into the SDLC through best practices implemented through the SDL. Ignoring the privacy concerns of users can invite blocked deployments, litigation, negative media coverage, and mistrust. We have incorporated privacy protection best practices into our SDL, which will be described in subsequent chapters.

2.8 The Importance of Metrics

In the words of Lord Kelvin, "If you cannot measure it, you cannot improve it."[53] This maxim holds true today as it applies to product security and the need to measure a software development organization's security posture accurately. Meaningful security metrics are critical as corporations grapple with regulatory and risk management requirements, tightening security budgets require shrewd security investments, and customers demand proof that security and privacy is being built into their products rather than through the historical post-release fixes.

Metrics tracking is like an insurance policy for your software projects and also assists in managing protection against vulnerabilities. As we have noted repeatedly, the cost of detecting a defect in successive stages of the SDLC is very high compared with detecting the same defect at the stage of the SDLC where the defect originated. Metrics can track these costs and provide significant help in various ROI (return-on-investment) calculations throughout the SDL/SDLC process. As shown in Figure1.1, it costs little to avoid potential security defects early in development, especially compared to costing 10, 20, 50, or even 100 times that amount much later in development. A visual representation of the cost of fixing defects at different stages of the SDLC as part of the SDL process is given in Figure 2.2. It can be argued that the cost of preventing just one or two defects from going live is worth the cost of tracking metrics. The ability to foresee defects and remediate them is a good indicator of a healthy software security program, but quality metrics throughout the SDL/SDLC process can help in managing and often avoiding excessive remediation costs.

One goal of the SDL is to catch defects throughout the process as a multistaged filtering process rather than through a single activity or point in time, thus minimizing the remaining defects that lead to vulnerabilities. Each defect removal activity can be thought of as a filter that removes some percentage of defects that can lead to vulnerabilities from the software product.[54] The more defect removal filters there are in the software development lifecycle, the fewer defects that can lead to vulnerabilities will remain in the software product when it is released. More important, early measurement of defects enables the organization to take corrective action early in the SDLC. Each time defects are removed, they are measured. Every defect removal point becomes a measurement point.

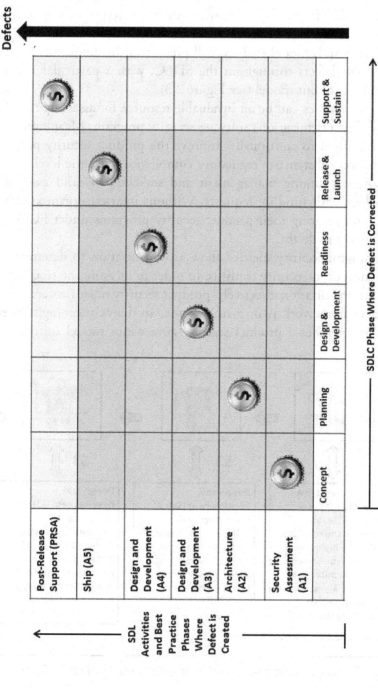

Cost to Correct Defects

SDL Activities and Best Practice Phases Where Defect is Created	Concept	Planning	Design & Development	Readiness	Release & Launch	Support & Sustain
Post-Release Support (PRSA)						$
Ship (A5)					$	
Design and Development (A4)			$			
Design and Development (A3)			$			
Architecture (A2)		$				
Security Assessment (A1)	$					

SDLC Phase Where Defect is Corrected →

Figure 2.2 Visual representation of the cost of fixing defects at different stages of the SDLC as part of the SDL process.

Defect measurement leads to something even more important than defect removal and prevention: It tells teams where they stand versus their goals, helps them decide whether to move to the next step or to stop and take corrective action, and indicates where to fix their process to meet their goals.[55] The SDL model that we will present in this book will focus on filtering out defects throughout the SDLC, with a particular focus on phases S1–S3 of our model (see Figure 2.3).

Security metrics can be an invaluable resource for assessing the effectiveness of an organization's software security program. Meaningful metrics can be used to continually improve the product security program's performance, substantiate regulatory compliance, raise the level of security awareness among management and stakeholders, and assist decision makers with funding requests. Without metrics, organizations are reduced to operating their product security programs under FUD: fear, uncertainty, and doubt.

Meaningful security metrics allow an organization to determine the effectiveness of its security controls. In order to measure the security posture of an organization effectively, product security must first ensure that the proper framework is in place in order to derive meaningful metric data. This includes a product security governance model suited to the

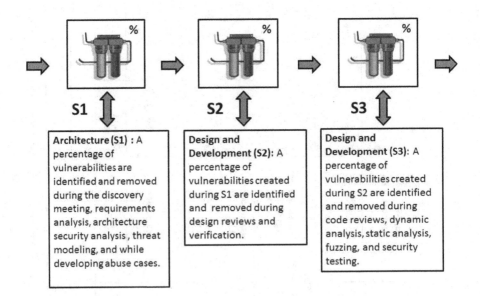

Figure 2.3   SDL phases S1–S3: defect identification and remediation filtering process.

entity's strategic and operational requirements. Such a model should support implementation of practical product security policies and procedures, consistent deployment of best practices and measures, and require strong executive management support across the organization. Best practices dictate a model under which security is managed as an enterprise issue—horizontally, vertically, and cross-functionally throughout the organization. This model is better suited to enable consistent monitoring, measurement, and reporting of an organization's product security posture.

For security to be measured effectively, it must be managed effectively. As companies struggle to protect valuable information assets and justify risk-based decision making, a centralized metrics reporting mechanism is crucial for producing meaningful metrics and providing an ongoing assessment of the state of product security within a software development organization.

Rather than include a separate chapter on metrics in this book, our approach will be to include metrics in each step of the SDL model presented. This will cumulate in a discussion of the use of SDL metrics in managing the overall corporate software security program.

2.9 Mapping the Security Development Lifecycle to the Software Development Lifecycle

Whatever form of SDL you use, whether it is one that already exists, one you developed yourself, or a combination of both, you must map it to your current SDLC to be effective. Figure 2.4 is a SDL activity and best practices model that the authors have developed and mapped to the typical SDLC phases. Each SDL activity and best practice is based on real-world experience and examples from the authors to showing the reader that security can be built into each of the SDLC phases—a mapping of security to the SDLC, if you will. If security is built into each SDLC phase, then the software has a higher probability of being secure by default, and later software changes are less likely to compromise overall security. Another benefit of this mapping is that you will have presumably worked with the owner(s) and stakeholders of the SDL, which will serve to build buy-in, efficiency, and achievable security in both the operational and business processes of the SDLC and will include the developers, product and program managers, business managers, and executives.

Subsequent chapters will describe each phase of the SDL in Figure 2.4 in detail and will be broken up as shown in Figures 2.5–2.10.

Security Assessment	A1	• Software security team is looped in early • Software security team hosts a discovery meeting • Software security team creates an SDL project plan (states what further work will be done) • Privacy Impact Assessment (PIA) plan initiated
Architecture	A2	• A2 Policy compliance analysis • SDL policy assessment & scoping • Threat modeling / architecture security analysis • Open source selection (if needed) • Privacy information gathering and analysis
Design & Development	A3	• A3 Policy compliance analysis • Security test plan composition • Static Analysis • Threat model updating • Design security analysis & review • Privacy implementation assessment
	A4	• A4 Policy compliance analysis • Security test case execution • Static analysis • Dynamic analysis • Fuzz testing • Manual code review • Privacy validation and remediation
Ship	A5	• A5 Policy compliance analysis • Final security review • Vulnerability scan • Penetration testing • Open source licensing review • Final privacy review
Post-Release Support	PRSA	• External vulnerability disclosure response • 3rd Party reviews • Post-release certifications • Internal review for new product combinations or cloud deployment • Security architectural reviews & tool-based assessments of current, legacy and M&A products and solutions

Typical SDLC Phases:

1	Concept
2	Planning
3	Design & Development
4	Readiness
5	Release & Launch
PRSA 1-5	Support & Sustain

Figure 2.4 Mapping the security development lifecycle to the software development lifecycle.

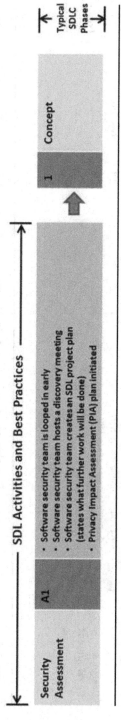

SDL Activities and Best Practices

Security Assessment	A1

A1
- Software security team is looped in early
- Software security team hosts a discovery meeting
- Software security team creates an SDL project plan (states what further work will be done)
- Privacy Impact Assessment (PIA) plan initiated

Typical SDLC Phases

1	Concept

Figure 2.5 Chapter 3: Security Assessment (A1): SDL activities and best practices.

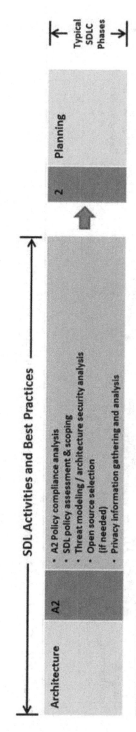

SDL Activities and Best Practices

Architecture	A2

A2
- Policy compliance analysis
- SDL policy assessment & scoping
- Threat modeling / architecture security analysis
- Open source selection (if needed)
- Privacy information gathering and analysis

Typical SDLC Phases

2	Planning

Figure 2.6 Chapter 4: Architecture (A2): SDL activities and best practices.

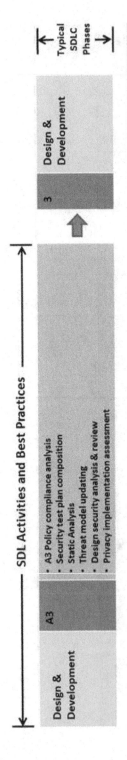

Figure 2.7 Chapter 5: Design and Development (A3): SDL activities and best practices.

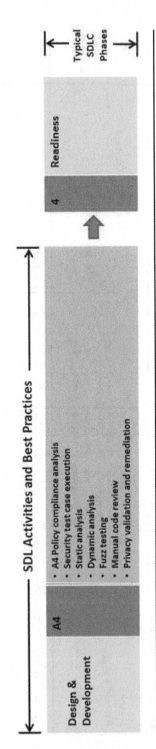

Figure 2.8 Chapter 6: Design and Development (A4): SDL activities and best practices.

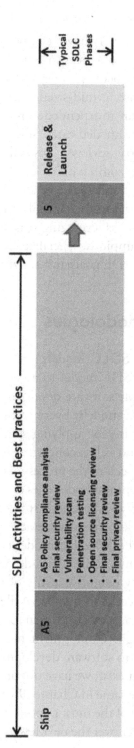

Figure 2.9 Chapter 7: Ship (A5): SDL activities and best practices.

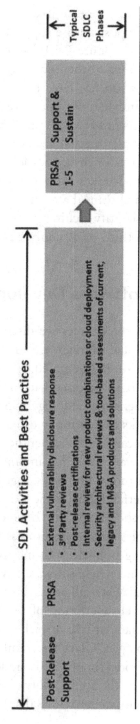

Figure 2.10 Chapter 8: Post-Release Support (PRSA1-5): SDL activities and best practices.

Please note that, unlike some of the SDLs you may have seen before, we include post-release support activities and best practices in our SDL, as shown in Figure 2.10. We have included this because most software security teams or their equivalent, especially those in mid-sized or small companies, do not have the luxury of having an independent Product Security Incident Response Team (PSIRT), a team dedicated solely to conduct security M&A assessments, third-party reviews, post-release certifications, internal reviews for new product combinations of cloud deployments, or review for legacy software that is still in use or about to be re-used. It takes some outside-the-box thinking to manage all of this with a small team. Later in the book we will discuss leveraging seasoned software security architects, software security champions, specialized software, and third-party contractors to accomplish SDL goals and activities.

2.10 Software Development Methodologies

Earlier in the chapter we discussed the various SDLC models and provided a visual overview of our mapping of our SDL model to a generic SDLC. It should be noted, however, that multiple software development methodologies are used within the various SDLC models. Every software development methodology approach acts as a basis for applying specific frameworks to develop and maintain software and is less concerned with the technical side but rather the organizational aspects of the process of creating software. Principal among these development methodologies are the Waterfall model and Agile together with its many variants and spin-offs. The Waterfall model is the oldest and most well known software development methodology. The distinctive feature of the Waterfall model is its sequential step-by-step process from requirements. Agile methodologies are gaining popularity in industry although they comprise a mix of traditional and newly software development practices. You may see Agile or traditional Waterfall or maybe a hybrid of the two. We have chosen to give a high-level description of the Waterfall and Agile development models and a variant or two of each as an introduction to software development methodologies. Given the number of models that exist, we have not only a generic model for our SDL model but will do the same in Chapter 9 when we describe the applicability of our SDL to a few of the most popular software development models that you may encounter over the next few years.

2.10.1 Waterfall Development

Waterfall development (see Figure 2.11) is another name for the more traditional approach to software development. This approach is typically higher-risk, more costly, and less efficient than the Agile approach that will be discussed later in this chapter. The Waterfall approach uses requirements that are already known, each stage is signed off before the next commences, and requires extensive documentation because this is the primary communication mechanism throughout the process. Although most development organizations are moving toward Agile methods of development, the Waterfall method may still be used when requirements are fully understood and not complex. Since the plan is not to revisit a phase using this methodology once it is completed, it is imperative that you do it right the first time: There is generally no second chance.

Although Waterfall development methodologies vary, they tend to be similar in that practitioners try to keep to the initial plan, do not have working software until very late in the cycle, assume they know everything upfront, minimize changes through a change control board (i.e., assume that change is bad and can be controlled), put most responsibility on the project manager (PM), optimize conformance to schedule and budget, generally use weak controls, and allow realization of value only upon completion. They are driven by a PM-centric approach under the belief that if the processes in the plan are followed, then everything

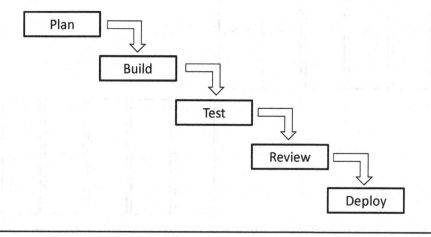

Figure 2.11   Waterfall software development methodology.

will work as planned. In today's development environment, most of the items listed in the previous sentence are considered negative attributes of the Waterfall methodology and are just a few of the reasons that industry is moving toward Agile development methodologies. The Waterfall approach may be looked on as an assembly-line approach which may be excellent when applied properly to hardware but which has shortcomings in comparison to Agile when it comes to software development.

2.10.1.1 Iterative Waterfall Development

The iterative Waterfall development model (see Figure 2.12) is an improvement on the standard Waterfall model. This approach carries less risk than a traditional Waterfall approach but is more risky and less efficient than the Agile approach. In the iterative Waterfall method, the overall project is divided into various phases, each executed using the traditional Waterfall method. Dividing larger projects into smaller identifiable phases results in a smaller scope of work for each phase, and the end deliverable of each phase can be reviewed and improved if necessary before moving to the next phase. Overall risk is thus reduced. Although the iterative method is an improvement over the traditional Waterfall method, you are more likely to face an Agile approach to software development

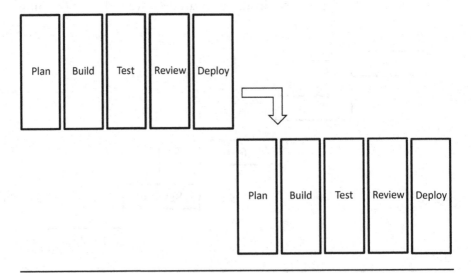

Figure 2.12   Iterative Waterfall software development methodology.

rather than either a standard or an iterative Waterfall methodology in today's environment.

2.10.2 Agile Development

The Agile approach is based on both iterative and incremental development methods. Requirements and solutions evolve through collaboration among self-organizing, cross-functional teams, and a solution resulting from every iteration is reviewed and refined regularly throughout the process. The Agile method is a time-boxed iterative approach that facilitates a rapid and flexible response to change, which in turn encourages evolutionary development and delivery while promoting adaptive planning, development, teamwork, collaboration, and process adaptability throughout the lifecycle of the project. Tasks are broken into small increments that require minimal planning. These iterations have short time frames called "time boxes" that can last from one to four weeks. Multiple iterations may be required to release a product or new features. A cross-functional team is responsible for all software development functions in each iteration, including planning, requirements analysis, design, coding, unit testing, and acceptance testing. An Agile project is typically cross-functional, and self-organizing teams operate independently from any corporate hierarchy or other corporate roles of individual team members, who themselves decide how to meet each iteration's requirements. This allows the project to adapt to changes quickly and minimizes overall risk. The goal is to have an available release at the end of the iteration, and a working product is demonstrated to stakeholders at the end of each iteration.

2.10.2.1 Scrum

Scrum (see Figure 2.13) is an iterative and incremental Agile software development method for managing software projects and product or application development. Scrum adopts an empirical approach, accepting that the problem cannot be fully understood or defined and focusing instead on maximizing the team's ability to deliver quickly and to respond to emerging requirements. This is accomplished through the use of co-located, self-organizing teams in which all disciplines can be

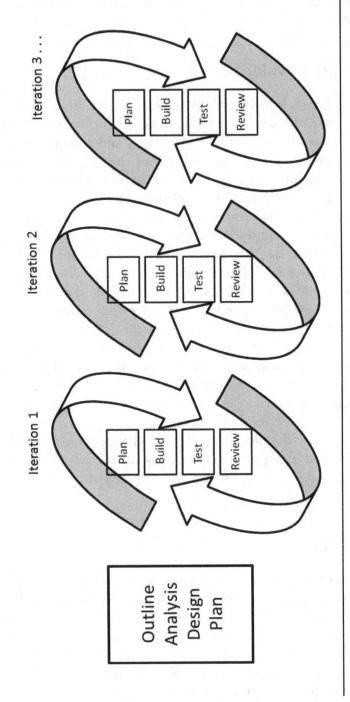

Figure 2.13 Scrum software development methodology.

represented. In contrast to traditional planned or predictive methodologies, this concept facilitates the ability to handle churn resulting from customers that change the requirements during project development. The basic unit of development for Scrum is called a "sprint," and a sprint can last from one week to one month. Each sprint is time-boxed so that finished portions of a product are completed on time. A prioritized list of requirements is derived from the product backlog, and if they are not completed during the sprint, they are left out and returned to the product backlog. The team demonstrates the software after each sprint is completed. Generally accepted value-added attributes of Scrum include its use of adaptive planning; that it requires feedback from working software early during the first sprint (typically two weeks) and often; that it stresses the maximization of good change such as focusing on maximizing learning throughout the project; that it puts most responsibility on small, dedicated tight-thinking adaptive teams that plan and re-plan their own work; that it has strong and frequent controls; optimizes business value, time to market, and quality; and supports realization of value earlier, potentially after every sprint.

2.10.2.2 Lean Development

In our experience, for those of you who have recently moved from or are in the process of moving from a Waterfall methodology for software development, Scrum is the most likely variant of Agile that you will encounter. Lean (see Figure 2.14) is another methodology that is gaining

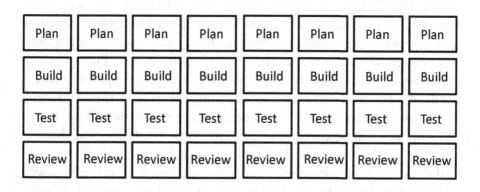

Figure 2.14   Lean software development methodology.

popularity and is thus worth mentioning. Unfortunately, there are many definitions of Lean, and it is a methodology that is evolving in many directions. Although Lean is similar to Scrum in that it focuses on features rather than groups of features, it takes this idea one step further in that, in its simplest form, you select, plan, develop, test, and deploy one feature before you select, plan, develop, test, and deploy the next feature. The objective is to further isolate risk to the level of an individual feature. This isolation has the advantage of focusing on eliminating "waste" when possible and doing nothing unless it is absolutely necessary or relevant. Lean development can be summarized by seven principles based on Lean manufacturing principle concepts: (1) eliminate waste, (3) amplify learning, (3) decide as late as possible, (4) deliver as fast as possible, (5) empower the team, (6) build integrity in, and (7) see the whole. One of the key elements of Lean development is to provide a model where you can see the whole, even when your developers are scattered across multiple locations and contractors. Although still considered related to Agile by many in the community, Lean software development has evolved into a related discipline rather than a specific subset of Agile.

2.3 Chapter Summary

In this chapter we described the importance and applicability of the SDL and its relation and inclusion into the SDLC. Throughout the discussion, we highlighted the models, methodologies, tools, human talent, and metrics for managing and overcoming the challenges to make software secure. Our SDL process encompasses a series of security-focused activities and best practices at each of the phases of our SDL. These activities and best practices include the development of threat models during software design, the use of static analysis code-scanning tools during implementation, and the conduct of code reviews, security testing, and metrics. Lastly, we discussed our model for mapping the SDL to the SDLC and the various popular software methodologies to which we will apply the elements and best practices of our SDL in Chapter 9. In the next chapter, we will start the process of walking through each step of our SDL model and show that incremental implementation of the elements the SDL will yield incremental improvements in an overall holistic approach to software security.

References

1. Microsoft Corporation (2012), Graphic for Microsoft SDL. Retrieved from http://www.microsoft.com/security/sdl/discover/default.aspx.
2. Addison-Wesley (2012), Software Security Series. Graphic for "Build Security in for Seven Touchpoints for Software Security." Retrieved from http://www.buildsecurityin.com/concepts/touchpoints.
3. OWASP (2012), OWASP: The Open Web Application Security Project—Security Code Review in the SDLC, Secure Code Review Process—Operational Process. Retrieved from https://www.owasp.org/index.php/Security_Code_Review_in_the_SDLC.
4. Cisco Systems (2012), Cisco Secure Development Lifecycle (CSDL) Graphics. Retrieved from http://www.cisco.com/web/about/security/cspo/csdl/index.html.
5. Microsoft Corporation (2012). Microsoft Security Development Lifecycle: The SDL Optimization Model Graphic. Retrieved from http://www.microsoft.com/security/sdl/learn/assess.aspx.
6. Microsoft Corporation (2012), "Microsoft SDL Optimization Model." Retrieved from http://www.microsoft.com/download/en/details.aspx?displaylang=en&id=2830.
7. Bsimm.com (2012), Building Security in Maturity Model.pdf. Graphic for the BSIMM Software Security Framework (SSF), p. 24. Retrieved from bsimm.com/download/dl.php.
8. OWASP (2012), "Software Assurance Maturity Model (SAMM)." Retrieved from https://www.owasp.org/index.php/Software_Assurance_Maturity_Model_(SAMM).
9. Businesswire.com (2012), "BSIMM4 Release Expands Software Security Measurement Tool and Describes New Activities." Retrieved from http://www.businesswire.com/news/home/20120918005298/en/BSIMM4-Release-Expands-Software-Security-Measurement-Tool.
10. Ibid.
11. OWASP (2012), "Software Assurance Maturity Model (SAMM)." Retrieved from https://www.owasp.org/index.php/Software_Assurance_Maturity_Model_(SAMM).
12. ISO (2013), "ISO/IEC 27034-1:201: Information Technology—Security Techniques—Application Security—Part 1: Overview and Concepts." Retrieved from http://www.iso.org/iso/catalogue_detail.htm?csnumber=44378.
13. Pickel, J. (May 2013), "ISO/IEC 27034—Why, What, and How." PowerPoint presentation at the 2013 Microsoft Software Development Conference, delivered on ebruary 25, 2013, San Francisco, CA.
14. Ashord, W. (May 13, 2013), "Microsoft Declares Conformance with ISO 27034." Computer Weekly.Com. Retrieved from http://www.computerweekly.com/news/2240184149/Microsoft-declares-conformance-with-ISO-27034-1.
15. SAFECode (2012), SAFECode "About Us" webpage. Retrieved from http://www.safecode.org/about_us.php.

16. SAFECode (2011), *Fundamental Practices for Secure Software Development, 2nd ed., A Guide to the Most Effective Secure Development Practices in Use Today,* February 8, 2011. Retrieved from www.safecode.org/publications/SAFECode_Dev_Practices0211.pdf.

17. U.S. Department of Homeland Security (2012), "Build Security In." Retrieved from https://buildsecurityin.us-cert.gov/bsi/home.html.

18. U.S. Department of Homeland Security (2012), "Background: Department of Homeland Security (DHS) National Cyber Security Division's (NCSD)." Retrieved from https://buildsecurityin.us-cert.gov/swa/cwe/background.html.

19. U.S. Department of Homeland Security (2012), "Software Assurance: Community Resources and Information Clearinghouse." Retrieved from https://buildsecurityin.us-cert.gov/swa/cwe.

20. U.S. National Institute of Standards and Technology (2012), "Introduction to SAMATE." Retrieved from http://samate.nist.gov/index.php/Introduction_to_SAMATE.html.

21. U.S. National Institute of Standards and Technology (2008), NIST Special Publication 800-64, Revision 2: *Security Considerations in the System Development Life Cycle,* October 2008. Retrieved from http://csrc.nist.gov/publications/nistpubs/800-64-Rev2/SP800-64-Revision2.pdf.

22. U.S. National Institute of Standards and Technology (2012), *National Vulnerability Database,* Version 2.2. Retrieved from http://nvd.nist.gov.

23. U.S. National Institute of Standards and Technology (2012), "NVD Common Vulnerability Scoring System Support v2." Retrieved from http://nvd.nist.gov/cvss.cfm?version=2.

24. MITRE Corporation (2012), Common Vulnerabilities and Exposures (CVE) homepage. Retrieved from http://cve.mitre.org.

25. MITRE Corporation (2012), "CVE Frequently Asked Questions." Retrieved from http://cve.mitre.org/about/faqs.html.

26. SANS Institute (2012), "Twenty Critical Security Controls for Effective Cyber Defense: Consensus Audit Guidelines." Retrieved from http://www.sans.org/critical-security-controls.

27. MITRE Corporation (2012), "CVE-Compatible Products and Services." Retrieved from http://cve.mitre.org/compatible/compatible.html.

28. MITRE Corporation (2012), "CVE Frequently Asked Questions." Retrieved from http://cve.mitre.org/about/faqs.html.

29. U.S. Department of Defense Cyber Security and Information Systems Information Analysis Center (CSIAC) (2012), CSIAC webpage. Retrieved from https://www.thecsiac.com/group/csiac.

30. Goertzel, K., et al., for Department of Homeland Security and Department of Defense Data and Analysis Center for Software (2008), *Enhancing the Development Life Cycle to Produce Secure Software: A Reference Guidebook on Software Assurance,* Version 2, October 2008. Retrieved from https://www.thedacs.com/techs/enhanced_life_cycles.

31. Goertzel, K., et al. (2008), *Software Security Assurance: State-of-the-Art Report*

(SOAR), July 31, 2008. Retrieved from http://iac.dtic.mil/iatac/download/security.pdf.

32. Cert.org (2013), Carnegie Mellon cert.org webpage. Retrieved from http://www.cert.org.

33. SecurityFocus (2013), Bugtraq website. Retrieved from http://www.securityfocus.com/archive/1.

34. SecurityFocus (2013), Security website. Retrieved from http://www.securityfocus.com.

35. National Institute of Standards and Technology (2013), National Vulnerability Database webpage. Retrieved from http://web.nvd.nist.gov/view/vuln/search.

36. Codenomicon (2012), Codenomicon website. Retrieved at http://www.codenomicon.com.

37. Peachfuzzer.com (2012), Peach Fuzzing Platform webpage. Retrieved from http://peachfuzzer.com/Tools.

38. Coverity (2012), Coverity Static Analysis webpage. Retrieved from http://www.coverity.com/products/static-analysis.html.

39. HP (2012), HP Fortify Static Code Analyzer webpage. Retrieved from http://www.hpenterprisesecurity.com/products/hp-fortify-software-security-center/hp-fortify-static-code-analyzer.

40. IBM (2012), IBM Security AppScan Source webpage. Retrieved from http://www-01.ibm.com/software/rational/products/appscan/source.

41. Klocwork (2012), Klocwork webpage. Retrieved from http://www.klocwork.com/?utm_source=PPC-Google&utm_medium=text&utm_campaign=Search-Klocwork&_kk=klocwork&gclid=CMy0_q6svbICFUjhQgodOGwAFg.

42. Parasoft (2012), Static Analysis webpage. Retrieved from http://www.parasoft.com/jsp/capabilities/static_analysis.jsp?itemId=547.

43. Veracode (2012), Veracode webpage. Retrieved from http://www.veracode.com.

44. Hewlett-Packard (2012), Webinspect webpage. Retrieved from http://www.hpenterprisesecurity.com/products/hp-fortify-software-security-center/hp-webinspect.

45. Hewlett-Packard (2012), QAinspect webpage. Retrieved from http://www.hpenterprisesecurity.com/products/hp-fortify-software-security-center/hp-qainspect.

46. IBM (2012), IBM Security AppScan Enterprise webpage. Retrieved from http://www-01.ibm.com/software/awdtools/appscan/enterprise.

47. Veracode (2012), Veracode webpage. Retrieved from http://www.veracode.com.

48. White Security (2012), "How the WhiteHat Sentinel Services Fit in Software Development Lifecycle." Retrieved from (SDLC)https://www.whitehatsec.com/sentinel_services/SDLC.html.

49. Denning, P. J. (December 1976), "Fault Tolerant Operating Systems." *ACM Computing Surveys,* vol. 8, no. 4, pp. 359–389. DOI:10.1145/356678.356680.

50. Saltzer, J., and Schroeder, M. (September 1975), "The Protection of Information in Computer Systems." *Proceedings of the IEEE,* vol. 63, no. 9, pp. 1278–1308. DOI:10.1109/PROC.1975.9939.

51. Microsoft Corporation (2012), "Elevation of Privilege (EOP) Card Game." Retrieved from http://www.microsoft.com/security/sdl/adopt/eop.aspx.
52. Microsoft Corporation (2012), *Microsoft Security Development Lifecycle (SDL), Version 3.2*. Retrieved from http://www.microsoft.com/en-us/download/details.aspx?id=24308.
53. Quotationsbook.com (2012), Lord Kelvin quote. Retrieved from http://quotationsbook.com/quote/46180.
54. U.S. Department of Homeland Security (2012), "Build Security In." *Secure Software Development Life Cycle Processes* online doc. Retrieved from https://buildsecurityin.us-cert.gov/bsi/articles/knowledge/sdlc/326-BSI.html.
55. Ibid.

Chapter 3

Security Assessment (A1): SDL Activities and Best Practices

In this chapter, we will introduce the reader to the first phase of our security development lifecycle. This phase (A1) is called Security Assessment. We will describe different activities within this phase, why it is important, and then walk the reader through key success factors, deliverables, and metrics from this phase.

Security Assessment (A1) is the first phase of our SDL (see Figure 3.1). This is the phase where the project team identifies the product risk profile and the needed SDL activities; in some SDLs it is called the discovery phase. An initial project outline for security milestones and controls is developed and integrated into the development project schedule to allow proper planning as changes occur. Throughout this phase, four principal questions should be addressed to determine what is required to ensure the security of the software:

1. How critical is the software to meeting the customers' mission?
2. What security objectives are required by the software [e.g., confidentiality, integrity, and availability (CIA), as described in Chapter 1]?

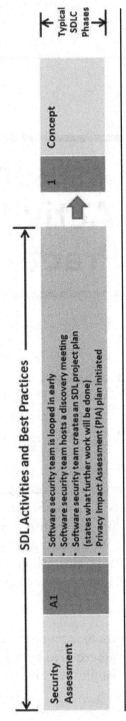

Figure 3.1 Security Assessment (A1): SDL activities and best practices.

3. What regulations and policies are applicable in determining what is to be protected?
4. What threats are possible in the environment where the software will be operating?

During the initial kick-off meeting, all key stakeholders should discuss, identify, and have a common understanding of the security privacy implications, considerations, and requirements. The initial set of key security milestones, including time frames or development triggers that signal a security step is approaching, are also outlined in these discussions to enable the developers to plan security requirements and associated constraints into the project. It also reminds project leaders that many decisions being made have security implications that should be weighed appropriately as the project continues. These discussions should also include the identification of all sources of security requirements, including relevant laws, regulations, and standards.

Privacy, often neglected as part of the SDL in the past, is assessed at this phase as well. The Privacy Impact Assessment (PIA) process evaluates issues and privacy impact rating related to the privacy of personally identifiable information in the software and will be initiated during this stage of the development process.

3.1 Software Security Team Is Looped in Early

SDLCs typically have formalized kick-off meetings, and it is important that the software security team is included, to ensure that security is a key element of the SDLC and is built into the process. An in-person or live web conference meeting will give attendees and stakeholders an important opportunity to gauge understanding and awareness. Bringing the security team into the development process early is the most cost-effective way to enable risk identification, planning, and mitigation. Early identification and mitigation of security vulnerabilities and misconfigurations will result in lower cost of security control implementation and vulnerability mitigation; provide awareness of potential engineering challenges caused by mandatory security controls; and identification of shared security services and reuse of security strategies and tools to reduce development cost while improving security posture through proven methods and techniques. The early involvement of the security team will enable the developers to plan security requirements and associated constraints into the project. It also reminds project leaders that many decisions being made have security implications that should be weighed appropriately, as the project continues. Early planning and awareness will result in cost and time saving through proper risk management planning. Security discussions should be performed as part of, not separate from, the development project to ensure solid understandings among project personnel of business decisions and their risk implications to the overall development project.[1]

3.2 Software Security Hosts a Discovery Meeting

The discovery meeting is essentially a SDL kick-off meeting where the key SDLC stakeholders get on the same page at the beginning of the process so that security is built in rather than bolted on post-release. Security planning in the discovery meeting should include preparations for the entire system life cycle, including the identification of key security milestones and deliverables, and tools and technologies. Special consideration should be given to items that may need to be procured, such as software security testing and assessment tools, and the potential use of third-party software security architects or engineers if staff augmentation is needed or the customer requires third-party attestation. Other resource impacts such as active testing, accreditation, and required training must be considered as well. A series of milestones or security meetings should be planned to discuss each of the security considerations throughout the system development. The outcomes of the discovery meeting are typically in terms of decisions that are made for future activities, which are followed later in the SDL by actual security or privacy activities. A project schedule should integrate security activities to ensure proper planning of any future decisions associated with schedules and resources. All meeting participants and stakeholders should walk away from this meeting with common understanding of the security implications, considerations, and requirements for the software.

The following four questions should be addressed in this phase to determine the security controls that will be required for the software being developed:

1. How critical is the system to meeting the organization's mission?
2. What are the security objectives required by the software in terms of confidentiality, integrity, and availability (CIA)?
3. What regulations and policies are applicable in determining what is to be protected?
4. What threats are possible in the environment where the system will be operating?

Key tasks during the discovery meeting include the following:

- Develop an initial project outline for security milestones, which will be integrated into the development project schedule and will allow proper planning as changes occur.
- Identify the sources for the security requirements, such as relevant laws, regulations, standards, and customer requirements.
- Identify any required certification and/or accreditation requirements and the resources required for them.
- Identify any third-party or open-source software that will be required.
- Identify the common security controls that will be used for the software being developed, including those that will be needed if the software is to be used in a SaaS/cloud environment or as part of a larger solution using multiple software products.
- Identify and define the required security reporting metrics in both tactical and strategic (business) terms.
- Develop an initial framework of key security milestones, including time frames or development triggers that will signal a security step is approaching.
- Define the security responsibilities of the core software security team, the software security champions, developers, privacy team, and any other stakeholders required to support security during the SDL/SDLC process.
- Identify and document the software security design, architecture, and security coding practices to be used.
- Identify the security testing and assessment techniques that will be used.
- Lay out a pre-privacy impact assessment process, including determination of information categorization and identification of known

special handling requirements to transmit, store, or create information such as personally identifiable information, and preliminary identification of any privacy requirements.

- When possible, project artifacts such as meeting minutes, briefings, and role identifications should be standardized and provided to developers for proper level-of-effort planning. This should be an ongoing process throughout the SDL.

3.3 Software Security Team Creates an SDL Project Plan

This can actually be considered initial project planning because the formal plan will be finalized as an outcome of the design phase, which will be covered in the next chapter. At this stage, the SDL project plan should outline security milestones based on the information gained during the discovery phase in 3.1 and integrate them into the overall SDLC schedule to allow proper planning as changes occur. As in the discovery phase, activities may be more in terms of decisions translated into milestones that will be followed by security activities. This project plan integrates the common understanding of security expectations identified in the discovery phase reflecting the initial schedule of security and privacy activities or decisions.

3.4 Privacy Impact Assessment (PIA) Plan Initiated

There are a number of methods for privacy protection and management. In the past, however, privacy tools have generally been applied in an ad-hoc way, or in a piecemeal fashion to address immediate issues; as with security, these issues are typically addressed post-release. Just as with security, treating privacy as a secondary consideration or as an issue for future exploration during system design does not provide an effective level of privacy protection. Addressing components of privacy issues and not through a holistic design and implementation leads to further potential privacy issues. Privacy must be a fundamental design consideration that is integrated into every phase of SDLC.

There are a growing number of privacy regulatory requirements on a variety of levels—state, federal, and international—resulting in a patchwork of compliance requirements that have serious penalties for non-compliance. Rather than devote an entire chapter to recent and upcoming privacy requirements and the potential ramifications of each, we will discuss the best practices needed to adequately cover a majority of what you will face in terms of privacy, regulatory, and policy compliance. Software programs are designed to integrate with the user's computer, and therefore may be able to access and store personal information. Software developers must adhere to the guidelines and privacy policies that relate to the operating systems and platforms for which their software is designed. The bottom line is that when customers entrust your company with sensitive information, every employee is obligated to protect that information. As with security, privacy violations have significant implications for the trust customers have in you, which in turn will affect your company's reputation and the jpotential revenue from the software you develop.

Before you can begin developing a Privacy Impact Assessment (PIA), you will need to evaluate what regulatory legislation or policies are applicable to the software you are developing. In some models, this is called the data sensitivity assessment. Since most developers do not have a background in law, and regulators generally do not have a background in software development, understanding the issues surrounding regulatory compliance can be difficult and frustrating. It is often very difficult for developers to understand fully the language and requirements described by legislation, and it is often not easy to pin down explicit software requirements. To successfully translate regulations into requirements, it will be necessary to engage with your corporate legal counsel and any external legal privacy experts who may be on retainer. If you happen to have a chief privacy officer (CPO), this person can be an ideal partner who can offer you the resources and training you will need to meet the challenge of building privacy into the SDL and ultimately the SDLC.

Microsoft's *Privacy Guidelines for Developing Software Products and Services*[2] and NIST Special Publication 800-64 Revision 2: *Security Considerations in the System Development Life Cycle*[3] are among the most popular references for developing a PIA in your SDL—You can use either in its entirety or as a template to develop your own. No matter what methodology you use, the following should be included in your PIA:

- **Summary of the Legislation:** Explains the act from a developer's point of view, telling you what you need to know in order to understand its implications on your application development.

- **Required Process Steps:** Explains in more depth which requirements are relevant to software developers. Generally speaking, this section describes what types of data are considered sensitive and how they need to be protected.
- **Technologies and Techniques:** Explains strategies and techniques for meeting the legislative requirements. These are separated into five main categories: Confidentiality, Integrity, Availability, Auditing and Logging, and Authentication.
- **Additional Resources:** Provides links where you can gather more information on the legislation in question.[4]

The primary task of the PIA process is the determination of need in the system along with an initial definition of the problem to be a solved. The PIA created at this phase is only a preliminary version for initial system specifications and requirements, and is designed to guide developers in assessing privacy through the early stages of development. For simplicity, we have included only the privacy design principles requirements analysis and part of the initial PIA analysis. At its core, this stage of the PIA is the planning, documentation, and assessment of preliminary requirements for personally identifiable information (PII) and personal information used by the software and includes or accesses the following:

- **Education of stakeholders.** All stakeholders should be educated on the "four C's" of privacy design (comprehension, consciousness, control, and consent) at the Security Assessment (A1) discovery and kick-off meeting. The architects and developers should be asking whether they need to collect the data, have a valid business need to do so, and whether the customer will support the software's business purpose for collecting their PII.
- **Additional software interaction.** External system processes, other systems interacting with the new software and their use of PII, personal information, and system users.
- **Collection of PII.** The purposes and requirements for the collection of PII.
- **PII storage retention.** Proposed personal information retention periods and reasons for the lengths of those periods.
- **Access.** Determine what entities will have access to the PII and personal information and the preliminary design for separation of duty/tasks/roles/data in the software.

- **Privacy management tools.** Identification of privacy management tools and system processes that may be needed to manage personal information in the software and the solution it may be part of. This is particularly important if the software is going to be a component of an SaaS- or cloud-based solution.
- **Security safeguards.** The setting of requirements for security safeguards that will be used to protect PII and personal information.
- **Integrity of the data.** Determine that PII and personal information is kept up to date and accurate.
- **Assess whether there are any conflicts between security and privacy requirements.** If so, they need to be addressed and resolved at this stage of the development process. This step includes the categorization of the level of privacy and security protection that the software will require.
- **Apply the principle of least privilege.** Essentially, this entails limiting access to "need to know."Access to user data should be limited to those who have a legitimate business purpose for accessing the data. In addition, nonusers such as administrators or database managers should only be given access to the smallest amount of user data needed to achieve the specific business purpose. This must include third parties that have access to the data or to which it is transferred: They should only be given the specific data they need to fulfill their business purpose. Data protection provisions, including retention and destruction requirements, are typically required of third parties through contract agreements.
- **Websites and Web services.** All externally facing websites must have a link to a privacy statement on every page. This includes pop-ups that collect PII. Whenever possible, the same privacy statement should be used for all sites within a domain.
- **The use of cookies.** PII and identifiers that facilitate tracking may be stored in cookies as small files which are stored on a user's computer. They are designed to hold a modest amount of data specific to a particular client and website, and can be accessed either by the Web server or the client computer. Privacy guidelines for cookie usage apply to locally stored text files that allow a server-side connection to store and retrieve information, including HTTP cookies (e.g., Web cookies) and Flash cookies (e.g., Flash Shared Objects). Persistent cookies must not be used where a session cookie would satisfy the purpose. Persistent cookies should expire within the

shortest timeframe that achieves the business purpose. PII stored in a persistent cookie must be encrypted.

- **IP addresses.** The customer's IP address is always sent with the data as part of the communication protocol when it is transferred over the network. As of the date of this writing, there is still a lot of debate and discussion as to whether or not an IP address is PII. The fact that privacy regulators are even discussing this is a warning sign that we may need to consider the possibility that this information will fall into the category of PII in the foreseeable future. Storing an IP address with PII should be avoided if anonymity is required in order to avoid correlation between the two. If possible, the IP address should be stripped from the payload to reduce its sensitivity by limiting the number of digits. The IP address can also be discarded after translating it to a less precise location.

- **Customer privacy notification.** Software that collects user data and transfers it must provide and give notice to the customer. These are also called disclosure notices and must inform users of the type of information that software will collect and how it will be used. Depending on the type of software, an opt-out clause may be required to allow users the ability to withhold certain types of personal information if they so choose. The type of notice and consent required depends on the type of user data being collected and how it will be used. Customers must also be presented with a choice of whether they want to share this information or not. All notices must be written in clear, easy-to-read language. There are two types of notification, prominent and discoverable. A "Prominent Notice" is one that is designed to catch the customer's attention and invites customers to inspect the current privacy settings, learn more about their options, and make choices. A "Discoverable Notice" is one the customer has to find. This can be done by selecting a privacy statement link from a Help menu in a software product or by locating and reading a privacy statement on a website. This notification typically includes the type of data that will be stored, how it will be used, with whom it will be shared, how it is protected, available user controls including the update process if the PII is stored and reusable, and company contact information. If you are developing a product to be used by another company or as an original equipment manufacturer (OEM), the customer company typically has specific privacy statements that third-party software developers are required to include. Other companies may require that software that is designed to work with their products contain a privacy statement that informs users that their information will not be sold to other companies or displayed publicly. Software developers must inform users of the software's method of safeguarding users' personal information in the privacy policy and notification. As we will discuss later in the book, this can be done via a valid SSL certificate, or using other security and encryption methods. As with other privacy-related areas, regulatory and other requirements are dynamic, and you should consult your privacy expert or legal counsel for the latest guidance for your software.

- **Children's privacy.** Care must be taken to consider children's privacy, since they may lack the discretion to differentiate when disclosing their PII that doing so may put them at risk. This has become particularly important with the advent of collaboration and sharing features found in social software. Parental controls are typically added to products, websites, and Web services to help protect the privacy of children. Special efforts must be made to ensure that parents retain control over whether their children can reveal PII. There are numerous privacy requirements for those offering websites and Web Services that target children and/or collect the age of their customers. There are numerous existing and forthcoming state, local, and international requirements for this area. Make sure you consult your privacy expert and/or corporate counsel (or equivalent) if you have software that will fall into this area.

- **Third parties.** Two types of third parties must be considered when assessing your privacy requirements. One type of third party is authorized to act on the company's behalf and uses data in accordance with the company's privacy practices. An independent third party follows its own privacy practices and uses customer information for its own purposes, which require a contract specifying data protection requirements. This requires a software provision for the customer to provide opt-in consent. The customer must provide opt-in consent before PII is shared with an independent third party. Only a Discoverable Notice is required if PII is transferred via a third party authorized to act on the company's behalf.

- **User controls.** User controls give users the ability to manage and control the privacy of their data and change their settings. These controls should be intuitive and easy to find. The data may reside on a computer, within a Web service, or on a mobile device. A webpage is used as the privacy site for Web services. Privacy controls for mobile devices can be on the device itself or via a computer-based user interface or a website that links to the device.

- **Privacy controls required for software used on shared computers.** It is common for software used in home or small office/home office (SOHO) environments to be shared by multiple users. Software designed for use in these environments that also collects or stores PII must provide controls over which users have access to the data. These controls may include strict computer/file/document access control and file permissions or encryption. Controls must also be a default setting and not opt-in. Shared folders must be clearly marked or highlighted.
- **Collaboration, sharing, and social software privacy features.** This is an area with very complex challenges in that content can be shared among a community, and in some cases, linked community members and shared friends or contacts. Software that supports these types of applications should provide controls and notifications to help prevent inadvertent sharing of PII with unintended audiences.
- **Security.** Security, of course, is the topic of this book, and a critical element of both privacy and quality. The security requirements will depend on the type of user data collected and whether it will be stored locally, transferred, and/or stored remotely. The end goal for security controls and measures is to protect PII from loss, misuse, unauthorized access, disclosure, alteration, and destruction. The controls and measures include not only software controls such as access controls and encryption in transfer and storage but also physical security, disaster recovery, and auditing. Compensating controls may be needed when standard protection is not possible due to business needs, such as the use of PII as a unique identifier or an IP address or e-mail address used for routing.
- **Privacy Impact Ratings.** The Privacy Impact Rating (P1, P2, or P3) is a practice used in the Microsoft SDL. It measures the sensitivity of the data your software will process from a privacy point of view. Early awareness of all the required steps for deploying a project with

high privacy risk may help you decide whether the costs are worth the business value gained. General definitions of privacy impact are as follows:

- o **P1 High Privacy Risk.** The feature, product, or service stores or transfers PII or error reports, monitors the user with an ongoing transfer of anonymous data, changes settings or file type associations, or installs software.
- o **P2 Moderate Privacy Risk.** The sole behavior that affects privacy in the feature, product, or service is a one-time, user-initiated; anonymous data transfer (for example, the user clicks a link and goes out to a website).
- o **P3 Low Privacy Risk.** No behaviors exist within the feature, product, or service that affect privacy. No anonymous or personal data is transferred, no PII is stored on the machine, no settings are changed on the user's behalf, and no software is installed.[5]

The risk assessment questionnaire and risk ranking system developed by Microsoft can be a great tool in assessing the risk and prioritizing the work to remediate those risks in the SDL.

In summary, the purpose of the PIA is to provide details on where and to what degree privacy information is collected, stored, or created within the software that you are developing. The PIA should continue to be reviewed and updated as major decisions occur or the proposed use of the software and scope change significantly.

3.5 Security Assessment (A1) Key Success Factors and Metrics

3.5.1 Key Success Factors

Setting success criteria for any SDL phase will make it more effective and will help in performing post-mortem afterwards to understand what worked and what didn't. Table 3.1 outlines success criteria suggested by the authors. However, each environment is different, and security teams are in the best position to understand success criteria within their own environment.

Table 3.1 Key Success Factors

Key Success Factor	Description
1. Accuracy of planned SDL activities	All SDL activities are accurately identified.
2. Product risk profile	Management understands the true cost of developing the product.
3. Accuracy of threat profile	Mitigating steps and countermeasures are in place for the product to be successful in its environment.
4. Coverage of relevant regulations, certifications, and compliance frameworks	All applicable legal and compliance aspects are covered.
5. Coverage of security objectives needed for software	"Must have" security objectives are met.

Success Factor 1: Accuracy of Planned SDL Activities

The Security Assessment (A1) phase is the first phase of our SDL and therefore is mostly discovery in nature. It sets the tone and direction of future SDL activities. It is during this phase that a rough outline of needed SDL activities is decided, as well as what emphasis should be placed on each SDL activity (code review, threat modeling, etc.). Though one can always course correct identified SDL activities and their importance later, a key measure of success of this phase is how many revisions are made to initial requirements and the direction of the SDL. Though this is not measurable at the start, once the SDL cycle is complete, one should go back to the initial planning documents to identify deviations from it and reasons those variances happened. This should help in estimating future SDL activities more accurately.

Success Factor 2: Product Risk Profile

Another key success factor is a product risk profile. Based on software, its importance to customers (its use in their environment), data processed through the software, and relevant regulations and target market/countries, a basic product risk profile can be prepared. The profile should include risk arising out of customer expectations and use of the product, regulatory compliance, as well as security changes needed to cater to different markets. This will also help articulate real cost to management.

Success Factor 3: Accuracy of Threat Profile

Too many times, software is developed without a complete understanding of its intended use or the environment in which it will operate. Though a product may be designed for certain uses, customers often add their own enhancements and then use it in ways that were not thought through before. Another example is APIs exposed to the public. In most cases, APIs exposed increase over a period of time (often after software is released). However, the threat profile from exposure of these APIs is not always considered or done correctly. In other cases, software depends on open-source (or closed-source) software that was not considered in defining the threat profile for the product.

Thus, one of the critical success factors to take away from this phase is the accuracy of the threat profile. The profile should cover not only perceived use cases but also research on customer integrations and security exposure through dependency on other products or software.

Success Factor 4: Coverage of Relevant Regulations, Certifications, and Compliance Frameworks

One key criterion for success of this phase is whether all key regulations, compliance frameworks, and certifications for the product (or libraries) have been identified. This success factor depends on understanding product objectives and customer uses. One can easily make the mistake of thinking that certain regulations will not be applicable because their use cases are not considered valid. Customers, however, often have a different take on this. A cloud product that a customer uses to interact with other customers might not need to be compliant with HIPAA from one viewpoint. However, for a customer, it is crucial that this product, if not compliant with HIPAA, at least does not create issues that may result in noncompliance.

Compliance frameworks are another thing to watch out for. Depending on how the product is used (in-house or in the cloud), different permutations are expected by customers. If customers are going for an ISO 27001 certification and are using your product in a cloud environment, they will expect a demonstrable and verifiable operational and product security posture. If customers are paying for your service using credit cards, not only they but your environment may fall under the regulations of payment card industry standards. Though we are focusing on product security here, operational security is equally important.

Finally, many times, while covering regulations, compliance frameworks, and certifications, security and development teams fail to look closely at dependencies. For example, if the product needs to comply with the Federal Information Processing Standards (FIPS), how will using an open-source library affect compliance? If the product needs to obtain Certification A, will dependent software make or break this certification? These questions need to be carefully considered to prevent future fire fighting.

Success Factor 5: Coverage of Security Objectives Needed for Software

Finally, one should look at how many of the security objectives were actually met at the conclusion of this phase. If some objectives were not met, why not? One may start out with a laundry list of security objectives, but they often compete with other product features and product management may shoot them down. An example might be logging. If one of the key security objectives is to detect and respond to threats as they happen, one thing that can aid in doing this is logging. However, the feasibility of logging (and logging securely) may compete with other requirements (operational efficiency, other product features). One could insist on logging events securely by encrypting them and transporting them safely to a central repository. However, depending on resources and other competing demands, such logging might not make it to the final list.

Before closing out this phase, it is a good idea to see whether any security objectives were not met in their entirety; if not, were these really important to have, or were they just "nice to have." This knowledge should help future product SDL cycles. Having too many "nice to haves" may actually undermine the credibility of the security team.

3.5.2 Deliverables

In each of our SDL phases, we will outline a key set of deliverables for that phase. The idea is to make sure that all required activities have a tangible documented outcome. Often we see only verbal or nonofficial documents created and kept by a project management team. In our opinion, formal documentation should be created and kept in a central repository with appropriate sign-offs and versioning.

Table 3.2 Deliverables for Phase A1

Deliverable	Goal
Product risk profile	Estimate actual cost of the product.
SDL project outline	Map SDL to development schedule.
Applicable laws and regulations	Obtain formal sign-off from stakeholders on applicable laws.
Threat profile	Guide SDL activities to mitigate threats.
Certification requirements	List requirements for product and operations certifications.
List of third-party software	Identify dependence on third-party software.
Metrics template	Establish cadence for regular reporting to executives.

Key deliverables for Phase A1 are listed in Table 3.2 and discussed below.

- **Product risk profile.** The product risk profile helps management see the actual cost of the product from different perspective, including selling it in different markets and liabilities that might be incurred if it is a SaaS/cloud product.
- **SDL project outline (for security milestones and mapping to development schedule).** An essential outcome of this phase is an SDL project outline or plan. The SDL plan should include security milestones that will be met during each phase, mapped to the development plan/schedule. Reporting should be set up to keep track of progress on the project.
- **Applicable laws and regulations.** This deliverable is a comprehensive review of laws and regulations that may be applicable to the product. The legal department should be heavily involved in preparing this documentation and, for laws/regulations that are not applicable, clearly articulate our understanding as to why those were not applicable.
- **Threat profile.** This deliverable articulates our assumptions about the environment in which the product will operate and potential threats in that environment. This will be helpful in later stages to focus our SDL activities to ensure the product is as secure as possible under the threat profile developed by the team. It will also be

useful for post-mortem in case we missed a threat/scenario in the SDL phases.

- **Certification requirements.** This deliverable should articulate clearly certifications needed for the product (e.g., FIPS) and resulting requirements. In the case of SaaS/cloud software, it should identify operational controls that will be needed for the software to be certified by various frameworks.
- **List of third-party software.** Purpose of this list is to identify all third-party components to be used with our software and thereby incorporate them in our threat profile. It should also help us to finalize the list of changes/requirements required for certifications.
- **Metrics template.** This deliverable is a template on metrics that we plan to report to management on a periodic basis.

3.5.3 Metrics

In the SDL model we propose, we outline, in each and every phase, metrics that should be measured. First, however, we would like to point out a few things we have learned in our professional careers.

We should decide what to measure upfront and stick to those decisions as much as possible. While we understand we may have to modify metrics as we go along, we should resist the temptation to overhaul metrics every now and then. The metrics template should be put together with its audience in mind. However, there is a tendency among executives to ask for a slightly different set of metrics as the project moves along. We should try to educate and make executives aware of why the metrics were chosen and their importance. Often that should take care of conflicting suggestions on metrics. In a nutshell, identify a set of metrics that is appropriate for your audience and stick to it. In the long term, metrics will provide you guidance on your overall progress so whatever set of metrics you choose, it will serve you well.

Here are our suggestions for metrics for this phase:

- Time in weeks when software security team was looped in
- Percent of stakeholders participating in SDL
- Percent of SDL activities mapped to development activities
- Percent of security objectives met

3.6 Chapter Summary

We have described the importance and best practices for addressing security and privacy at the very beginning of the SDL/SDLC process. By now, it should be clear that security and privacy are fundamental aspects of quality required to have a secure software development process and that the optimal time to define the requirements for these two areas is during the initial planning stage described in this chapter. Defining and establishing these requirements allows the team to identify key milestones and deliverables for integration of security and privacy into the software in a manner that will minimize disruption to plans and schedules. Identification of the key stakeholders and security roles for the SDL/SDLC, assessment and specification of minimum security and privacy requirements for the software to run in its planned operational environment, the overall SDL plan, and an agreed-upon security vulnerability identification/remediation work item tracking system are the key elements of the Security Assessment (A1) phase described in this chapter. It should be clear that both security and privacy risk assessments are mandatory components of a SDL. These are key elements in defining functional aspects of the software that will require a deeper review later in the development process.

Toward the end of the chapter we discussed key success factors and their importance, deliverables from this phase, as well as metrics that should be collected from this phase.

The best practices discussed in this chapter will serve as the groundwork and baseline for the future phases of our SDL model. The next phase, Architecture (A2), will be discussed next, in Chapter 4.

References

1. Kissel, R., et al. (2008), U.S. Department of Commerce, NIST Special Publication 800-64 Revision 2: *Security Considerations in the System Development Life Cycle.* Retrieved from http://csrc.nist.gov/publications/nistpubs/800-64-Rev2/SP800-64-Revision2.pdf.
2. Microsoft Corporation (2008), *Privacy Guidelines for Developing Software Products and Services, Version 3.1.* Retrieved from www.microsoft.com/en-us/download/details.aspx?id=16048.
3. Kissel, R., et al. (2008), U.S. Department of Commerce, NIST Special Publication 800-64 Revision 2: *Security Considerations in the System Development Life Cycle.*

Retrieved from http://csrc.nist.gov/publications/nistpubs/800-64-Rev2/SP800-64-Revision2.pdf.

4. Security Innovation, Inc. (2006), *Regulatory Compliance Demystified: An Introduction to Compliance for Developers.* Retrieved from http://msdn.microsoft.com/en-us/library/aa480484.aspx.

5. Microsoft Corporation (2012), "Appendix C: SDL Privacy Questionnaire." Retrieved from http://msdn.microsoft.com/en-us/library/windows/desktop/cc307393.aspx.

Chapter 4

Architecture (A2): SDL Activities and Best Practices

During the second phase of the security development lifecycle, security considerations are brought into the software development lifecycle to ensure that all threats, requirements, and potential constraints on functionality and integration are considered (see Figure 4.1). At this stage of the SDL, security is looked at more in terms of business risks, with inputs from the software security group and discussions with key stakeholders in the SDLC. Business requirements are defined in the security terms of confidentiality, integrity, and availability, and needed privacy controls are discussed for creation, transmission, and personally identifiable information (PII). SDL policy and other security or privacy compliance requirements are also identified at this stage of the SDL. This ensures that security and privacy discussions are performed as part of, rather than separate from, the SDLC, so that there are solid understandings among project personnel about business decisions and their risk implications for the overall development project. A cost analysis for development and support costs required for security and privacy consistent with business needs is also done as part of the requirements analysis. As discussed previously,

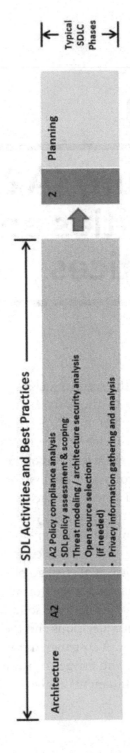

Figure 4.1 Architecture (A2): SDL activities and best practices.

the planning and awareness of security, privacy, and risk management early in the SDLC through the proper used of an SDL will result in significant cost and time savings.

Perhaps the most important, complex, and difficult part of the SDL starts during this phase of the SDL. As discussed previously, threat modeling and architectural security analysis typically fall into the domain of the senior software security architects and requires the most experience and expertise of any of the tasks within the SDL. Fortunately, tools are currently available and in the process of being developed that can assist this phase, and help leverage and scale a skill set that is typically a limited resource in a software security group.

Additional security training that may be needed for key developers to understand the current threats and potential exploitations of their products, as well as training for secure design and coding techniques specific to the software being developed and for the systems with which the software will be interacting, are identified at this stage of the SDL. This enables the developers to work more efficiently with the software security architects and others from the software security group to create more secure designs and empower them to address key issues early in the development processes.

4.1 A2 Policy Compliance Analysis

The purpose of a software security policy is to define what needs to be protected and how it will be protected, including reviewing and incorporating policies from outside the SDL that may impact the development process. These might include policies governing software or applications developed or applied anywhere in the organization.During this phase, any policy that exists outside the domain of the SDL policy is reviewed. Corporate security and privacy policies will likely instruct designers and developers on what the security and privacy features need to be and how they must be implemented. Other policies may include those that govern the use of third-party and open-source software or the protections and control of source code and other intellectual property within and outside the organization. Assuming the software security group is separate from the centralized information security group, it is important that both groups collaborate on all policies and guidelines related to the development and post-release security support and response of software from that organization. It is also important to collaborate with the privacy function of the company, whether it is a centralized group or outside legal counsel.

4.2 SDL Policy Assessment and Scoping

The SDL also provides an invaluable guide for software developers setting a security standard for their organization and should offer a roadmap for implementation without disrupting the core business of producing quality software applications. Unless the senior leadership of the development organization and the management team support this model, the SDL will likely fail. It must be driven by a policy that is signed off, promulgated, and provides support by the software development management team and ideally by the CEO. An organization should have a documented and repeatable SDL policy and guideline that supports the SDLC including its business needs and as a complement to the engineering and development culture that it supports. The culture and maturity of the organization is very important to consider in the development of the SDL policy, so that you ensure it will be both feasible and practical to implement. The management style, complexity of people, process, and technology needs, including the overall architecture of the product, will help determine how granular or objective in focus the guidelines will be. The amount of outsourced development, if any, will need to be assessed as part of this process as well. An internal development team will require more detailed procedures, while an outsourced function will require more contractual objects, service levels, and detailed deliverables. The vulnerabilities and risk of using outsourced development resources will be covered later in the book.

4.3 Threat Modeling/Architecture Security Analysis

4.3.1 Threat Modeling

As discussed previously, threat modeling requires a special set of skills, experience, and mindset: The people on the team who do this must be able to think like an adversary. A senior software security architect or one of the more seasoned software security champions typically runs this aspect. The developers and team members who are pulled into this process must know not only how to develop or build software, but also how to deconstruct or take apart the software and its architecture while thinking like an adversary.

Microsoft first documented its threat modeling methodology in 1999, and its method has evolved into an industry standard since that time.[1] This was not the first time anyone threat-modeled at Microsoft, of course, but rather the first time the methodology was formalized or considered as an abstracted engineering activity. The threat risk modeling process has five steps, enumerated below and shown graphically in Figure 4.2. They are

1. Identify security objectives.
2. Survey the application.
3. Decompose it.
4. Identify threats.
5. Identify vulnerabilities.

Following these five steps will help you understand what assets you need to protect, from whom you need to protect them, how you can protect them, what is the implementation priority, and what risk you will have to live with if a few of the threats are not included in the implementation scope.

The focus of threat modeling should not be simply on the software product itself, but include the context of the business and the user. The implementation priorities can be limited to the software product itself after the threat modeling, analysis, and architectural security risk analysis are completed. Besides the cost savings achieved by building security in early in the process, another advantage is to take into account the business and user needs and requirements so you can balance out and make security decisions that are cost-efficient and relevant to the competiveness of the product in addition to facilitating expected and required security and privacy controls.

The user context influences not only the scope of threats and vulnerabilities, it may also strongly affect priorities for implementation. For example, if you are storing customers' credit card data in your hosting

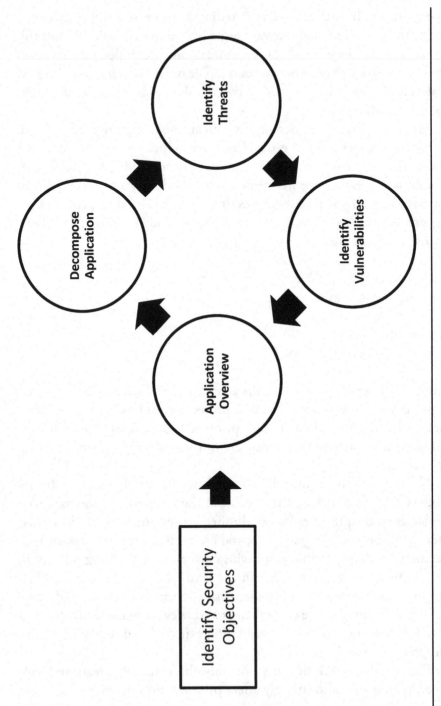

Figure 4.2 The five steps of threat modeling.

environment, then the threat of data stealing by your internal support staff or employees will be much more critical to mitigate then an outside attack from an unknown community. To put this into perspective from a practical threat modeling perspective, some of the scenarios on which you should focus with regard to this user-centric view include considering any possibility that an unauthorized user of your software product could gain access; whether there is any possibility that this same unauthorized user could escalate his privileges; and whether either an authorized or unauthorized user could gain access to admin functions or provide direct access to contents of back-end databases and then misuse the authority. One of the worst-case scenarios would be an unauthorized user who could compromise the Web/front-end server and obtain escalated privileges on all resources available on the server; this would provide the ability to exploit the trust relation to obtain unauthorized access to critical information from access/event logs or configuration files. During the threat modeling process, you must always think like an attacker, assume that all inputs to your software product could be malicious, and that all trust boundaries may be breached at the first level, that is, the first interaction layer between the software product and the end user.[2]

The goal of threat modeling is to gain an understanding of the software application by decomposing it and understanding how it interacts with external entities. This is achieved by information gathering and documentation into a clearly defined structure, which ensures that the correct information is collected. From a security perspective, the key goal in threat modeling is to gain an understanding of what success looks like, and in order to accomplish that, you need a baseline of security success criteria. A very useful list of such items appeared in *MSDN Magazine* in 2006 and is reproduced here:

Design Principles

- Open design: Assume the attackers have the sources and the specs.
- Fail-safe defaults: Fail closed; no single point of failure.
- Least privilege: No more privileges than what is needed.
- Economy of mechanism: Keep it simple, stupid.
- Separation of privileges: Don't permit an operation based on a single condition.
- Total mediation: Check everything, every time.

- Least common mechanism: Beware of shared resources.
- Psychological acceptability: Will they use it?

Security Properties

- Confidentiality: Data is only available to the people intended to access it.
- Integrity: Data and system resources are only changed in appropriate ways by appropriate people.
- Availability: Systems are ready when needed and perform acceptably.
- Authentication: The identity of users is established (or you're willing to accept anonymous users).
- Authorization: Users are explicitly allowed or denied access to resources.
- Nonrepudiation: Users can't perform an action and later deny performing it.[3]

The key steps involved in threat modeling are[4]

1. Break down your product architecture using data flow diagrams
2. Use STRIDE threat categories to identify what threats are applicable to each element of the data flow diagram.
3. Map all threats with relevant vulnerabilities as applicable in the context of the usage scenario.
4. Rank threats. Assign a risk rating to each threat and vulnerability to understand the impact; this will help define the priority for fixing. Use DREAD or other methodologies.
5. Define the mitigation plan/countermeasures for each of the vulnerabilities identified.
6. Fix the vulnerabilities that are not acceptable to the business in order of priority as decided in the preceding steps.

4.3.2 Data Flow Diagrams

The first step of the threat modeling process is to develop a visual representation of the threat flows in the form of a diagram typically drawn during a whiteboard session. It is important to provide a structure for this process. Providing structure helps avoid mistakes. Without a good diagram, you likely won't have a good threat model. It is important to understand, first, that this exercise is about data flow and not the code flow. This is a mistake often made by developers on the team because they live, breath, and eat code development and are not typically focused on the data security of the code they are developing. It should be no surprise that the diagram produced in this stage of the threat modeling process is called a data flow diagram or DFD. The focus of the DFD is on how data moves through the software solution and what happens to the data as it moves, giving us a better understanding of how the software works and its underlying architecture by providing a visual representation of how the software processes data. The visual representation is hierarchical in structure, so it allows you to decompose the software architecture into subsystems and then lower-level subsystems. At a high level, this allows you to clarify the scope of the application being modeled, and at the lower levels it allows you to focus on the specific processes involved when processing specific data.

Before you get start developing your DFD, it is always a good idea to understand the element images you are going to use. The basic elements and symbols that are typically used in DFDs are shown in Figure 4.3. You build the DFD by connecting these various elements as data flows and applying boundaries between the elements where appropriate.

Our first example of the use of a DFD is a data flow diagram for threat modeling of a Web application, as shown in Figure 4.4. This data flow diagram represents the process by which customers and remote employees access corporate marketing data from a corporate website. The first and most obvious security control differentiates between file access by an employee of the company versus file access by a customer. The employee data might contain company IP information authorized only for company employees and, depending on their role, very sensitive competitive marketing and pricing data authorized only for employees who have a "need to know."

The DFD in Figure 4.4 is for illustrative purposes only and does not represent the best way to develop an application. Examining the flow diagram more closely, we notice the following:

- There is no segmentation between data for employees and customers.
- There does not seem to be two-factor authentication for remote employees (e.g., VPN) before they access data on the site.

Element Type	Type Description	Element Symbol
External Element	An element outside your control and external to your software application but may be called to or interact with the software being modeled via an entry point.	□
Process	This represents a task that handles data within the software. This task may process or perform a task based on the data.	○
Multiple Processes	This is used to represent a collection of sub-processes for the data and typically indicates that another DFD will be involved in which case its sub-processes are broken down and extended into an additional DFD.	◎
Data Store	This represents where data is stored but not modified.	‖
Data Flow	This represents the movement of the data within the software and its direction of movement is represented by the arrow.	⟋
Trust Boundary	A trust boundary occurs when one component doesn't trust the component on the other side of the boundary. Trust boundaries always exist between elements running at different privilege levels. There can also be trust boundaries between different components running at the same privilege level.	⌒

Figure 4.3 DFD element types.

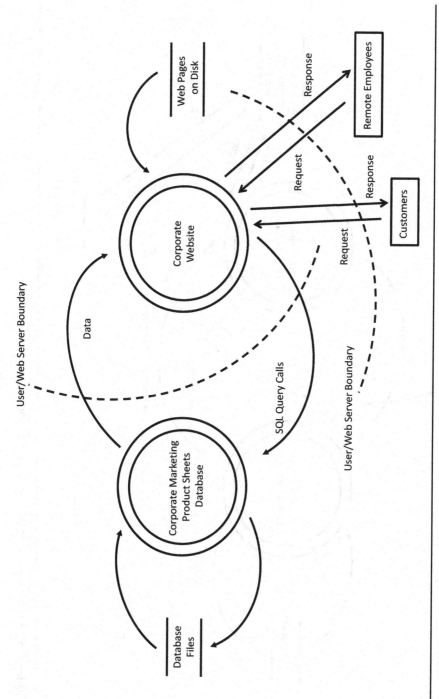

Figure 4.4 Example data flow diagram for application threat modeling.

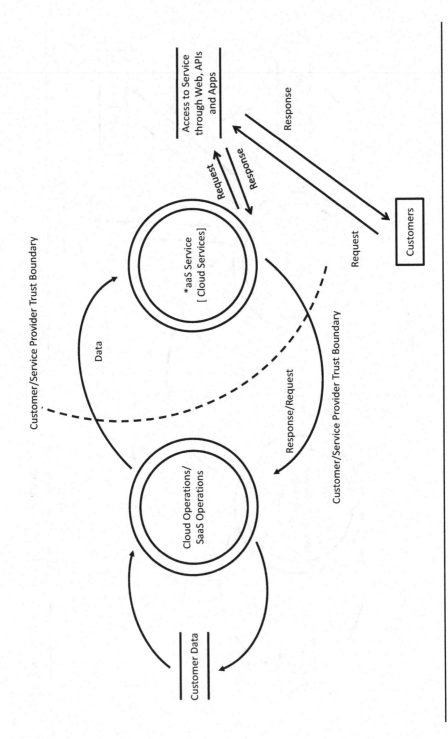

Figure 4.5 Example data flow diagram for a cloud-based application.

- Tiered structure that should be part of Web applications is not developed fully (or at least not part of this DFD). This might simplify the diagram but may also hide some use cases and flows.

The DFD in Figure 4.5 is an example of *aaS based services provided to customers. Instead of a traditional Web application, this DFD shows an example of how customers access services through a cloud provider. The most obvious security control in this case is protecting customer data through cloud operations. Customers can access service in multiple ways—through API calls, Web applications, or custom application development.

Examining the flow diagram more closely, we notice the following:

- There is no distinction between application access through an API or the Web.
- Cloud operations is a high-level abstraction for more detailed cloud operations architecture.
- The DFD does not tell us anything about segmentation between different customers.
- It also does not show how secure the data is—i.e., is it encrypted, are Web servers talking only to database servers in a cluster or is communication any-any?

Getting the DFD right is key to getting the threat model right. Spend enough time on yours, making sure all the pieces of your system are represented. Each of the elements (processes, data stores, data flows, and interactors) has a set of threats to which it is susceptible, as you can see in Figure 4.6. This chart, along with your DFD, gives you a framework for investigating how your system might fail.[5]

The DFD process requires not only that you think like an attacker but possibly like multiple attackers, particularly if your software product is going to be operating in the could or a SaaS environment. Once the DFD is completed, you should have an accurate overview of the how data is processed by the software, including how it moves and what happens to it within the application and others that may be associated with it. The high levels of the DFD clarify the scope of the application, and the lower levels clarify processes involved when specific data is being processed.

	Data Flow	Data Store	Process	External
Spoofing			✓	✓
Tampering	✓		✓	
Repudiate		✓*	✓	✓
Information Disclosure	✓	✓	✓	
Denial of Service	✓	✓	✓	
Elevate Privilege			✓	

Figure 4.6 Threats affecting elements. (*For data stores that are logs, there is concern about repudiation issues, and attacks on the data store to delete the logs. A set of questions to make these threats more concrete and accessible should be used to make this assessment more complete.[35])

4.3.3 Architectural Threat Analysis and Ranking of Threats

4.3.3.1 Threat Determination

The first step in determining threats is to adopt a methodology by which you can categorize them. This provides the ability to systematically identify sets of threat categories within the software application in a structured and repeatable manner. STRIDE is a method of threat categorization that was popularized by Microsoft a number of years ago and will be used in this chapter as an example of a threat determination tool, but it is certainly not the only methodology that can be used. Each letter in the acronym STRIDE helps classify attacker goals:

- **S**poofing
- **T**ampering
- **R**epudiation
- **I**nformation disclosure
- **D**enial of service
- **E**levation of privilege[6]

The first step in STRIDE is to decompose your system into relevant components, then analyze each component for susceptibility to the threats, and finally, mitigate the threats. The process is then repeated until you are comfortable with any remaining threats. The system is then considered secure, since you have now broken your software application and system down to individual components and mitigated the threats to each. Of course, this methodology has its flaws in that the individual components of the software and system can be part of a larger system and you are only as secure as your weakest link. Individual components of a software product and system may not be susceptible to a threat in isolation but may be once it is part of a larger system. This is particularly true for software products that were not designed to be used on the Internet, in the cloud or SaaS environment.

General threats and the security controls they may affect within each of the STRIDE categories include the following:

- Spoofing: A threat action that is designed to illegally access and use another user's credentials, such as username and password—*Authentication*

- Tampering: Threat action aimed to maliciously change/modify persistent data, such as persistent data in a database, and the alteration of data in transit between two computers over an open network, such as the Internet—*Integrity*
- Repudiation: Threat action aimed to perform illegal operations in a system that lacks the ability to trace the prohibited operations—*Nonrepudiation*
- Information disclosure: Threat action to read a file that one was not granted access to, or to read data in transit—*Confidentiality*
- Denial of service: Threat aimed to deny access to valid users, such as by making a Web server temporarily unavailable or unusable—*Availability*
- Elevation of privilege: Threat aimed to gain privileged access to resources for gaining unauthorized access to information or to compromise a system—*Authorization*[7]

4.3.3.2 Threat Analysis

After you have completed the DFD, you should identify the design and implementation approaches for input validation, authentication, authorization, configuration management, and the other areas where applications are most susceptible to vulnerabilities, creating what is called a security profile.

A practical example of the kind of questions that are typically asked in analyzing each aspect of the design and implementation of your software application is the following.[8] We divide these into broad categories of input validation, authentication, authorization, configuration management, sensitive data, session management, cryptography, exception management, parameter manipulation, and audit and logging.

Input Validation

Rationale behind this is that tall user input should be considered untrusted and should be validated before being used in software. Below are relevant questions to ask for input validation:

1. Is all input data validated?
2. Could an attacker inject commands or malicious data into the application?

3. Is data validated as it is passed between separate trust boundaries (by the recipient entry point)?
4. Can data in the database be trusted?
5. Would you prefer whitelisting or blacklisting of user input?

Authentication

All of user interactions (and software/API) interactions with overall system should be thought through and validated through authentication. None of the services and functionality should be available without validating if user/system/API/component is legitimate. Whether or not it can use the functionality takes us into authorization. Typically questions to ask for authentication are as follows:

1. Are credentials secured if they are passed over the network?
2. Are strong account policies used?
3. Are strong passwords enforced?
4. Are you using certificates? Are there any wild card certificates in use?
5. Are password verifiers (using one-way hashes) used for user passwords?
6. How do system components authenticate to each other (e.g. how does a service authenticate to a database)?
7. During boot process for the service/application, how do system components authenticate to each other?
8. Are keys used for authentication instead of password?

Authorization

Many a times we would like to restrict users/systems/API/components from accessing certain functionality in a software system. Authorization enables us to do just that i.e. prevent certain operations to certain agents. Questions typically related to authorization are as follows:

1. What gatekeepers are used at the entry points of the application?
2. How is authorization enforced at the database?
3. Is a defense-in-depth strategy used?
4. Do you fail securely and only allow access upon successful confirmation of credentials?

Configuration Management

Configuration management enables us to harden software, systems, services and devices and lock them down thus reducing risk to the environment. Components of configuration management include hardening standards and guidelines, reviewing application dependencies on services, looking at user and administrator interfaces, security change management and so on. Questions are along the following lines:

1. What administration interfaces does the application support?
2. How are they secured?
3. How is remote administration secured?
4. What configuration stores are used and how are they secured?
5. Have hardening standards been developed for the software stack (OS, DB, Application)?
6. Does software system provide a way to detect variances from approved security configuration changes?
7. Do all groups (IT, QA, Engineering, Operations) only use approved (golden master) software images for different components such as OS, DB, Web, and Application servers?
8. Do approved images are used across entire lifecycle from development to deployment?

Sensitive Data

This aspect deals with awareness around type of data handled by application and systems. In many cases, we have found that developers and operations teams are not aware or educated enough on type of data their application will handle (either by design or mistake) and if protection is enough for data elements.

1. What sensitive data is handled by the application?
2. What regulatory/compliance requirements are applicable to data/ data elements?
3. How is it secured over the network and in persistent stores? Is this good enough given legal/regulatory requirements?
4. What type of encryption is used and how are encryption keys secured?
5. Are sensitive data elements present in logs, source code or configuration (e.g., XML) files?

Session Management

Securely establishing and mainlining integrity of session is one of the key components of today's applications specifically web applications. Once user is authenticated, a session is established. This can result in multiple scenarios where session can be abused. Session management focuses on preventing such abuses. Questions asked for this aspect are typically along the following lines:

1. How are session cookies generated?
2. How are they secured to prevent session hijacking?
3. How is persistent session state secured?
4. Where is session information stored? On server or the client side?
5. How is session state secured as it crosses the network?
6. How does the application authenticate with the session store?
7. Are credentials passed over the wire and are they maintained by the application? If so, how are they secured?
8. How are multiple sessions from a user/component handled?

Cryptography

Everyone uses cryptography. Cryptography tends to provide a sense of security for most developers and users. However, proper use of cryptography is not that common in our experience. Using cryptography to solve the wrong problem can often cause frustration and even exposure. When dealing with cryptography, it is best to stick with well-tested, publicly available algorithms and libraries. Questions on cryptography can include the following:

1. What is the problem cryptography is going to solve (confidentiality, integrity or both)?
2. What algorithms and cryptographic techniques are used?
3. Are there any proprietary or in-house algorithms used?
4. How long are encryption keys and how are they secured?
5. Does the application put its own encryption into action?
6. How often are keys recycled? Are certificates checked for their validity? Are certificates checked against revocation lists?

Parameter Manipulation

Application often passes parameters to communicate with the other side. Parameters range from (not so important) iterators, variable names and values to session tokens. Man-in-the middle (MITM) attacks and deliberate parameter tampering makes it important for us to device mechanism to detect if parameters received are indeed safe and can be used as designed. Imperative here is on the receiver side—like input validation, do not blindly trust parameters.

1. Does the application detect tampered parameters?
2. Does the application rely on only client-side validation or there is server side validation as well?
3. Does it validate all parameters in form fields, view state, cookie data, and HTTP headers?
4. Are parameters directly used in database queries?
5. Are parameters directly reflected back to the browser?

Exception Management

Gracefully handling error conditions and exceptions is critical to software applications. Often, developers miss such conditions or handle them incorrectly. Side affects from improper error handling/exception management range from denial of service or information leakage. Sample questions to probe this aspect are as follows:

1. How does the application handle error conditions?
2. Is there a default catch for exceptions?
3. Are exceptions ever allowed to propagate back to the client?
4. Are generic error messages that do not contain exploitable information used?
5. Do exceptions log any sensitive information to logs?
6. Are built-in capabilities from programming languages used for this purpose or developers rely on in-house modules?

Auditing and Logging

Audit and logging is critical for multiple reasons. Security being one of them, audit trail in case of legal issues being another. Operations/ debugging is often the driver for audit/logging though increasingly attention is being paid to security aspect as well. Below are sample questions that can be asked to get a sense of audit and logging.

1. Does your application audit activity across all tiers on all servers?
2. How are log files secured?
3. Does application log any sensitive information (e.g. credentials, data elements, session tokens)?
4. Are log files transported securely (e.g. TCP/TLS)?
5. Is retention period clearly defined for log files? Does it align with regulatory and legal requirements?
6. How often are logs rotated?
7. Are trigger levels defined for certain types of events?

Now that you have a visual representation of the threat and have answered questions as above, the next step is to identify the threats that may affect your software application. This is also where you bring together elements of the software security group and the development team for a whiteboard meeting to brainstorm cost-effective and practical solutions to the vulnerabilities that have been identified in threat modeling. The goals of the attacker are addressed in relation to the threats and questions during the STRIDE assessment. This is done from a somewhat higher architectural and multifunctional perspective given the makeup of the brainstorming team. It is also common practice to use any available categorized threat list and apply it to any of the vulnerabilities identified earlier.

The use of attack trees and attack patterns is a traditional approach to threat assessment that can help you identify additional potential threats. Although attack patterns represent commonly known attacks, their combination with attack trees can be used for a greater depth of analysis highlighting areas you may have missed in your initial analysis or through the use of categorized lists of known threats. Since attack trees are in a hierarchical, structured, and flow diagram style, they give a great visual representation of attacks and help focus efforts on potential additional approaches to avoiding or mitigating such attacks. They are also useful for the creation of test plans and the assessment of security costs. Since the primary focus of attack patterns, attacker techniques, and STRIDE is on the goals of the attacker, using them in combination with attack trees helps bring a holistic approach to this process, especially when used in face-to-face brainstorming sessions.

Before you move on to the next stage of the threat modeling and architectural risk assessment process and start assigning values to the risk, it

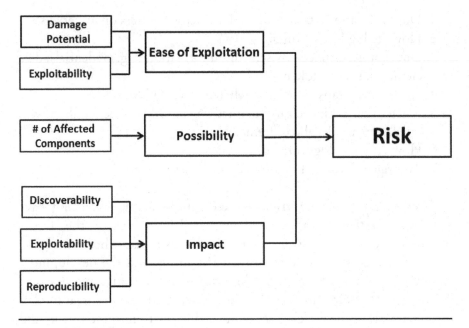

Figure 4.7 Risk assessment process.

is important to be sure you have addressed risk with regard to the ease of exploitation, possibility, and impact. A visual representation of what knowledge you must have before moving on to the next step is given in Figure 4.7. If you don't have the information required to address an area of risk, you will need to go back through the process and fill in the gaps in your knowledge and understanding.

4.3.3.3 Ranking the Threats

During the final stage of the threat modeling and architecture security analysis, the threats are ranked from a risk perspective. Given that it may not be economically feasible to mitigate all of the identified threats, they are ranked from the highest to lowest risk. Some threats may also be ignored because of the very limited likelihood that they will occur in addition to the limited harm the vulnerabilities would cause if they were exploited. A prioritized list of threats by risk will significantly help the priority and importance of mitigation. At a high level, these risks will typically be ranked as high, medium, and low. A typical risk probability formula used in industry shows the risk and consequence of a particular vulnerability as equal to the probability of the threat occurring multiplied by the damage potential. That is,

Risk = Probability × Damage Potential

A 10-scale measurement is typically used in risk probability calculations, with the number 1 representing a threat or component of a threat that is least likely to occur and the number 10 representing that which is most likely to occur. The same 1-to-10 ranking system is used for assigning damage potential, with 1 indicating the least damage potential and 10 the most.

As an example of the mechanics involved, a threat that is moderately likely to occur, with a probability risk score of 5, and a high damage potential of 10 has a risk equal to that of a threat having a probability risk score of 10 and a medium damage risk potential of 5. Mathematically,

If **Probability** = 5 and **Damage Potential** = 10, then **Risk** = 5 × 10 = 50%
If **Probability** = 10 and **Damage Potential** = 5, then **Risk** = 10 × 5 = 50%

As you can see from this example, 100 can be divided into three ranges of numbers to indicate a high, medium, or low risk rating. Obviously, your level of priority to fix the vulnerabilities will start with the highest priority of risk, which likely means that immediate mitigation is required. Then you would tackle vulnerabilities of medium risk, which should be done shortly thereafter but with less priority. The priority of low risks,as noted previously, will depend on the level of effort, exposure, and financial or legal risk also associated with the risk.

4.3.3.4 DREAD

Although many different risk models can be used when assessing vulnerabilities during the software development process, the DREAD model used by Microsoft is one the most popular. The acronym DREAD stands for **D**amage potential, **R**eproducibility, **E**xploitability, **A**ffected users, and **D**iscoverability. Answers to questions used to establish a risk rating for each of these elements produces a number from 0 -10; the higher the number, the more serious is the risk. These numbers are used as a classification scheme for quantifying, comparing, and prioritizing the amount of risk presented by each evaluated threat and calculating the overall risk in numeric form so that threats can be ranked and sorted with any other risks found in the software application.

The DREAD algorithm, shown below, is used to compute a risk value, which is an average of all five categories:

$$\text{Risk\_DREAD} = (\underline{D}\text{AMAGE} + \underline{R}\text{EPRODUCIBILITY} + \underline{E}\text{XPLOITABILITY} + \underline{A}\text{FFECTED USERS} + \underline{D}\text{ISCOVERABILITY})/5^9$$

Here are some examples of how you arrive at the risk rating for a given threat by asking questions to quantify the DREAD categories:[10]

Damage Potential

- If a threat exploit occurs, how much damage will be caused?
  - 0 = nothing
  - 5 = individual user data is compromised or affected
  - 10 = complete system or data destruction

Reproducibility

- How easy is it to reproduce the threat exploit?
  - 0 = very hard or impossible, even for administrators of the application
  - 5 = one or two steps required; may need to be an authorized user
  - 10 = just a Web browser and the address bar is sufficient, without authentication

Exploitability

- What is needed to exploit this threat?
  - 0 = advanced programming and networking knowledge, with custom or advanced attack tools
  - 5 = malware exists on the Internet, or an exploit is easily performed using available attack tools
  - 10 = just a Web browser

Affected Users

- How many users will be affected?
  - o 0 = none
  - o 5 = some users, but not all
  - o 10 = all users

Discoverability

- How easy is it to discover this threat?
  - o 0 = very hard to impossible; requires source code or administrative access
  - o 5 = can figure it out by guessing or by monitoring network traces
  - o 9 = details of faults like this are already in the public domain and can be easily discovered using a search engine
  - o 10 = the information is visible in the Web browser address bar or in a form

The next step is to classify your threat ratings as low (value = 1), medium (value = 2), or high (value = 3) for each category of DREAD based on your answers. Answers that would indicate a low, medium, or high risk for each DREAD category are shown below:[11]

Damage Potential

Low (value = 1): Leaking trivial information.

Medium (value = 2): Leaking sensitive information.

High (value = 3): The attacker can subvert the security system; get full trust authorization; run as administrator; upload content.

Reproducibility

Low (value = 1): The attack is very difficult to reproduce, even with knowledge of the security hole.

Medium (value = 2): The attack can be reproduced, but only with a timing window and a particular race situation.

High (value = 3): The attack can be reproduced every time and does not require a timing window.

DREAD Category	Low Risk (1)	Medium Risk (2)	High Risk (3)	Subtotal Risk Scores
Damage Potential (D)				
Reproducibility (R)				
Exploitability (E)				
Affected Users (A)				
Discoverability (D)				
				Total Risk Score

Figure 4.8 DREAD threat rating table.

Exploitability

Low (value = 1): The attack requires an extremely skilled person and in-depth knowledge every time to exploit.

Medium (value = 2): A skilled programmer could make the attack, and then repeat the steps.

High (value = 3): A novice programmer could make the attack in a short time.

Affected Users

Low (value = 1): Very small percentage of users, obscure feature; affects anonymous users.

Medium (value = 2): Some users, nondefault configuration.

High (value = 3): All users, default configuration, key customers.

Discoverability

Low (value = 1): The bug is obscure, and it is unlikely that users will work out damage potential.

Medium (value = 2): The vulnerability is in a seldom-used part of the product, and only a few users should come across it. It would take some thinking to see malicious use.

High (value = 3): Published information explains the attack. The vulnerability is found in the most commonly used feature and is very noticeable.

These numbers can then be put into a matrix similar to the one shown in Figure 4.8. After you count and sum the values for a given threat, the result will fall in the range of 5 to 15. Threats with overall ratings of 12 to 15 are typically considered high risk, those with ratings from 8 to 11 as medium risk, and and those with ratings from 5 to 7 as low risk.

4.3.3.5 Web Application Security Frame

The Web Application Security Frame, also called the Application Security Frame (ASF), uses categories to organize common security vulnerabilities focused on Web software applications. If you use these categories when you review your application design to create a threat model, you can systematically reveal the threats and vulnerabilities specific to your application architecture. There are nine frame categories; sample questions used in the process are listed below.

Web Application Security Frame Categories and Assessment Questions[12]

- **Input and Data Validation**

  How do you know that the input your application receives is valid and safe? Input validation refers to how your application filters, scrubs, or rejects input before additional processing. Consider constraining input through entry points and encoding output through exit points. Do you trust data from sources such as databases and file shares?

- **Authentication**

  Who are you? Authentication is the process whereby an entity proves the identity of another entity, typically through credentials, such as a user name and password.

- **Authorization**

  What can you do? Authorization is how your application provides access controls for resources and operations.

- **Configuration Management**

  Who does your application run as? Which databases does it connect to? How is your application administered? How are these settings secured? Configuration management refers to how your application handles these operational issues.

- **Sensitive Data**

  How does your application handle sensitive data? Sensitive data refers to how your application handles any data that must be protected either in memory, over the network, or in persistent stores.

- **Session Management**

  How does your application handle and protect user sessions? A session refers to a series of related interactions between a user and your Web application.

- **Cryptography**
  How are you keeping secrets (confidentiality)? How are you tamper-proofing your data or libraries (integrity)? How are you providing seeds for random values that must be cryptographically strong? Cryptography refers to how your application enforces confidentiality and integrity.

- **Exception Management**
  When a method call in your application fails, what does your application do? How much do you reveal? Do you return friendly error information to end users? Do you pass valuable exception information back to the caller? Does your application fail gracefully?

- **Auditing and Logging**
  Who did what and when? Auditing and logging refer to how your application records security-related events.

4.3.3.6 The Generic Risk Model

Microsoft threat modeling processes such as STRIDE and DREAD may not be appropriate for your application, and you may want to use other threat risk models or modify the Microsoft processes for your own use, adopting the most appropriate threat modeling methodologies for your own organization. Using qualitative values such as high, medium, and low can also help avoid the ranking becoming too subjective, as with the numbering system used in DREAD.

These examples help in the calculation of the overall risk values by assigning qualitative values such as high, medium, and low to likelihood and impact factors. Here too, using qualitative values rather than numeric ones as in the DREAD model helps avoid the ranking becoming overly subjective.

An example of a more subjective model is the Generic Risk Model, which takes into consideration the likelihood (e.g., the probability of an attack) and the impact (e.g., damage potential) and is represented mathematically as[13]

$$\text{Risk} = \text{Likelihood} \times \text{Impact}$$

The likelihood or probability is defined by the ease of exploitation, which depends mainly on the type of threat and the system characteristics, and by the possibility to realize a threat, which is determined by the existence of an appropriate countermeasure. The following is a set of considerations for determining ease of exploitation:

1. Can an attacker exploit this remotely?
2. Does the attacker need to be authenticated?
3. Can the exploit be automated?

The impact depends mainly on the damage potential and the extent of the impact, such as the number of components that are affected by a threat. Examples to determine the damage potential are

1. Can an attacker completely take over and manipulate the system?
2. Can an attacker gain administration access to the system?
3. Can an attacker crash the system?
4. Can the attacker obtain access to sensitive information such as secrets, PII

Examples to determine the number of components that are affected by a threat include:

1. How many data sources and systems can be impacted?
2. How "deep" into the infrastructure can the threat agent go?

4.3.3.7 Trike

An alternative threat modeling methodology to STRIDE and DREAD is Trike. Trike is a unified conceptual framework for security auditing from a risk management perspective through the generation of threat models in a reliable, repeatable manner.[14] Trike uses a threat modeling framework that is similar to the Microsoft threat modeling methodologies. However, Trike differs in that it uses a risk-based approach with distinct implementation, threat, and risk models, instead of using the STRIDE/DREAD aggregated threat model (attacks, threats, and weaknesses).[15]

Trike is distinguished from other threat modeling methodologies by the high levels of automation possible within the system, the defensive perspective of the system, and the degree of formalism present in the methodology.[16] The latest version of the Trike tool can be downloaded at the Source Forge website at http://sourceforge.net/projects/trike/files/trike.

A security auditing team can use it to describe the security characteristics of a system from its high-level architecture to its low-level implementation details. The goal of Trike is to automate the repetitive parts of threat modeling. Trike automatically generates threats (and some attacks) based on a description of the system, but this requires that the user describe the system to Trike and check whether these threats and attacks apply.[17] A key element of Trike is the empowerment, involvement, and communications with the key stakeholders with complete progress and task status transparency so that they know the level of risk and can evaluate acceptance of the risk throughout the software development process.

4.3.3.8 PASTA (Process for Attack Simulation and Threat Analysis)

In 2011, a new application threat modeling methodology developed by Marco Morana and Tony Uceda Velez was presented. PASTA is a seven-step process that is applicable to most application development methodologies and is platform-agnostic. It not only aligns business objectives with technical requirements it also takes into account compliance requirements, business impact analysis, and a dynamic approach to threat management, enumeration, and scoring. The process begins with a clear definition of business objectives, security and compliance requirements, and business impact analysis. Similar to the Microsoft process, the application is decomposed into components, with use case diagrams and DFDs to illustrate the threat model with which threat and vulnerability analysis can be performed. The next step involves use of threat trees, abuse cases, scoring systems, and enumerations for further reference in analysis. Following this, the threat model is viewed from an attacker perspective by attack modeling in attack trees and attack surface analysis. In the final step, risk and business impact can be qualified and quantified, and necessary countermeasures identified. This process combines the best of various threat modeling approaches, with the attack trees serving as an attacker-centric means of viewing a threat, as well as, in combination with risk and impact analysis, helping to create an asset-centric means of planning a mitigation strategy. The threat trees, with mapping of threats to existing vulnerabilities, work in favor of easy and scalable threat management. Beyond the technical aspects, the risk and business impact analysis take threat modeling beyond just a software development exercise to involve participation of key decision makers in the vulnerability management process. What differentiates this methodology from Trike is that it focuses on involving risk management steps in the final stage of the process. This ensures that it is not limited to a specific risk estimation formula.[18]

The seven-step PASTA Threat Modeling Methodology is as follows:[19]

1. Define Objectives

   - Identify business objectives
   - Identify security and compliance requirements
   - Business impact analysis

2. Define Technical Scope

   - Capture the boundaries of the technical environment
   - Capture infrastructure, application, and software dependencies

3. Application Decomposition

   - Identify uses cases and define application entry points and trust levels
   - Indentify actors, assets, services, roles and data sources
   - Data flow diagramming and trust boundaries

4. Threat Analysis

   - Probabilistic attack scenarios analysis
   - Regression analysis on security events
   - Threat intelligence correlation and analytics

5. Vulnerability and Weakness Analysis

   - Queries of existing vulnerability reports and issues tracking
   - Threat to existing vulnerability mapping using threat trees
   - Design flaw analysis using use and abuse cases
   - Scorings (CVSS/CWSS) and enumerations (CWE/CVE)

6. Attack Modeling

- Attack surface analysis
- Attack tree development and attack library management
- Attack to vulnerability and exploits analysis using attack trees

7. Risk and Impact Analysis

- Qualify and quantify business impact
- Countermeasure identification and residual risk analysis
- ID risk mitigation strategies

There is also fairly new threat-modeling tool called ThreatModeler, developed by MyAppSecurity, Inc., that supports the PASTA methodology. ThreatModeler is a threat modeling product which brings a mind mapping approach to threat modeling. It allows companies to scale their threat modeling initiative across thousands of applications easily and effortlessly. ThreatModeler automatically generates threats and classifies them under various risk categories. It provides a centralized threat management platform where organizations can define threats related to network, host, applications, mobile, Web services, etc., and associate attributes such as technical impacts, business impacts, and threat agents to better understand a threat and prioritize mitigation strategies.[20,21]

Although its original focus was on banking malware threats, PASTA certainly has applicability across all software applications and will fit well into most SDLCs. It will be interesting to see how widely it is accepted in industry over the next few years.

4.3.3.9 CVSS

Another risk assessment methodology that is very popular and is used extensively by corporate product security incident response teams (PSIRTs) and internal software security groups to classify externally discovered software vulnerabilities is the U.S. government's Common Vulnerability Scoring System (CVSS). The National Infrastructure Advisory Council (NIAC) commissioned CVSS to support the global Vulnerability Disclosure Framework. CVSS is currently maintained by the Forum of Incident Response and Security Teams (FIRST),[22] and was a joint effort involving many companies, including CERT/CC, Cisco Systems, DHS/MITRE, eBay, Internet Security Systems, Microsoft, Qualys, and Symantec. The CVSS model is designed to provide end users with an overall composite score representing the severity and risk of a vulnerability. It is derived from metrics and formulas. The metrics are in three distinct categories that can be quantitatively or qualitatively measured. Base metrics contain qualities that are intrinsic to any given vulnerability; these qualities do not change over time or in different environments. Temporal metrics contain characteristics of a vulnerability that evolve over the lifetime of the vulnerability. Environmental metrics contain characteristics of a vulnerability that are related to an implementation in a specific user's environment. Scoring is the process of combining all metric values according to specific formulas and based on a series of measurements called metrics based on expert assessment which is described below:[23]

- Base scoring is computed by the vendor or originator with the intention of being published, and, once set, is not expected to change. Base scoring is also computed from confidentiality, integrity, and availability. This is the foundation that is modified by the temporal and environmental metrics. The base score has the largest bearing on the final score and represents vulnerability severity.
- Temporal scoring is also computed by vendors and coordinators for publication, and modifies the base score. It allows for the introduction of mitigating factors to reduce the score of a vulnerability and is designed to be reevaluated at specific intervals as a vulnerability ages. The temporal score represents vulnerability urgency at specific points in time.
- Environment scoring is optionally computed by end-user organizations and adjusts the combined base-temporal score. This adjusted combined score should be considered the final score and represents a moment in time, tailored to a specific environment. User organizations should use this score to prioritize responses within their own environments.

A useful tool is the the Common Vulnerability Scoring System Version 2 Calculator, which can be found on the National Institute of Standards and Technology (NIST) National Vulnerability Database website at http://nvd.nist.gov/cvss.cfm?calculator&version=2.

The CVSS has become an industry standard for assessing the severity of computer system security vulnerabilities. It establishes a measure of how much concern vulnerability should warrant compared to other vulnerabilities so that mitigation efforts can be prioritized. As of the writing of this book, the current version of CVSS is version 2.

The CVSS is typically used by an internal software security group to respond to a security researcher or other source that has notified you that your software product has vulnerability. This provides the ability to keep your severity ratings normalized, consistent, and accurate. The scores are also used in the communication to the customers acknowledging that there is a vulnerability in the product that they have purchased, the severity of the vulnerability, and what your company is doing to mitigate that vulnerability, including any patch releases for the vulnerability. In turn, a security researcher will likely use the CVSS ranking system to provide a risk rating to the company within whose software product they have found a vulnerability, so that the vendor has a good idea of the severity of the vulnerability that is being disclosed and the details of what to verify with its product development team.

It should be noted that the CVSS is not a threat modeling methodology and is not used to find or reduce the attack surface or to help specify risks within a piece of code. It is, rather, a risk scoring system and it adds complexities that don't exist in STRIDE and DREAD. It is used to calculate risks that are identified post-product release in addition to environmental factors.

4.3.3.10 OCTAVE

OCTAVE (Operationally Critical Threat, Asset, and Vulnerability Evaluation) is a very complex risk methodology approach originating from Carnegie Mellon University's Software Engineering Institute (SEI) in collaboration with the SEI Computer Emergency Response Team (CERT). OCTAVE focuses on organizational risk, not technical risk. It comprises a suite of tools, techniques, and methods for risk-based information security strategic assessment and planning. There are three OCTAVE methods: (1) the original OCTAVE method, which forms the basis for the OCTAVE body of knowledge; (2) OCTAVE-S, for smaller organizations; and (3) OCTAVE-Allegro, a streamlined approach for information security assessment and assurance. All of the methods have specific catalogs of practices, profiles, and worksheets to document the modeling outcomes. OCTAVE methods are founded on the OCTAVE criteria—a standard approach for a risk-driven and practice-based information security evaluation. The OCTAVE criteria establish the fundamental principles and attributes of risk management that are used by the OCTAVE methods.[24]

OCTAVE is a valuable structured approach to documenting and measuring overall IT security risk, particularly as it relates to corporate IT and business risk management and when documenting risks surrounding complete systems becomes necessary. Although a software security professional may be involved in a portion of the assessment as a software or process for building software security into the development process may be within its scope, it is not valuable for modeling, defining, and ranking specific risks and vulnerabilities within the SDL process. As with CVSS scoring, OCTAVE does not include threat risk modeling and is used primarily to enumerate risk. It is also much more complex than most other risk assessment and scoring methodologies in that it consists of 18 volumes with many worksheets to work through. The comprehensive version of OCTAVE (unlike OCTAVE-S for small organizations) defines "likelihood" assuming that the threat will always occur, which is not applicable to many large organizations. For these reasons, it is not likely to be an approach that is used throughout the software development lifecycle.

4.3.3.11 AS/NZS ISO 31000:2009

The Australian/New Zealand Standard AS/NZS 4360, first issued in 1999 and revised in 2004, was the world's first formal standard for documenting and managing risk and is still one of the few formal standards for managing it.[25] AS/NZS ISO 31000:2009 is a newer standard published November 20, 2009, for managing risk and supersedes AS/NZS 4360:2004.[26]

ISO 31000:2009 provides principles and generic guidelines on risk management and can be used by any public, private, or community enterprise, association, group, or individual, and is not specific to any industry or sector. It can be applied throughout the life of an organization, and to a wide range of activities, including strategies and decisions, operations, processes, functions, projects, products, services, and assets. It can also be applied to any type of risk, whatever its nature, whether having positive or negative consequences. Although ISO 31000:2009 provides generic guidelines, it is not intended to promote uniformity of risk management across organizations. The design and implementation of risk management plans and frameworks will need to take into account the varying needs of a specific organization, its particular objectives, context, structure, operations, processes, functions, projects, products, services, or assets, and specific practices employed. It is intended that ISO 31000:2009 be utilized to harmonize risk management processes in existing and future standards. It provides a common approach in support of standards dealing with specific risks and/or sectors, and does not replace those standards.[27]

ISO 31000:2009 does not define the methodology to perform a structured threat risk modeling exercise or a structured approach to specify software application security risks and works best in evaluating business or systemic risks rather than for technical risks. As with OCTAVE, this methodology is likely to be used by a centralized corporate risk management team. Software security professionals may be involved in a portion of the assessment because their software or process for building software security into the development process may be in scope, but it is not likely that this methodology will be used in the SDL as a primary risk methodology because it is not valuable for modeling, defining, and ranking specific risks and vulnerabilities within the SDLC process.

4.3.4 Risk Mitigation

Before you move onto the risk mitigation phase you will need to make a master list of high-risk vulnerabilities during the threat modeling process, including STRIDE or an equivalent. This will give you a priority list from which to work as you follow through your mitigation plan.

There are four ways you can plan mitigation and address threats:[28]

1. Redesign the process to eliminate the threat.
2. Apply a standard mitigation as per general recommendations.
3. Invent a new mitigation strategy (risky and time-consuming)
4. Accept vulnerabilities with low risk and high effort to fix them.

Vulnerability threats that have no countermeasures in STRIDE or Application Security Frame (ASF) are categorized, and countermeasured for specific threats are identified for each of the categories they fall into. OWASP has two checklists that, although not inclusive, can serve as a great guideline for this activity. Both lists can be found at https://www. owasp.org/index.php/Application_Threat_Modeling and is also described below with corresponding mitigation techniques.

STRIDE Threat & Mitigation Techniques List[29]

Spoofing identity
- Appropriate authentication
- Protect secret data
- Don't store secrets

Tampering with data
- Appropriate authorization
- Hashes
- MACs
- Digital signatures
- Tamper-resistant protocols

Repudiation
- Digital signatures
- Timestamps
- Audit trails

Information disclosure
- Authorization
- Privacy-enhanced protocols
- Encryption
- Protect secrets
- Don't store secrets

Denial of service
- Appropriate authentication
- Appropriate authorization
- Filtering
- Throttling
- Quality of service

Elevation of privilege
- Run with least privilege

ASF Threat and Countermeasures List[30]

Authentication

1. Credentials and authentication tokens are protected with encryption in storage and transit.
2. Protocols are resistant to brute force, dictionary, and replay attacks.
3. Strong password policies are enforced.
4. Trusted server authentication is used instead of SQL authentication.
5. Passwords are stored with salted hashes.
6. Password resets do not reveal password hints and valid usernames.

Authorization

1. Strong ACLs are used for enforcing authorized access to resources.
2. Role-based access controls are used to restrict access to specific operations.
3. The system follows the principle of least privilege for user and service accounts.
4. Privilege separation is correctly configured within the presentation, business, and data access layers.

Configuration management

1. Least privileged processes are used and service accounts with no administration capability.
2. Auditing and logging of all administration activities is enabled..
3. Access to configuration files and administrator interfaces is restricted to administrators

Data protection in storage and transit

1. Standard encryption algorithms and correct key sizes are used.
2. Hashed message authentication codes (HMACs) are used to protect data integrity.
3. Secrets (e.g., keys, confidential data) are cryptographically protected both in transport and in storage.
4. Built-in secure storage is used for protecting keys.
5. No credentials and sensitive data are sent in clear text over the wire.

Data validation/parameter validation

1. Data type, format, length, and range checks are enforced.
2. All data sent from the client is validated.
3. No security decision is based on parameters (e.g., URL parameters) that can be manipulated.
4. Input filtering via white list validation is used.
5. Output encoding is used.

Error handling and exception management

1. All exceptions are handled in a structured manner.
2. Privileges are restored to the appropriate level in case of errors and exceptions.
3. Error messages are scrubbed so that no sensitive information is revealed to the attacker.

User and session management

1. No sensitive information is stored in clear text in the cookie.
2. The contents of the authentication cookies is encrypted.
3. Cookies are configured to expire.
4. Sessions are resistant to replay attacks.
5. Secure communication channels are used to protect authentication cookies.
6. User is forced to re-authenticate when performing critical functions.
7. Sessions are expired at logout.

Auditing and logging

1. Sensitive information (e.g., passwords, PII) is not logged.
2. Access controls (e.g., ACLs) are enforced on log files to prevent unauthorized access.
3. Integrity controls (e.g., signatures) are enforced on log files to provide nonrepudiation.
4. Log files provide for audit trail for sensitive operations and logging of key events.
5. Auditing and logging is enabled across the tiers on multiple servers.

After you have identified the software threats and associated mitigation strategies and ranked the risks, it is possible to identify a mitigation threat profile for each threat that has been identified through the threat modeling/architecture security analysis process. The following criteria are used to categorize your final list from this process:

- **Fully mitigated threats:** Threats that have appropriate counter-measures in place and do not expose vulnerability or cause impact.
- **Partially mitigated threats:** Threats partially mitigated by one or more countermeasures, which represent vulnerabilities that can only partially be exploited and cause a limited impact.
- **Nonmitigated threats:** Threats that have no countermeasures and represent vulnerabilities that can be fully exploited and cause an impact[31]

Now that you have categorized your threats in one of the three categories above, you have a choice to make concerning what strategy you are going to pursue. Your choices of action will likely fall under one of the following five options:

1. Do nothing: for example, hope for the best.
2. Inform about the risk: for example, warn your user population about the risk.
3. Mitigate the risk: for example, by putting countermeasures in place.
4. Accept the risk: for example, after evaluating the impact of the exploitation (business impact).
5. Transfer the risk: for example, through contractual agreements and insurance.[32]

Your decision as to which of the strategies listed above will be used will depend on several factors:

- The impact an exploitation of a threat can have
- The likelihood of its occurrence
- The costs for transferring (i.e., costs for insurance) or avoiding (i.e., costs or losses due to redesign) it.[33]

Risk in this sense is an identified threatening situation due to the potential presence of an actor, motivation, and vulnerability with a significant probability and business impact. The risk of a threat is not the issue, but rather an identified risk that has been ranked in severity with a significant business consequence as the result of the outcome of a threat. The probability of the threat is considered separately because it is affected by the motivation of the actor and the specifics and external factors affecting the vulnerability. Business impact is also a key element of risk that is affected by both the type of actor, which can be state, industrial, or criminal, and the specifics of the vulnerability. This can be visualized as shown in Figure 4.9.

In this section we have shown some of the options and standard methodologies that can be used to assess your threats, rank your risk, and develop a risk mitigation plan. The process we have described is visualized in Figure 4.10.

The bottom line is that risk assessment is about business risk and results in trade-offs as it relates to security risk to the software, the system it interacts with, and the overall business risk management strategy. It is important for security professionals to know this, and that is why we have included two popular overall business risk assessment methodologies that focus on information security risk, specifically, OCTAVE and AS/NZS ISO 31000:2009. As with the ecosystem the software is part of, the risk assessment methodology used for secure software development will also have points of intersection with the overall business risk management methodology, and those areas need to be taken into account as part of the software risk analysis.

Ultimately this will be a business decision. This is why one decision may be to fix vulnerabilities only where the cost to fix is less than the potential business impact that might result from exploitation of the vulnerability, or why another decision may be made to accept the risk when the loss of some security controls (e.g., confidentiality, integrity, and availability) risks only a small degradation of the service, not a loss of a critical business function.[34]

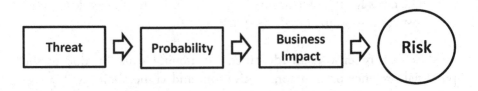

Figure 4.9 Elements of risk.

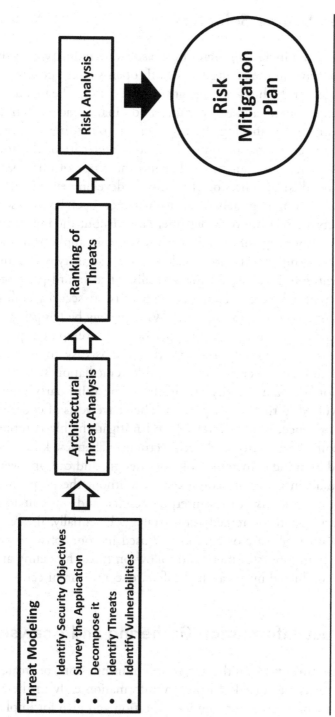

Figure 4.10 A holistic approach for software security risk assessment.

4.4 Open-Source Selection

There has been an increasing trend in the software industry over the last few years to draw on the strengths of both open-source and proprietary software to deliver the highest value at the lowest cost. The blend of both is called "mixed source" and is becoming a dominant practice in industry. Understanding and managing the licensing of your software assets will be critical as open source becomes an ever-greater part of the software development landscape, but this is beyond the scope of our discussion and will be handled by others on the software development team.

There is an ongoing debate as to whether open-source software increases software security or is detrimental to it, but the bottom line is that you are importing software into your software application or solution that your company did not develop or have security oversight over. This will require an extensive review, typically called a third-party security assessment, that will be conducted by your software security architect, a third party, or a combination of both. While it may be tempting to rely on tools and a cursory review of the open-source development processes, without the proper training and experience it is easy to misinterpret results, and difficult to create an actionable remediation strategy. That is why senior software security architects or the third-party equivalent must be involved in this review process. They have years of code security auditing experience, routinely review and mitigate highly complex and advanced software security and architectural challenges, know how to identify and examine vulnerable points in design, and can uncover flaws that may result in a security compromise. Without the proper training and experience it is easy to misinterpret results, and difficult to create any necessary actionable remediation strategy. Essentially, the review of any open-source software or component used in your software product will require both tool assessment and follow-on threat modeling and risk assessment conducted by a seasoned software security architect.

4.5 Privacy Information Gathering and Analysis

It is important to consider if the system will transmit, store, or create information that may be considered privacy information early in the SDLC. The gathering of information and identification and plan for implementing proper safeguards and security controls, including processes to address privacy information incident handling and reporting requirements, is determined at this stage. This stage of the SDL is where the information gathering and analysis for the Privacy Impact Assessment (PIA) begins. The analysis phase determines how PII will be handled to ensure that it conforms to applicable legal, regulatory, and policy requirements regarding privacy; what the risks and effects of collecting, maintaining, and disseminating privacy information in identifiable form in the software and overall system being developed or one that it potentially interfaces with in a cloud or SaaS environment; and examine and evaluate protections and alternative processes for handling information to mitigate potential privacy risks.

4.6 Key Success Factors and Metrics

4.6.1 Key Success Factors

Success of this second phase of the SDL depends on how well the SDLC identifies the threats, requirements, and constraints in functionality and integration and mitigates the risk. Key success factors for this second phase are listed in Table 4.1.

Table 4.1 Key Success Factors

Key Success Factor	Description
1. Identification of business requirements and risks	Mapping of business requirements and risks defined in terms of CIA
2. Effective threat modeling	Identifying threats for the software
3. Effective architectural threat analysis	Analysis of threats to the software and probability of threat materializing
4. Effective risk mitigation strategy	Risk acceptance, tolerance, and mitigation plan per business requirements
5. Accuracy of DFDs	Data flow diagrams used during threat modeling

Success Factor 1: Identification of Business Requirements and Risks

During this phase, key stakeholders including the software security group help write out business risks and requirements. Business requirements are defined through the CIA pillars of information security. It is imperative for a successful SDL cycle that all requirements are identified and captured to the best extent possible.

Success Factor 2: Effective Threat Modeling

Though it is a complex and challenging task, on threat modeling rests the entire risk mitigation plan. Any gaps in a threat model will result in lack of effective security controls in the software and/or deployment.

Success Factor 3: Effective Architectural Threat Analysis

Architectural threat analysis enables identification of threats and ranks them in order of priority. It is essential that all threat vectors resulting in the risk are identified and prioritized.

Success Factor 4: Effective Risk Mitigation Strategy

The culmination of threat modeling and threat analysis is risk acceptance, tolerance, and a risk mitigation plan. It is imperative that business appetite for risk acceptance and tolerance be thoroughly vetted, including through legal and finance.

Success Factor 5: Accuracy of DFDs

DFDs are used during threat modeling to identify various components/ elements of interest. DFDs should be as detailed as possible. Any assumptions should be reviewed carefully. Specifically, trust boundaries (client/ server, private/public infrastructure, tiered architecture), etc., should be properly documented and reviewed.

4.6.2 Deliverables

Table 4.2 lists deliverables for this phase of the SDL.

Business Requirements

A formal business requirement is an artifact that lists software requirements and business risks mapped to the three pillars of information security: confidentiality, integrity, and availability.

Table 4.2 Deliverables for Phase A2

Deliverable	Goal
Business requirements	Software requirements, including CIA
Threat modeling artifacts	Data flow diagrams, elements, threat listing
Architecture threat analysis	Prioritization of threats and risks based on threat analysis
Risk mitigation plan	Plan to mitigate, accept, or tolerate risk
Policy compliance analysis	Analysis of adherence to company policies

Threat Modeling Artifacts

A critical component of this SDL phase, there are a few artifacts that come from this step. Key artifacts include data flow diagrams, technical threat modeling reports, high-level executive threat modeling reports, threat lists, and recommendations for threat analysis.

Architecture Threat Analysis

The key artifact from this step of the SDL is an artifact that outlines risks of threat materializing. Another one that should be required from this step is threat ranking/priority.

Risk Mitigation Plan

The risk mitigation plan outlines risks (and threats) to be mitigated, accepted, or tolerated. For each of these categories, it also outlines steps on mitigation risks. Finally, this report should be presented to business for sign-off before actual work on the project begins.

Policy Compliance Analysis

This artifact is a report on compliance with different security and nonsecurity policies within the company—for example, how does software to be developed comply with information security policy, data governance policy, data retention and cryptography policy, and so on.

4.6.3 Metrics

The following metrics should be collected and recorded for this second phase of the SDL cycle:

- List of business threats, technical threats (mapped to business threats), and threat actors
- Number of security objectives unmet after this phase
- Percent compliance with company policies (existing)
- Number of entry points for software (using DFDs)
- Percent of risk (and threats) accepted, mitigated, and tolerated
- Percent of initial software requirements redefined
- Number of planned software architectural changes (major and minor) in a product
- Number of software architectural changes needed based on security requirements

4.7 Chapter Summary

The primary goal of the Architecture (A2) phase of our DSL model is to identify the overall requirements and structure for the software from a security perspective. The key elements of this phase are threat modeling, documentation of elements of the software attack surface from an architectural perspective; definition of security architecture and design guidelines; continued security, SDL, and privacy policy and requirements compliance reviews; and software product security release requirements.

These best practices result in the definition of the overall structure of the software from a security perspective. They identify those components whose correct functioning is essential to security. They also identify the appropriate security design techniques applicable for the soft product architecture, including the application of least privilege, and minimize the attack surface of the software product and any supporting infrastructure. Although a higher layer may depend on the services of lower layers, the lower layers are forbidden from depending on higher layers. Although the security architecture identifies an overall perspective on security design, the specifics of individual elements of the architecture will be detailed in individual design specifications.

The identification and measurement of the individual elements of the attack surface provides the development and software security team with an ongoing metric for default security and enables them to detect instances where the software has been made susceptible to attack. During this phase, all exceptions to reducing the attack surface must be reviewed, because the goal is to maximize security as a default for a software product that is being developed. The Threat modeling uses a structured approach at a component-by-component level, identifying the assets that the software must manage and the interfaces by which those assets can be accessed. The likelihood of harm being done to any of the assets identified during threat modeling is estimated as a measure of risk. Countermeasures or compensating controls to mitigate the risk are also identified. Where appropriate and feasible, tools should be used that can capture the threat models in machine-readable form for storage and updating. Specific preship software security criteria are also identified at this stage of the SDL.

Toward the end of the chapter we discussed key success factors and their importance, deliverables from this phase, and metrics that should be collected from this phase.

References

1. Kohnfelder, L., and Garg, P. (1999), "The threats to our products." *Microsoft Interface,* April 1, 1999. Retrieved from http://blogs.msdn.com/sdl/attachment/9887486.Ashx.
2. cisodesk.com (2012), "SiteXposure: Threat Modeling Process—Overview." Retrieved from http://www.cisodesk.com/web-application-security/threat-modeling-overview.
3. Hernan, S., et al. (2006), "Threat Modeling: Uncover Security Design Flaws Using the STRIDE Approach." *MSDN Magazine.* Retrieved from http://msdn.microsoft.com/en-us/magazine/cc163519.aspx#S3.
4. cisodesk.com (2012), "SiteXposure: Threat Modeling—Practice." Retrieved from http://www.cisodesk.com/web-application-security/threat-modeling-in-practice.
5. Hernan, S., et al. (2006), "Threat Modeling: Uncover Security Design Flaws Using the STRIDE Approach." *MSDN Magazine.* Retrieved from http://msdn.microsoft.com/en-us/magazine/cc163519.aspx#S3.
6. http://msdn.microsoft.com/en-us/library/ee823878(v=cs.20).aspx.
7. OWASP (2012), *Application Threat Modeling.* Retrieved from https://www.owasp.org/index.php/Application_Threat_Modeling#Data_Flow_Diagrams.
8. Meier, J., et al. (June 2003), *Microsoft Corporation MSDN Library Doc: Improving Web Application Security: Threats and Countermeasures.* Retrieved from http://msdn.microsoft.com/en-us/library/ff648644.aspx.
9. OWASP (2012), *Threat Risk Modeling.* Retrieved from https://www.owasp.org/index.php/Threat_Risk_Modeling.
10. Ibid.
11. Meier, J., et al. (June 2003), *Microsoft Corporation MSDN Library Doc: Improving Web Application Security: Threats and Countermeasures.* Retrieved from http://msdn.microsoft.com/en-us/library/ff648644.aspx.
12. Microsoft MSDN (2012), *Cheat Sheet: Web Application Security Frame—Web*

Application Security Frame Categories. Retrieved from http://msdn.microsoft.com/
en-us/library/ff649461.aspx.

13. OWASP (2012), *Application Threat Modeling.* https://www.owasp.org/index.php/
Application_Threat_Modeling.

14. Saitta, P., Larcom, B., and Eddington, M. (2005), *Trike v.1 Methodology Document
[Draft].* Retrieved from http://octotrike.org/papers/Trike_v1_Methodology_
Document-draft.pdf.

15. OWASP (2012), *Threat Risk Modeling.* Retrieved from https://www.owasp.org/
index.php/Threat_Risk_Modeling.

16. Saitta, P., Larcom, B., and Eddington, M. (2005), *Trike v.1 Methodology Document
[Draft].* Retrieved from http://octotrike.org/papers/Trike_v1_Methodology_
Document-draft.pdf.

17. U.S. Department of Homeland Security—US CERT (2009), *Requirements and
Analysis for Secure Software—Software Assurance Pocket Guide Series: Development,
Volume IV Version 1.0, October 5, 2009.* Retrieved from https://buildsecurityin.
us-cert.gov/swa/downloads/RequirementsMWV1001AM091111.pdf.

18. MyAppSecurity (2012), *Comparison of Threat Modeling Methodologies: P.A.S.T.A
(Process for Attack Simulation and Threat Analysis).* Retrieved from http://www.
myappsecurity.com/threat-modeling/comparison-threat-modeling-methodologies.

19. Morana, M., and Ucedavelez, T. (2011), "OWASP Threat Modeling of Banking
Malware-Based Attacks Presentation," AppSec EU, June 10, 2011, Trinity College,
Dublin, Ireland. Retrieved from https://www.owasp.org/images/5/5f/Marco_
Morana_and_Tony_UV_-_Threat_Modeling_of_Banking_Malware.pdf.

20. Morana, M. (2011), "Writing Secure Software Blog: Attack Simulation and
Threat Analysis of Banking Malware-Based Attacks," June 10, 2011. Retrieved
from http://securesoftware.blogspot.com/2011/06/attack-simulation-and-threat-
analysis.html.

21. MyApp Security (2012), *ThreatModeler.* Retrieved from http://www.myappsecurity.
com.

22. FiRST (2012), FiRST Homepage. Retrieved from http://www.first.org.

23. FiRST (2012), "CVSS Frequently Asked Questions." Retrieved from http://www.
first.org/cvss/faq.

24. Software Engineering Institute–Carnegie Mellon (2012), *OCTAVE.* Retrieved
from http://www.cert.org/octave.

25. OWASP (2012), *Threat Risk Modeling.* Retrieved from https://www.owasp.org/
index.php/Threat_Risk_Modeling.

26. STANDARDS Australia–New Zealand (2012), *AS/NZS ISO 31000:2009 Risk
Management-Principles and Guidelines.* Retrieved from http://sherq.org/31000.pdf.

27. ISO (2012), *ISO 31000:2009—Risk Management—Principles and Guidelines.*
Retrieved from http://www.iso.org/iso/catalogue_detail?csnumber=43170.

28. Cisodesk (2012), *Threat Modeling—Practice Guide.* Retrieved from http://www.
cisodesk.com/web-application-security/threat-modeling-in-practice.

29. OWASP (2012), *Application Threat Modeling: STRIDE Threat & Mitigation
Techniques List.* Retrieved from https://www.owasp.org/index.php/Application_
Threat_Modeling.

30. OWASP (2012), *Application Threat Modeling: ASF Threat & Countermeasures List.* Retrieved from https://www.owasp.org/index.php/Application_Threat_Modeling.
31. OWASP (2012), *Application Threat Modeling.* Retrieved from https://www.owasp.org/index.php/Application_Threat_Modeling.
32. Ibid.
33. Ibid.
34. Ibid.
35. Shostack, A. (2008), "Experiences Threat Modeling at Microsoft." Retrieved from http://www.homeport.org/~adam/modsec08/Shostack-ModSec08-Experiences-Threat-Modeling-At-Microsoft.pdf.

Chapter 5

Design and Development (A3): SDL Activities and Best Practices

The design and development (A3) phase (see Figure 5.1) is when the end user of your software is foremost in your mind. During this phase you will do an analysis of policy compliance, create the test plan documentation, update your threat model if necessary, conduct a design security analysis and review, and do a privacy implementation assessment so you can make informed decisions about how to deploy your software securely and establish development best practices to detect and remove security and privacy issues early in the development cycle. You will perform static analysis during both the design and development (A3) and the ship (A4) phases of your SDL. We will provide a detailed description of static analysis in the next chapter. You will build the plan for how you will take your project through the rest of the SDL process, from implementation, to verification, to release. During the design and development (A3) phase you establish best practices for this phase using functional and design specifications.

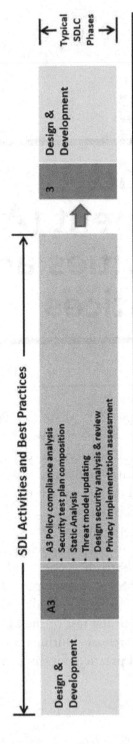

Figure 5.1 Design and Development (A3): SDL activities and best practices.

5.1 A3 Policy Compliance Analysis

A3 policy compliance analysis is a continuation of the A2 policy compliance review described in Chapter 4. During this phase, any policy that exists outside the domain of the SDL policy is reviewed. These might include policies from outside the development organization that set security and privacy requirements and guidelines to be adhered to when developing software or applications. Corporate security and privacy policies will likely instruct designers and developers on what the security and privacy features need to be and how they must be implemented. Other policies might focus on third-party and open-source software used as part of a software product, or on the protection and control of source code and other intellectual property within and outside the organization. Assuming the software security group is separate from the centralized information security group, it is important that both groups collaborate on all policies and guidelines related to the development and post-release security support and response of software from that organization. It is also important to collaborate with the privacy function of your company, whether it is a centralized group or outside legal counsel.

5.2 Security Test Plan Composition

Testing activities validate the secure implementation of a product, which reduces the likelihood of security bugs being released and discovered by customers and/or malicious users. Software assurance and competency from a security perspective is demonstrated by security testing and the use of artifacts, reports, and tools. The goal is not to test for insecurity, but rather to validate the robustness and security of the software products before making the product available to customers. These security testing methods do find security bugs, especially in products that may not have undergone critical secure development process changes. The results of security testing and evaluation may also uncover deficiencies in the security controls used to protect the software that is under development. A detailed plan of action and milestone schedule are required to document the corrective measures planned to increase the effectiveness of the security controls and provide the requisite security for the software prior to its release.

As with the risk analysis methodologies discussed in Chapter 4, a holistic approach is necessary for security testing to be effective. Security testing confirms that the software complies with security requirements through design and code analysis and software behavior investigation. In other words, security testing is conducted to demonstrate that the software functions as specified by the requirements, and every software requirement must be tested using at least one relevant test case. The number of requirements tested versus the total number of requirements can be traced from test cases to functional requirements; then the ratio of requirements tested to the total number of requirements will become a test requirement metric.

Another element of security testing is to identify software weaknesses so that security violations and noncompliance with security requirements that could cause the software to fail or be out of compliance with any of software security requirements are avoided. As discussed in the risk analysis ranking section, due to resource limitations, security test plan efforts typically focus only on software requirement items that are considered to be critical. A master test plan is used to outline the entire test process, and is augmented by detailed test plans for individual test stages and individual modules.

While traditional requirements-based testing is important to the correctness and adequacy of security functions implemented by software, no amount of testing can fully demonstrate that software is free from vulnerabilities; any such testing can only provide a small-scale view of what is needed to verify the security of the software. Even the most robustly specified security requirements are not likely to address all possible conditions under which the software may be forced to operate in the real world, including the behavior of software under anomalous and hostile conditions.

Generally, the shortcomings of requirements-based over risk-based software security testing can be summarized as follows:

- The changing nature of threats to the software you have in development may result in new attack methodologies both pre- and post-release.
- Your software may change its position as a functional component of a SaaS or cloud-based solution, which may also change the attack surface and thus require new security fixes or mitigations.

- In today's competitive and rapidly changing environment, the design assumptions on which the requirements were based may be obsolete by the time the software is ready for testing.
- Other factors often change frequently and likely more rapidly than your specification can keep up.
- If the software is going to use components acquired from a third party, the original architecture may not account for future versions that were not planned for in the initial implementation.
- The original design assumptions may not account for vulnerability susceptibilities due to design changes or new external attacker capabilities or exploits that may occur during the time taken to develop later versions of the software.

This list highlights why software risk-based security testing as described in this section should always augment traditional requirements-based testing.

As mentioned previously and used as a continuing theme throughout this book, problems found early in the software lifecycle by "building security in" are significantly easier and less costly to correct than problems discovered post-implementation or, worse, post-deployment. This is why it is imperative that a disciplined approach to security reviews and tests begin early in the SDL/SDLC process and continue post-release until the software reaches end of life.

Software security testing takes the perspective that the tester is the attacker. Test scenarios should be based on misuse and abuse possibilities developed through the methodologies and threat modeling described in Chapter 4, and should incorporate both known attack patterns as well as anomalous interactions that seek to invalidate assumptions made by and about the software and its environment. Comprehensive test scenarios, test cases, and test oracles should be derived. Be sure that all that misuse cases developed in the previous stage are executed and thoroughly tested. The testing of each development iteration, use case, and misuse case will identify major design flaws early in the SDL and should catch up to 95 percent of defects well before the last phase.[1]

The test environment should duplicate as closely as possible the anticipated execution environment in which the software will be deployed, and it should be kept entirely separate from the development environment. It should also provide for strict configuration management control to prevent tampering or corruption of test data, testing tools, the integrated test environment, as well as the test plan itself and both the raw and finalized test results. It is also important to ensure that each tool set and test technique is appropriate for the individual software vulnerabilities that are being tested.

Testing for both functionality and security requires execution of the code and validation/verification of the results. It is also not always automated, because human intervention by experienced software security architects is typically needed. Because of the complexities and interactions of software ecosystems such as SaaS or cloud environments, the knowledge of such experts is required so that a wider range of scenarios can be tested.

As mentioned previously, the test plan lays out what needs to be tested for functionality, protected for security, and how the application will react to specific attacks. The test plan is a joint effort by the project management, development, and security teams, among others, to specify the logistics of the test plan, including who will execute the testing and when testing will begin and end.

The following are common steps that can be used to implement a test plan regardless of the strategy, framework, or standard being used:

- **Define test scripts.** Scripts are very detailed, logical steps of instructions that tell a person or tool what to do during the testing. Functional testing scripts are step-by-step instructions that depict a specific scenario or situation that the use case will encounter as well as the expected results. Secure testing scripts are scripts created specifically to test the security of the application. The basis for these scripts comes from the threat models that were generated during the design phase. Misuse cases define what needs to be protected (assets) and what types of attacks can gain access to those assets. Secure test scripts define the acts of carrying out those attacks.
- **Define the user community.** Defining the user community helps testers identify acceptable levels of failures and risk.
- **Identify the showstoppers.** Defining the must-haves and the "what-if-available" scenarios should be in the use case. If not, a revisit to the requirements might be necessary so that these specifications can be documented.
- **Identify internal resources.** Internal resources come from the company's organization, including developers, analysts, software tools, and sometimes project managers.

- **Identify external resources.** External resources are tools or people who are hired on a temporary basis to come into a project, test the application, and report findings. External resources are best suited for security testing because they typically come highly trained in secure programming techniques and they are far removed from the code and any internal politics. If external resources are needed, the test plan needs to answer the following questions: (1) What are they going to test? (2) To whom will they report? and (3) With whom will they be working?[2]

Assessing the security properties and behaviors of software as it intersects with external entities such as human users, the environment, and other software and as its own components interact with each other is a primary objective of security testing. As such, it should verify that software exhibits the following properties and behaviors:

- Its behavior is predictable and secure.
- It exposes no vulnerabilities or weaknesses.
- Its error- and exception-handling routines enable it to maintain a secure state when confronted by attack patterns or intentional faults.
- It satisfies all of its specified and implicit nonfunctional security requirements.
- It does not violate any specified and implicit nonfunctional security requirements.
- It does not violate any specified security constraints.
- As much of its runtime-interpretable source code and byte code as possible has been obscured or obfuscated to deter reverse engineering.[3,4]

A security test plan should be included in the overall software test plan and should define all security-related testing activities, including the following:

- Security test cases or scenarios (based on abuse cases)
- Test data, including attack patterns
- Test oracle (if one is to be used)
- Test tools (white box, black box, static, and dynamic)
- Analyses to be performed to interpret, correlate, and synthesize the results from the various tests and outputs from the various tools.[5,6]

Software security testing techniques can be categorized as white box, gray box, or black box:

- **White box.** Testing from an internal perspective, i.e., with full knowledge of the software internals; the source code, architecture and design documents, and configuration files are available for analysis.
- **Gray box.** Analyzing the source code for the purpose of designing the test cases, but using black-box testing techniques; both the source code and executable binary are available for analysis.
- **Black box.** Testing the software from an external perspective, i.e., with no prior knowledge of the software; only binary executable or intermediate byte code is available for analysis.[7,8]

The commonly used security testing techniques can be categorized using the above as follows:

- **Source code analysis (white box).** Source-code security analyzers examine source code to detect and report software weaknesses that can lead to security vulnerabilities. The principal advantage that source-code security analyzers have over the other types of static analysis tools is the availability of the source code. The source code contains more information than code that must be reverse-engineered from byte code or binary. Therefore, it is easier to discover software weaknesses that can lead to security vulnerabilities. Additionally, if the source code is available in its original form, it will be easier to fix any security vulnerabilities that are found.
- **Property-based (white box).** Property-based testing is a formal analysis technique developed by the University of California Davis. Property-based testing validates that the software's implemented functionality satisfies its specifications. It does this by examining security-relevant properties revealed by the source code, such as the absence of insecure state changes. Then these security-relevant properties in the code are compared against the software's specification to determine if the security assumptions have been met.
- **Source-code fault injection (white box, gray box).** Fault injection is a technique used to improve code coverage by testing all code paths, especially error-handling code paths that may not be exercised

during functional testing. In fault injection testing, errors are injected into the software to simulate unintentional attacks on the software through its environment, and attacks on the environment itself. In source-code fault injection, the tester decides when environment faults should be triggered. The tester then "instruments" the source code by nonintrusively inserting changes into the program that reflect the changed environment data that would result from those faults. The instrumental source code is then compiled and executed, and the tester observes the ways in which the executing software's state changes when the instrumental portions of code are executed. This allows the tester to observe the secure and nonsecure state changes in the software resulting from changes in its environment. The tester can also analyze the ways in which the software's state change results from a fault propagating through the source code. This type of analysis is typically referred to as fault propagation analysis, and involves two techniques of source-code fault injection: extended propagation analysis and interface propagation analysis.

- **Dynamic code analysis (gray box).** Dynamic code analysis examines the code as it executes in a running application, with the tester tracing the external interfaces in the source code to the corresponding interactions in the executing code, so that any vulnerabilities or anomalies that arise in the executing interfaces are simultaneously located in the source code, where they can be fixed. Unlike static analysis, dynamic analysis enables the tester to exercise the software in ways that expose vulnerabilities introduced by interactions with users and changes in the configuration or behavior of environmental components. Because the software is not fully linked and deployed in its actual target environment, the testing tool essentially simulates these interactions and their associated inputs and environment conditions.

- **Binary fault injection (gray box, black box).** Binary fault injection is a runtime analysis technique whereby an executing application is monitored as faults are injected. By monitoring system call traces, a tester can identify the names of system calls, the parameters to each call, and the call's return code. This allows the tester to discover the names and types of resources being accessed by the calling software, how the resources are being used, and the success or failure of each access attempt. In binary fault analysis, faults are injected into the environment resources that surround the application.

- **Fuzz testing (black box).** Fuzzing is a technique that is used to detect faults and security-related bugs in software by providing random inputs (fuzz) to a program. As opposed to static analysis, where source code is reviewed line by line for bugs, fuzzing conducts dynamic analysis by generating a variety of valid and invalid inputs to a program and monitoring the results. In some instances, the result might be the program crashing.
- **Binary code analysis (black box).** Binary code scanners analyze machine code to model a language-neutral representation of the program's behaviors, control and data flows, call trees, and external function calls. Such a model may then be traversed by an automated vulnerability scanner in order to locate vulnerabilities caused by common coding errors and simple back doors. A source code emitter can use the model to generate a human-readable source code representation of the program's behavior, enabling manual code review for design-level security weaknesses and subtle back doors that cannot be found by automated scanners.
- **Byte code analysis (black box).** Byte code scanners are used just like source-code security analyzers, but they detect vulnerabilities in the byte code. For example, the Java language is compiled into a platform-independent byte code format that is executed in the runtime environment (Java Virtual Machine). Much of the information contained in the original Java source code is preserved in the compiled byte code, thus making de-compilation possible. Byte code scanners can be used in cases where the source code is not available for the software—for example, to evaluate the impact a third-party software component will have on the security posture of an application.
- **Black box debugging (black box).** Debuggers for low-level programming languages such as C or ASM are software tools that enable the tester to monitor the execution of a program, start and stop a program, set breakpoints, and modify values. Debuggers are typically used to debug an application when the source code or the compiler symbols are available. The source-code and compiler symbols allow information, the values of internal variable, to be tracked to discover some aspect of internal program behavior. However, sometimes only the binary is available, and the binary was compiled from code with no compiler symbols or debug flags set. This is typical in commercial software, legacy software, and software that

implements protective measures, such as code obfuscation, to prevent reverse engineering. In this case, traditional debugging is not possible. It should be noted that if the focus of debugging effort is on the software interaction with an external component, the binary may be all that is needed.

- **Vulnerability scanning (black box).** Automated vulnerability scanning of operating system and application-level software involves use of commercial or open-source scanning tools that observe executing software systems for behaviors associated with attack patterns that target specific known vulnerabilities. Like virus scanners, vulnerability scanners rely on a repository of "signatures," in this case indicating recognizable vulnerabilities. Like automated code review tools, although many vulnerability scanners attempt to provide some mechanism for aggregating vulnerabilities, they are still unable to detect complex vulnerabilities or vulnerabilities exposed only as a result of unpredictable (combinations of) attack patterns. In addition to signature-based scanning, most vulnerability scanners attempt to simulate the reconnaissance attack patterns used by attackers to "probe" software for exposed, exploitable vulnerabilities.
- **Penetration testing (black box).** The portion of security testing in which the evaluators attempt to circumvent the security features of a system. The evaluators might be assumed to use all systems design and implementation documentation, which can include listings of system source code, manuals, and circuit diagrams. The evaluators work under the same conditions as are applied to ordinary users.[9–12]

The test plan organizes the security testing process and outlines which components of the software system are to be tested and what test procedure is to be used on each one. The outline is more than just a list of high-level tasks to be completed; it should also include which artifacts are to be tested, what methodologies are to be used, and a general description of the tests themselves, including prerequisites, setup, execution, and what to look for in the test results. The risk analysis described previously is typically used to prioritize the tests, since it is usually not possible, given time and budget constraints, to test every component of the software. Security test planning is an ongoing process, and the details of the test process are fleshed out as additional information becomes available.

The developing organization may modify software because problems have been uncovered and then send the software back to be retested.

Therefore it is often inefficient for begin testing only after development is complete, so one component may be in testing while other components of the same system are still being developed. For larger projects, the test plan is typically broken down into test cycles. Given the examples above, test cycles may be created because of the need to retest software that was already tested once before; or test cycles may be created because the nature of the development effort requires that different modules be tested at different times.

Intercomponent dependencies, including those elements or software components in a SaaS or cloud environment that may interact with the software being developed, must be taken into account so that the potential need for retesting is minimized. A development organization typically has a very regimented development process, so the security team needs to be involved from the beginning of the SDLC process. The security team needs to specify early the order in which components should be tested, to ensure that each module is tested before other modules that might depend on it are developed and tested. The concept of "building security in" should be used not just to promote the security program; it must be strictly adhered to if the SDL is to be successful. This means the security team needs to be included in the general test plan discussions to ensure that the elements of security are included in the validation of the test environment and the test data, and how the test cases define the test condition. The *test condition* is what is actually going to be tested to see how the software is actually going to respond. Test cases are created during the test execution process and include information about the test pre-conditions and post-conditions, how it will be set up and terminated, and how the results will be evaluated.

Automation will be key to making the process run smoothly and most importantly, repeatable and should be used wherever possible. As mentioned, previously, this will not always be possible and the human element will be absolutely necessary, particularly the skills of senior software security architects. The test plan will be expected to provide as much guidance as possible to let the tester definitely know what they are looking for in each test and what the specific test preparations are

Michael and Radosevich, of Cigital, listed the following typical elements of a security test plan that can be used as a guideline for developing your own plan in their 2005 white paper titled "Risk-Based and Functional Security Testing":

- Purpose
- Software Under Test Overview
  - Software and Components
  - Test Boundaries
  - Test Limitations
- Risk Analysis
  - Synopsis of Risk Analysis
- Test Strategy
  - Assumptions
  - Test Approach
  - Items Not to Be Tested
- Test Requirements
  - Functionality Test Requirements
  - Security Test Requirements
  - Installation/Configuration Test Requirements
  - Stress and Load Test Requirements
  - User Documentation
  - Personnel Requirements
  - Facility and Hardware Requirements
- Test Environment
- Test Case Specifications
  - Unique Test Identifier
  - Requirement Traceability (what requirement number from requirement document does test case validate)
  - Input Specifications
  - Output Specifications/Expected Results
  - Environmental Needs
  - Special Procedural Requirements
  - Dependencies Among Test Cases
- Test Automation and Testware
  - Testware Architecture
  - Test Tools
  - Testware
- Test Execution
  - Test Entry Criteria
  - QA Acceptance Tests
  - Regression Testing
  - Test Procedures, Special Requirements, Procedure Steps

- o Test Schedule
- o Test Exit Criteria
- Test Management Plan
- Definitions and Acronyms[13]

5.3 Threat Model Updating

After working through the threat modeling process described in Chapter 4, it is important to know when you are done with the process. This will involve answering a few questions such as the following, whose answers will likely depend on competing business and security risk interests and may require some trade-offs:

1. Have you accounted for all the policies, laws, or regulations relevant to the software that you are developing, and accounted for and gained approval for the level of effort for each of these requirements?
2. Have all your stakeholders reviewed the security assessment and risks identified as a result of the threat modeling process? The appropriate architects, developers, testers, program managers, and others who understand the software should have been asked to contribute to threat models and to review them. Broad input and reviews should have been solicited to ensure that the threat models are as comprehensive as possible. It is also important that all stakeholders agree on the threats and risks that have been identified. If this is not the case, implementing appropriate counter-measures may prove to be difficult.
3. Have you accounted for and have your stakeholders agreed to the availability of time and resources required as both a result of the threat modeling process and any resulting mitigation and testing?
4. Have you ranked your threats and risks according to consensus from stakeholders? If you were a buy of this software, would you agree with this ranking?

5.4 Design Security Analysis and Review

In a 1974 paper, Saltzer and Schroeder of the University of Virginia addressed the protection of information stored in a computer system by focusing on hardware and software issues that are necessary to support information protection.[14] The paper presented the following 11 security design principles:

1. **Least privilege.** The principle of least privilege maintains that an individual, process, or other type of entity should be given the minimum privileges and resources for the minimum period of time required to complete a task. This approach eliminates the opportunity for unauthorized access to sensitive information.
2. **Separation of duties.** This principle requires that completion of a specified sensitive activity or access to sensitive objects is dependent on the satisfaction of multiple conditions. Separation of duties forces collusion among entities in order to compromise the system.
3. **Defense in depth.** This is the application of multiple layers of protection, such that a subsequent layer will provide protection if a previous layer is breached.
4. **Fail safe.** This means that if a system fails, it should fail to a state where the security of the system and its data are not compromised. In the situation where system recovery is not done automatically, the failed system should permit access only by the system administrator and not by users, until security controls are reestablished.
5. **Economy of mechanism.** This promotes simple and comprehensible design and implementation of protection mechanisms, so that unintended access paths do not exist or can be readily identified and eliminated.
6. **Complete mediation.** This is where every request by a subject to access an object in a computer system must undergo a valid and effective authorization procedure. This mediation must not be suspend or become capable of being bypassed, even when the information system is being initialized, undergoing shutdown, being restarted, or is in maintenance mode. Complete mediation entails: (a) identification of the entity making the access request; (b) verification that the request has not changed since its initiation; (c) application of the appropriate authorization procedures; and (d) reexamination of previously authorized requests by the same entity.
7. **Open design.** There has always been discussion of the merits and strength of security of designs that are kept secret versus designs that are open to scrutiny and evaluation by the community at large. For most purposes, an open-access control system design that has

been evaluated and tested by a large number of experts provides a more secure authentication method than one that has not been widely assessed.

8. **Least common mechanism.** This principle states that a minimum number of protective mechanisms should be common to multiple users, as shared access paths can be sources of unauthorized information exchange. Shared access paths that provide unintentional data transfers are known as covert channels. The least common mechanism promotes the least possible sharing of common security mechanisms.

9. **Psychological acceptability.** This refers to the ease of use and intuitiveness of the user interface that controls and interacts with the access control mechanisms. The user must be able to understand the user interface and use it without having to interpret complex instructions.

10. **Weakest link.** As in the old saying, "A chain is only as strong as its weakest link," the security of an information system is only as good as its weakest component. It is important to identify the weakest mechanisms in the security chain and layers of defense and improve them so that risks to the system are mitigated to an acceptable level.

11. **Leveraging existing components.** In many instances, the security mechanisms of an information system are not configured properly or used to their maximum capability. Reviewing the state and settings of the extant security mechanisms and ensuring that they are operating at their optimum design points will greatly improve the security posture of an information system. Another approach that can be used to increase system security by leveraging existing components is to partition a system into defended subunits. Then, if a security mechanism is penetrated for one subunit, it will not affect the other subunits and damage to the computing resources will be minimized.[15,16]

Designing good software isn't easy, and building security in makes it even more difficult. Although some software flaws may not matter from a user perspective, from a security perspective they may matter because an attacker may be able induce failures by setting up the highly specific conditions necessary to trigger a flaw. Something that may have had a low probability of happening randomly and dismissed as irrelevant may be significant if an attacker can take advantage of it. In the summary of Saltzer and Schroeder's design principles, the principles are stated clearly but they lack the success criteria for security. We fortunately do have a general idea of what security looks like and can avoid failure in this area by incorporating the long-accepted properties of confidentiality, integrity, and availability into the design principles. There are of course different views of security, from that of a software developer, who may think of security primarily in terms of quality; to that of a network administrator, who may think of security in terms of firewalls, IDS/IPS systems, incident response, and system management; or even those of managers and academics, who may think of security mostly in terms of the classic design principles described above or in terms of various security models. All these viewpoints are important in building secure systems and relevant to modeling the overall threat to your software. You must stay focused on the ultimate prize when designing security in: the potential exploitation of the software you are developing.

Detailed design artifacts are used to build each software component needed to satisfy the use case requirements required to effectively design your software for security. A thorough analysis of each software artifact for possible vulnerabilities is conducted for every feature, property, and service that exists in every component. As a result of analyzing each software component for the use cases and in misuse case scenarios identified through the processes described in Chapter 4, developers will be able to design appropriate countermeasures up front and transparently, so that the entire team is able to see how software security is being handled in the application. As a result, the use case concepts can be converted to actual software requirement specifications. As the developers review the specific application software they are developing, they should also assess any vulnerabilities found in the associated ecosystem it will support, including its network, architecture, and supporting software. It is also important for the development security team to stay current with the latest vulnerabilities that may affect your specific software and associated ecosystem, both pre- and post-release, to prepare for new potential planes of attack previously unknown or discovered, both internally and externally. It will be much easier and less expensive to fix or develop a countermeasure to an identified risk as the software is being designed and developed than after it is released. Although the secure design of the code is critical and of upmost importance, mistakes will be made, new attack methodologies will be discovered and will continue to drive the need to research and assess new methods of attack and vulnerabilities long after the product has shipped and likely until it reaches end of life. This of course is why it is so important to minimize the attack surface through the methods described in Chapter 4, combined with good design principles to maximize the limitation of severity of any security flaws that may be missed in the code. The design as organized framework will be a strategy breaking down the problem into smaller parts that are more easily solved. Threat modeling will be key to your success and process in this endeavor, as it will typically identify a secure design issue that might have gone unnoticed until much later. The data flow diagram results will be used next, along with the brainstorming of attacks and review of known checklists. Apply whatever combined methodology works best for you, conduct all the necessary research, and apply it early in your design to minimize any component failing late in the development process.

5.5 Privacy Implementation Assessment

The authors believe that the most concise, clear, and field-tested privacy implementation assessment processes, procedures, and guidelines for software development are available from Microsoft and are contained in three primary documents:

1. Microsoft's *Privacy Guidelines for Developing Software Products and Services*, Version 3.1; September 2008[17]
2. Microsoft MSDN's *SDL—Process Guidance—Appendix C: SDL Privacy Questionnaire*[18]
3. Microsoft's *Simplified Implementation of the Microsoft SDL*[19]

The process and guidance by which you determine your Privacy Impact Rating and estimate the work required to be compliant is described in Microsoft's *Privacy Guidelines for Developing Software Products and Services*, Version 3.1; September, 2008,[20] and their *SDL—Process Guidance—Appendix C: SDL Privacy Questionnaire.*[21] The ratings (P1, P2, or P3) represent the degree of risk your software presents from a privacy perspective. You need to complete only the steps that apply to your rating, based on the following guidelines:

- **P1: High Privacy Risk.** The feature, product, or service stores or transfers personally identifiable information (PII), changes settings or file type associations, or installs software.

- **P2: Moderate Privacy Risk.** The sole behavior that affects privacy in the feature, product, or service is a one-time, user-initiated, anonymous data transfer (for example, the user clicks on a link and the software goes out to a website).
- **P3: Low Privacy Risk.** No behaviors exist within the feature, product, or service that affect privacy. No anonymous or personal data is transferred, no PII is stored on the machine, no settings are changed on the user's behalf, and no software is installed.[22]

The questions are designed to help you complete the privacy aspects of the SDL, and you can complete some sections, such as the initial assessment and a detailed analysis, on your own. It is recommended that you complete other sections, such as the privacy review, together with your privacy advisor.[23]

One of the best ways to protect a customer's privacy is not to collect his or her user data in the first place. The questions that should constantly be asked by architects, developers, and administrators of data collection systems include:

- "Do I need to collect this data?"
- "Do I have a valid business purpose?"
- "Will customers support my business purpose?"[24]

The development organization must keep in mind that for customers to have control over their personal information, they need to know what personal information will be collected, with whom it will be shared, and how it will be used. In addition:

- Customers must provide consent before any personal information is transferred from their computer; and
- If customers' personal information is transferred over the Internet and stored remotely, they must be offered a mechanism for accessing and updating the information.[25]

The guidelines developed in the Microsoft *Privacy Guidelines for Developing Software Products and Services*, Version 3.1,[26] are based on the core concepts of the Organization for Economic Co-operation and Development (OECD) Fair Information Practices[27] and privacy laws such as the EU Data Protection Directive,[28] the U.S. Children's Online Privacy Protection Act of 1998 (COPPA),[29] and the U.S. Computer Fraud and Abuse Act[30] and its amendments. The Microsoft *Privacy Guidelines for Developing Software Products and Services*[31] document is divided into two main sections. Section 1 provides an introduction to key privacy concepts and definitions. Section 2 enumerates detailed guidelines for specific software product and website development scenarios. The table of contents for the *Privacy Guidelines for Developing Software Products and Services* is provided below to show the breadth and scope of the guidance in the document.

Table of Contents

As part of the design requirements activities, additional privacy actions include the creation of privacy design specifications, specification review, and specification of minimal cryptographic design requirements. Design specifications should describe privacy features that will be directly exposed to users, such as those that require user authentication to access specific data or user consent before use of a high-risk privacy feature. In addition, all design specifications should describe how to securely implement all functionality provided by a given feature or function. It is good practice to validate design specifications against the application's functional specification. The functional specification should include (1) an accurate and complete description of the intended use of a feature or function, and (2) a description of how to deploy the feature or function in a secure fashion.[32]

Security controls that help to protect PII data must consider all aspects of data protection, including, but not limited to, access controls, data encryption in transfer and storage, physical security, disaster recovery, and auditing. In many cases, the same security controls that are essential to protecting critical business data, including confidential and proprietary information, from compromise and loss are the same that will be used to protect personal information of customers and employees and should be leveraged whenever possible. This can only be determined after identifying, understanding, and classifying the PII data that the organization collects, stores, or transfers, according to the guidance described in this section.

5.6 Key Success Factors and Metrics

5.6.1 Key Success Factors

Success of this third phase of the SDL depends on a security test plan, design security analysis review, and privacy implementation assessment. It is during this phase that a plan for the rest of the SDL process from implementation to testing is built. Table 5.1 lists key success factors for this third phase.

Success Factor 1: Comprehensive Security Test Plan

During this phase, security architects and the assessment team define various aspects of the software that need to be tested and the types of testing that need to be scheduled and planned both before and after release of the software. The security test plan should map code development phases to the type of testing. For example, with every check-in associated static analysis, a comprehensive static analysis is a must after final code commit. Once the software enters the pre-release cycle, vulnerability assessments, gray box testing, and binary testing should be scheduled. One of the

Table 5.1 Key Success Factors

Key Success Factor	Description
1. Comprehensive security test plan	Mapping types of security testing required at different stages of SDLC
2. Effective threat modeling	Identifying threats to the software
3. Design security analysis	Analysis of threats to various software components
4. Privacy implementation assessment	Effort required for implementation of privacy-related controls based on assessment
5. Policy compliance review (updates)	Updates for policy compliance as related to Phase 3

most critical success factors of this phase and the overall SDL is that the security test plan is able to eliminate most security vulnerabilities before the product is deployed.

Success Factor 2: Effective Threat Modeling

If new threat or attack vectors are identified during this phase, the threat model and artifacts need to be updated to make sure the risk mitigation plan is comprehensive.

Success Factor 3: Design Security Analysis

Along with accuracy of security test plans, review of software design from a security viewpoint is perhaps the most important success factor during the first three phases of the SDL. It is important to minimize the attack surface and improve design principles to maximize the limitation of severity of any security flaws that may be missed in the code.

Success Factor 4: Privacy Implementation Assessment

It is imperative that your estimate of work required in adhering to privacy policies and practices both within the company and outside it are as accurate as possible. This will enable significant cost savings down the road. For example, if privacy practices require that PII data be encrypted across the board, it is critical that this need is identified during the design phase. Once the software is in the execution and release stages, it is often cost-prohibitive to do this. The authors have seen Fortune 500 companies where such decisions are taken during service pack release. By then, however, it is extremely difficult to fix the problem accurately. It is also very expensive. Another example of the problem is network segmentation. In a cloud/SaaS-based environment, this is an important decision to make. Often there will be multiple products hosted out from this shared environment. How to best protect one product from another is an important question for the design phase.

Success Factor 5: Policy Compliance Review (Updates)

If existing policies are updated or additional policies are identified, it is a good idea to review compliance against the new set of requirements. An example of an updated policy might be inclusion of any remaining privacy-related policies or forward-looking strategies.

5.6.2 Deliverables

Table 5.2 lists deliverables for this phase of the SDL.

Updated Threat Modeling Artifacts

Updated data flow diagrams, a technical threat modeling report, a high-level executive threat modeling report, threat lists, and recommendations

Table 5.2 Deliverables for Phase A3

Deliverable	Goal
Updated threat modeling artifacts	Data flow diagrams, elements, threat listing
Design security review	Modifications to design of software components based on security assessments
Security test plans	Plan to mitigate, accept, or tolerate risk
Updated policy compliance analysis	Analysis of adherence to company policies
Privacy implementation assessment results	Recommendations from privacy assessment

for threat analysis based on any new requirements/inputs to attack vectors need to be created.

Design Security Review

This is a formal specification that lists changes to software components and software design based on security review from security architects and assessments.

Security Test Plans

This is a formal security test schedule that maps different stages of the SDL process to different types of security testing (static analysis, fuzzing, vulnerability assessments, binary testing, etc.)

Updated Policy Compliance Analysis

Policy compliance analysis artifacts (see Chapter 4) should be updated based on any new requirements or policies that might have come up during this phase of the SDL.

Privacy Implementation Assessment Results

This is a roadmap to implement recommendations from the privacy implementation assessment. It should be based on privacy risk (high, medium, or low).

5.6.3 Metrics

Since some of the success factors and deliverables are similar to those for Phase 2 of the SDL, the same metrics should be collected and recorded:

- Threats, probability and severity
- Percent compliance with company policies (updated)
  - Percent of compliance in Phase 2 versus Phase 3
- Entry points for software (using DFDs)
- Percent of risk accepted versus mitigated
- Percent of initial software requirements redefined

- Percent of software architecture changes
- Percent of SDLC phases without corresponding software security testing
- Percent of software components with implementations related to privacy controls
- Number of lines of code
- Number of security defects found using static analysis tools
- Number of high-risk defects found using static analysis tools
- Defect density (security issues per 1000 lines of code)

Note that if too many controls related to privacy need to be implemented in the software components, you might want to review the design of the components.

5.7 Chapter Summary

During our discussion of design and development (Phase A3), we described the importance of an analysis of policy compliance, creation of the test plan documentation, updates to the threat modeling discussed in the last chapter if necessary, completion of a design security analysis and review, and a privacy implementation assessment. Out of all of this, best practices are created from the functional and design specifications that have been created that will be used throughout the remainder of the SDL process. Toward the end of the chapter, we discussed key success factors, deliverables, and metrics for this phase.

References

1. McConnell, S. (1996), *Rapid Development*. Microsoft Press, Redmond, WA.
2. Grembi, J. (2008), *Secure Software Development: A Security Programmer's Guide*. Course Technology, Boston, MA.
3. Krutz, R., and Fry, A. (2009), *The CSSLP Prep Guide: Mastering the Certified Secure Software Lifecycle Professional*. Wiley, Indianapolis, IN.
4. Information Assurance Technology Analysis Center (ITAC)/Data and Analysis Center for Software (DACS) (2007), *Software Security Assurance State-of-the-Art Report (SOAR)*. Available at http://iac.dtic.mil/csiac/download/security.pdf.
5. Krutz, R., and Fry, A. (2009), *The CSSLP Prep Guide: Mastering the Certified Secure Software Lifecycle Professional*. Wiley, Indianapolis, IN.

6. Information Assurance Technology Analysis Center (ITAC)/Data and Analysis Center for Software (DACS) (2007), *Software Security Assurance State-of-the-Art Report (SOAR)*. Available at http://iac.dtic.mil/csiac/download/security.pdf.

7. Krutz, R., and Fry, A. (2009), *The CSSLP Prep Guide: Mastering the Certified Secure Software Lifecycle Professional*. Wiley, Indianapolis, IN.

8. Information Assurance Technology Analysis Center (ITAC)/Data and Analysis Center for Software (DACS) (2007), *Software Security Assurance State-of-the-Art Report (SOAR)*. Available at http://iac.dtic.mil/csiac/download/security.pdf.

9. Krutz, R., and Fry, A. (2009), *The CSSLP Prep Guide: Mastering the Certified Secure Software Lifecycle Professional*. Wiley, Indianapolis, IN.

10. Information Assurance Technology Analysis Center (ITAC)/Data and Analysis Center for Software (DACS) (2007), *Software Security Assurance State-of-the-Art Report (SOAR)*. Available at http://iac.dtic.mil/csiac/download/security.pdf.

11. Fink, G., and Bishop, M. (1997), "Property-Based Testing: A New Approach to Testing for Assurance." *SIGSOFT Software Engineering Notes,* vol. 22, no. 4, pp. 74–80.

12. Goertzel, K., et al. (2008), *Enhancing the Development Life Cycle to Produce Secure Software. Version 2.0.* U.S. Department of Defense Data and Analysis Center for Software, Rome, NY.

13. Michael, C., and Radosevich, W. (2005), "Risk-Based and Functional Security Testing." Cigital white paper, U.S. Department of Homeland Security. Updated 2009-07-23 by Ken van Wyk. Available at https://buildsecurityin.us-cert.gov/bsi/articles/best-practices/testing/255-BSI.html#dsy255-BSI_sstest.

14. Saltzer, J., and Schroeder, M. (1974), "The Protection of Information in Computer Systems." Fourth ACM Symposium on Operating Systems Principle, October 1974.

15. Ibid.

16. Grembi, J. (2008), *Secure Software Development: A Security Programmer's Guide*. Course Technology, Boston, MA.

17. Microsoft Corporation (2008), *Privacy Guidelines for Developing Software Products and Services*, Version 3.1; September 2008. Available at http://www.microsoft.com/en-us/download/details.aspx?id=16048.

18. Microsoft Corporation (2012). MSDN, *SDL—Process Guidance—Appendix C: SDL Privacy Questionnaire*. Available at http://msdn.microsoft.com/en-us/library/cc307393.aspx.

19. Microsoft (2011), *Simplified Implementation of the Microsoft SDL*. Available at http://www.microsoft.com/en-us/download/details.aspx?id=12379.

20. Microsoft Corporation (2008), *Privacy Guidelines for Developing Software Products and Services*, Version 3.1; September 2008. Available at http://www.microsoft.com/en-us/download/details.aspx?id=16048.

21. Microsoft Corporation (2012), MSDN, *SDL—Process Guidance—Appendix C: SDL Privacy Questionnaire*. Available at http://msdn.microsoft.com/en-us/library/cc307393.aspx.

22. Microsoft (2011), *Simplified Implementation of the Microsoft SDL*. Available at http://www.microsoft.com/en-us/download/details.aspx?id=12379.

23. Microsoft Corporation (2012), MSDN, *SDL—Process Guidance—Appendix C: SDL Privacy Questionnaire*. Available at http://msdn.microsoft.com/en-us/library/cc307393.aspx.
24. Microsoft Corporation (2008), *Privacy Guidelines for Developing Software Products and Services*, Version 3.1; September 2008. Available at http://www.microsoft.com/en-us/download/details.aspx?id=16048.
25. Ibid.
26. Ibid.
27. Organisation for Economic Co-operation and Development (1980), *OECD Guidelines on the Protection of Privacy and Transborder Flows of Personal Data: Background*. Available at http://oecdprivacy.org.
28. *Official Journal of the European Communities* (2001), "REGULATION (EC) No 45/2001 OF THE EUROPEAN PARLIAMENT AND OF THE COUNCIL of 18 December 2000 on the Protection of Individuals with Regard to the Processing of Personal Data by the Community Institutions and Bodies and on the Free Movement of Such Data." Available at http://eurlex.europa.eu/LexUriServ/LexUriServ.do?uri=OJ:L:2001:008:0001:0022:en:PDF.
29. United States Government (1998), *Children's Online Privacy Protection Act of 1998 (COPPA)*. 15 U.S.C. §§ 6501–6506 (Pub.L. 105-277, 112 Stat. 2581-728, enacted October 21, 1998). Available at http://www.ftc.gov/ogc/coppa1.htm.
30. Doyle, C. (2008), *CRS Report for Congress—Cybercrime: A Sketch of 18 U.S.C. 1030 and Related Federal Criminal Laws*, Updated February 25, 2008. Available at http://fpc.state.gov/documents/organization/103707.pdf.
31. Microsoft Corporation (2008), *Privacy Guidelines for Developing Software Products and Services*, Version 3.1; September 2008. Available at http://www.microsoft.com/en-us/download/details.aspx?id=16048.
32. Microsoft (2011), *Simplified Implementation of the Microsoft SDL*. Available at http://www.microsoft.com/en-us/download/details.aspx?id=12379.

Chapter 6

Design and Development (A4): SDL Activities and Best Practices

In this chapter we will describe the SDL activities for the design and development (A4) phase of our security development lifecycle (see Figure 6.1). This phase can be mapped to the "readiness" phase in a typical software development lifecycle. We start with the continuation of policy compliance analysis for this phase and then move on to describe the elements of security test case execution. Building on the proper process for security testing that should have already been created, documented, and tested, analysis will continue until necessary tuning is identified in order to accomplish the required security level. We then describe the use of automated tools such as static, dynamic, and fuzz test tools to help automate and enforce security practices efficiently and effectively at a low cost. Static analysis analyzes the source code prior to compiling, provides a scalable method of security code review, and helps ensure that secure coding policies are being followed. Dynamic analysis monitors application behavior and ensures that the software functionality works

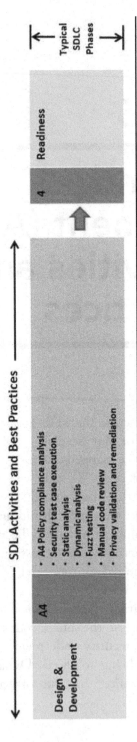

Figure 6.1 Design and Development (A4): SDL activities and best practices.

as designed. Fuzz testing induces program failure by deliberately introducing malformed or random data to an application and can be used as an effective and low-cost way of finding potential security issues prior to release and potentially throughout the SDL process. Fuzz testing is a specialized form of dynamic analysis. By using the latest version of these automated tools, the latest known automated security analysis, vulnerabilities, and recommended protections will be identified. After these multiple automated tools have been used to quickly analyze the flaws and vulnerabilities in the software, the code is then reviewed manually, every issue validated, and the code inspected to overcome the limitations of automated tools and techniques. As part of this process, attack surface and threat model reviews will ensure that any new attack vectors that have been created by any design or implementation changes have been identified and mitigated. Finally, we discuss the need, value, and process for privacy validation and remediation to be conducted during this phase of the SDL.

6.1 A4 Policy Compliance Analysis

This is a continuation of the A3 policy compliance review described in the previous chapter. As you will see, we continue to perform policy compliance analysis during different phases and review it again and again. It is of paramount importance that you persist through this and not make an assumption that you have covered everything in previous iterations. You will be surprised how often things are missed during initial phases/iterations of this step.

During this phase, any policy that exists outside the domain of the SDL policy is reviewed (or reviewed again). This may include policies from outside the development organization that carry security and privacy requirements and guidelines to be adhered to when developing software or applications anywhere within the organization. Often, too, policies are updated during the development process, and new requirements are added. Thus it is best to obtain a list of updated policies and make sure you have incorporated any additional requirements.

Corporate security and privacy policies will likely instruct designers and developers on what the security and privacy features need to be and how they must be implemented. Other policies may focus on the use of third-party and open-source software used as part of a software product or on the protections and control of source code and other intellectual property within and outside the organization. Assuming the software security group is separate from the centralized information security group, it is important that the two groups collaborate on all policies and guidelines related to the development and post-release security support by the organization. It helps the information security group to fine-tune its policies not only for corporate security policies/practices but also for software development. It is also important to collaborate with the privacy function of your company, whether it be a centralized group or outside legal counsel. If the company identifies potential new markets, privacy policies and practices (for that particular market) may be updated.

6.2 Security Test Case Execution

Security testing is a time-consuming process that requires proper preparation, consistency, and coordination with all stakeholders, as well as a deep understanding of what you are actually testing. It starts early and continues throughout the SDLC process. The approach for security testing is different from other forms of testing in that its purpose is to identify various vulnerabilities in a software design which are exposed and due to improper design or coding issues. The premise of this book is to secure at the source, and testing at this level will prevent many of the vulnerabilities that are typically found only when the software is exposed at the network level. Security, especially at the design level, can help us identify potential security problems and their impact before they are part of a larger system and network and perhaps cost-prohibitive to fix. Software security is a dynamic risk management exercise in that you are balancing the costs of potential assurance remedies against the skills and resources of adversaries—and there are always intelligent adversaries who are focused on breaking and exploiting your software. Thus, the security test itself must assess the probability of occurrence of an event based on exploiting a vulnerability and the risk associated with each potential occurrence.

In a typical SDLC cycle, software goes through quality assurance (QA) testing that includes unit, performance, system, and regression testing. If the software passes through test criteria for this QA testing, it will be given a "Go" by the QA team. Basically, this means that the software has been tested for quality and is good to go. From the authors' point of view, QA testing is not complete unless all security tests have been performed and the security test acceptance criteria are all met. Software cannot be a quality product unless it has been comprehensively tested for security issues. Treating security testing as an add-on is a mistake that many companies still make. Once QA testing is complete, the software goes to the security team for security testing. In our opinion, routine security testing should be part of the QA cycle. The QA team should treat security testing just like any other testing, and should create test cases and perform both manual and automated testing just as they would any other testing. The QA team, however, often does not have the skills to execute security test cases, which therefore often means that the QA team relies on the security team to perform *all* testing. This approach is not very effective and takes time away from the security team, which has to perform basic security tests instead of looking at advanced threats/corner cases. QA security testing is not meant to replace security testing by the security team. Instead, it should be looked upon as enabling the security team to focus on advanced testing. Below are a few examples of issues that QA security testing should look for:

- Plaintext passwords/weak passwords in configuration files
- Default accounts on the stack (Apache, Tomcat, operating systems)
- Sensitive information in log files
- Input validation (XSS, SQLi)
- Parameter tampering for Web applications
- Insecure services used by the software team (e.g., Telnet)
- Security configurations for various services (e.g., NFS)

The QA team should focus not just on application but also on the stack on which the software will run. This means testing various configurations of operating systems and related services, Web servers, etc., from a security point of view. Before QA gives the "Go" for a product, the entire stack (application, operation system, Web servers, storage) should have been tested for basic security issues.

Security test case execution is carried out from two primary perspectives:

1. Security mechanisms are tested to ensure that their functionality is properly implemented; and

2. Security testing is conducted in relation to understanding and simulating the attacker's approach as identified during threat modeling and other associated risk-based analyses.

Typically, three specific test type categories are performed on a software product and its associated system(s):

1. **Benchmarks.** These tests are used to compare estimates to actual results.
2. **Scheduled tests.** These tests include mandatory requirements to validate the security of the software and associated system(s) being tested, which must be conducted regardless of whether security issues or vulnerabilities are detected or tuning is required.
3. **Exploratory tests.** Exploratory testing emphasizes the personal freedom and responsibility of the individual tester to continually optimize the quality of his or her work by treating test-related learning, test design, test execution, and test result interpretation as mutually supportive activities that run in parallel throughout the project.[1] The tester actively controls the design of the tests, and those tests are performed while testing to design new and better tests.

A successful security test execution plan assumes that:

- You have done a detailed risk analysis to evaluate the software and the system(s) with which it will be associated. This process was detailed in the Chapter 5.
- Test assets have been developed as part of the risk management plan and the development of a security engineering/development test strategy.

Successful security test execution includes the following:

- Baseline and benchmark tests have been performed to ensure that obvious security issues have been identified early in the testing cycle.
- Automated test scripts have been validated as correct.
- Re-benchmarking testing has been conducted after tuning.
- A basis for future test comparison has been created.
- The results of the security test case execution have been analyzed.

o *Test execution results have been evaluated.* Your seasoned software security architects have a key role here, as they apply their skills and experience to compare the evaluation to previous tests, finding and analyze patterns including identification of obvious or potential security issues and/or the effects of the tuning effort, and apply their past experiences to the evaluation. Since this evaluation is more an art than a science, the software security architects should also involve the testers and developers in the analysis after the architects' initial review and evaluation to optimize the results of the analysis toward driving tuning efforts.

o *You have determined whether security test case execution acceptance criteria have been met.* This is a result of comparing the results from the most recent test, or suite of tests, to the acceptance criteria. If all of the results meet or exceed the security test execution criteria, then the test is complete; if not, the team should continue to evaluate the results.

o *You have determined whether the security test case execution results are conclusive.* If the results do not meet the acceptance criteria, then the test is likely inconclusive because the test results are not reproducible and you are unable to determine what is causing the security issue in the software. If results are inconclusive, an exploratory test will be needed.

o *You have determined whether tuning is required at this point.* At this stage, either a security issue has been detected or more tests are needed to validate compliance with additional acceptance criteria. Either the last test will be executed again to see whether the results are reproducible, or you will move on to tuning.

o There are some tests where no security issues are found and no tuning is required, but the software must be tested because there it is mandatory to validate the security of the software and its associated system(s) against specifically known software security issues and vulnerabilities.

Successful security test case execution completion criteria include the following:

• The specific target security requirements and goals of the software that has been tested have been met.

- When a situation outside the control of the software security group or its equivalent cannot be resolved, the security testing may be deemed complete as a result of any one of the following situations, if the company stakeholders responsible for the development of the software accept the risk:
  o The situation preventing the software security group or its equivalent from achieving its security test case criteria is outside the group's control or contractual obligations.
  o The predetermined engagement end date is reached and company stakeholders responsible for the development of the software accept the risk of not meeting the security criteria. In many cases this is accepted if a commitment to fix the vulnerability is scheduled for the next update of the product and/or patch release.
  o The software security group or its equivalent and all other stakeholders agree that the application performs acceptably, even though some security requirements or goals have not been achieved. As with the previous situation, this is typically not accepted unless the commitment to fix the vulnerability is scheduled for the next update of the product and/or patch release.

6.3 Code Review in the SDLC/SDL Process

Code review can be especially productive for identifying security vulnerabilities during software development. A properly conducted code review can do more for the security of your code than nearly any other activity. A code review allows you to find and fix a large number of security issues before the code is tested or shipped. There are four basic techniques for analyzing the security of a software application: automated scanning, manual penetration testing, static analysis, and manual code review. All of these methodologies, of course, have strengths, weaknesses, sweet spots, and blind spots. Collectively, these four types of security code reviews are likely the fastest and most accurate way to find and diagnose many security problems while being less expensive or time-consuming than they are warranted to be. If planned for and managed correctly, code reviews are very cost-effective, especially if they are built into the SDLC as part of the process, thereby avoiding the expensive process of handling, locating, and fixing security vulnerabilities during later stages of development or after

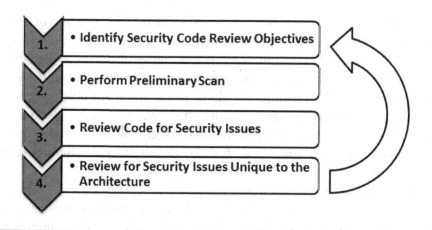

Figure 6.2   Four-step code review cycle.

software product release. Experienced and empowered security personnel who are knowledgeable about the four basic techniques of code review should be employed to ensure that the various techniques are mixed and matched as appropriate to create the most cost-effective and well managed plan for identifying all potential and known significant security issues in the software being developed. The human element in the process will also help apply context to the security vulnerabilities found by the automated tools. This holistic approach will be able to find problems or potential issues, prove that they are exploitable, and verify them by examining the code. Another advantage of this approach is that it facilitates the experience and education of the development team in the use of security best practices, which will help prevent future security issues. The process can be broken down into four primary steps as shown graphically in Figure 6.2 and described below.

1. Identify Security Code Review Objectives

During this step, goals and constraints are established for the review as the bases for an overall plan. As with most projects, if there is no basis for a plan, there will likely be a failed project. This is particularly the case when large amounts of code and/or complex SaaS/cloud applications are involved. A focused code review is an effective code review. This is why it is important to review the code with specific goals, time limits, and knowledge of the issues you want to uncover. This will significantly increase your chances for success while reducing the amount of time required for review. Having a plan will allow the reviewers to focus on reviewing the code each time there is a meaningful change rather than trying to find all of the security issues at once, or waiting until the end of the project and reviewing everything at one time. For efficiency, you should also identify any stated security objectives that are already known prior to review, so you can differentiate between vulnerability types that have elevated priority and others that may be out of scope based on your security objectives.

Security code review is most successful if it is planned and executed in the context of other security-related efforts such as threat modeling as described in the previous chapter. Threat modeling helps to identify a critical area of code that then becomes a subject of detailed review, and its results can likewise be used to validate or question security assumptions specified in a threat model and help to understand the application's functionality, technical design, and existing security threats and countermeasures. A security code review should begin with a review of the threat models and design specifications, then move on to source code.

The ideal flow of activities for code review success is perhaps best described by the steps identified by Chmielewski et al. in MSDN Magazine:

(a) *Threat Modeling:* Understand code and data flows; identify high-risk areas and entry points.
(b) *Code Reviews:* Document all findings in an appropriate way, as well as the process itself.
(c) *Resolve Problems:* Cooperate with owners of code on applying fixes and further efforts.
(d) *Learn the Lesson:* Update tools, educate development teams, improve processes, and plan future iterations.[2]

For an effective security code review, set goals and constraints for the following.

- *Time:* Set a time limit. This helps you to avoid spending too much time on a single issue. Performing multiple, smaller reviews is more effective than doing one long review.
- *Types of issues:* Determine what types of issues you are looking for. For example, consider:

- o General issues that affect confidentially, integrity, and availability
- o Issues related to your application's security quality-of-service requirements
- o Issues related to your application's compliance requirements
- o Issues related to the technologies your application uses
- o Issues related to the functionality your application exposes
- o Issues you found during threat modeling
- *Out-of-scope items:* Identify what you will not be looking for. Explain why these things are out of scope.[3]

2. Perform Preliminary Scan

Static analysis is used to find an initial set of security issues and to improve your understanding of where you will be most likely to find security issues when you review the code more fully and to discover hot spots where additional security issues are likely to be discovered in later steps. This is typically done with automatic scans, manual scans, or a combination of both, depending on the review objectives and time limitations of the code review plan. Automated scans have an advantage in their ability to quickly identify "low-hanging fruit" across large sets of applications. The results from these scans are used in creating a prioritized list of potential security vulnerabilities and security mechanisms to review and investigate.

An automatic scan can be used to supplement a manual review, as an extra check to go through large volumes of code that would be cost- and/ or time-prohibitive to do manually, to target areas to focus on for manual reviews, and to find security issues that may have been missed during manual review. Automatic scanning tools are typically good at finding security issues that are a result of single lines of code, finding security issues that span multiple lines of code in a single function, and may find problems that manual reviews will miss. Although automatic scanning can supplement a manual review, it should not be used to replace it because of the contextual problems and inability to find security issues over multiple functions such as those found in SaaS/cloud applications. Another issue with automated tools is the number of false positives and negatives that are found, which may require significant efforts to tune down to a reasonable number. On the positive side, these types of results will force you to gain a better understanding of the code, including controls and data flow, by forcing you to review why a false positive is false. Another risk of using automated tools is the possible sense of security in believing there are no security issues in your software if no security issues are identified as a result of the scan. A significantly sized and complex software product should never be assumed to be free of security vulnerabilities. All possible steps should be taken to limit the number of coding errors and reduce their practical impact, but something is always missed. Automated security tools are able to identify more and more coding errors, but some vulnerabilities will still be missed and either not detected or hidden among large numbers of false positives. Manual source code analysis is not a replacement for these tools, but it helps maximize the identification of vulnerabilities when integrated with them. As mentioned throughout this book, it requires a holistic approach to security, including a human element, to ensure that both false positives are false and that the code is really free of security vulnerabilities in spite of being given what appears to be a clean bill of health by the automated tools. Using both methods together enables reviewers to identify more software security vulnerabilities both efficiently and cost-effectively. For these reasons, automated review combined with a manual review is the best approach.

To catch the simpler issues, available security tools should be run against the code before manual review begins. To avoid finding already-known issues, all previously identified security vulnerabilities should be fixed. A manual scan is then conducted to gain a better understanding of the code and to recognize patterns; the results of the scan will identify areas that merit further analysis as the reviewers analyze the code for security issues in Step 3 below. This effort, however, should be a small percentage of the total code review time and should focus on answering the following questions:

- *Input data validation:* Does the application have an input validation architecture? Is validation performed on the client, on the server, or both? Is there a centralized validation mechanism, or are validation routines spread throughout the code base?
- *Code that authenticates and authorizes users:* Does the application authenticate users? What roles are allowed, and how do they interact? Is there custom authentication or authorization code?
- *Error-handling code:* Is there a consistent error-handling architecture? Does the application catch and throw structured exceptions? Are there areas of the code with especially dense or sparse error handling?

- *Complex code:* Are there areas of the code that appear especially complex?
- *Cryptography:* Does the application use cryptography?
- *Interop:* Does the application use interop to call into native code?[4]

3. Review Code for Security Issues

The results from Step 2 are typically used to focus the analysis of the reviewer during Step 3.

4. Review for Security Issues Unique to the Architecture

This is where the software security architect or seasoned software security champion come into play. In some cases, a third party may be used if you don't have the expertise in-house. This allows experts to apply their knowledge of the business logic, use and abuse cases, and prior experience to identify vulnerabilities while reducing the likelihood of false positives and false negatives. Static analysis tools are incapable of finding application flaws and business logic vulnerabilities and require the context and application understanding of a human analyst to identify. Having seasoned security professionals involved throughout the SDLC process will balance the developers' tendency to overlook certain coding errors even though they wrote the specific fragments of code and usually understand them best. Seasoned security experts can also help in understanding the technological context of the code, including not only the specific technologies that are used in the software product, but also operating-system and third-party dependencies as well as tools used in development. From a security perspective, these security experts can identify relationships between a product and other systems, applications, or services. In the context of security, it is possible for them to determine what components a product relies on, as well as what other software depends on the product, and how these relationships can be used to determine how a product affects the rest of the system and how it may be affected by it. Human errors are typically the cause of most security problems; given the current shortcomings of automated tools, humans should also be part of the solution. For example, a small coding error can result in a critical vulnerability that ends up compromising the security of an entire system or network or may result from a sequence of errors that occur during the course of the development cycle where a coding error is introduced and goes undetected during the testing phases, and available defense mechanisms do not stop a successful attack. This is just another example of why the human element is necessary in the process, to be able to assess these types of situations which are currently beyond the capabilities of automated software security tools.

The basic design of a product may also contain flaws, and it should be noted that some coding errors, although they may affect product reliability, are not actual vulnerabilities. Remember that the ultimate goal of security code reviews is to find code vulnerabilities that are accessible by an attacker and that may allow the attacker to bypass a security boundary.

6.4 Security Analysis Tools

The final goal of the security code review process is to improve the overall security of the product and to provide output that can be used by the development team to make changes and/or mitigations that will achieve improved software product security compared to what existed at concept commit for the start of the SDLC/SDL process. In this section we discuss the details of what functions and roles static analysis, dynamic analysis, fuzz testing, and manual code review have in this overall process. Before we begin, however, it is important to recognize that each approach has certain practical advantages and limitations.

Advantages of Static Code Analysis

1. Access to the actual instructions the software will be executing
   * No need to guess or interpret behavior
   * Full access to all of the software's possible behaviors
2. Can find exact location of weaknesses in the code
3. Can be conducted by trained software assurance developers who fully understand the code
4. Allows quick turnaround for fixes
5. Relatively fast if automated tools are used
6. Automated tools can scan the entire code base.
7. Automated tools can provide mitigation recommendations, reducing research time.

8. Permits weaknesses to be found earlier in the development lifecycle, reducing the cost to fix[5,6]

Limitations of Static Code Analysis

1. Requires access to source code or at least binary code and typically needs access to enough software artifacts to execute a build
2. Typically requires proficiency in running software builds
3. Will not find issues related to operational deployment environments
4. Time-consuming if conducted manually
5. Automated tools do not support all programming languages.
6. Automated tools produce false positives and false negatives.
7. There are not enough trained personnel to thoroughly conduct static code analysis.
8. Automated tools can provide a false sense of security that everything is being addressed.
9. Automated tools are only as good as the rules they are using to scan with.
10. Does not find vulnerabilities introduced in the runtime environment[7,8]

Advantages of Dynamic Code Analysis

1. Limited scope of what can be found
   - Application must be footprinted to find the test area.
   - That can cause areas to be missed.
   - You can only test what you have found.
2. No access to actual instructions being executed
   - The tool is exercising the application.
   - Pattern matching on requests and responses.
3. Requires only a running system to perform a test
4. No requirement to have access to source code or binary code
5. No need to understand how to write software or execute builds
   - Tools tend to be more "fire and forget."
6. Tests a specific operational deployment
   - Can find infrastructure, configuration, and patch errors that static analysis tools will miss.
7. Identifies vulnerabilities in a runtime environment
8. Automated tools provide flexibility on what to scan for.

9. Allows for analysis of applications without access to the actual code
10. Identifies vulnerabilities that might have been false negatives in the static code analysis
11. Permits validation of static code analysis findings
12. Can be conducted on any application[9,10]

Limitations of Dynamic Code Analysis

1. Automated tools provide a false sense of security that everything is being addressed.
2. Automated tools produce false positives and false negatives.
3. Automated tools are only as good as the rules they are using to scan with.
4. As for static analysis, there are not enough trained personnel to thoroughly conduct dynamic code analysis.
5. It is more difficult to trace the vulnerability back to the exact location in the code, taking longer to fix the problem.[11,12]

If you have no access to source or binaries, are not a software developer, and don't understand software builds, or you are performing a "pen test" or other test of an operational environment, you will likely choose to use a dynamic tool; otherwise, you will likely use a static analysis tool. Ideally, you should use both when possible.

Advantages of Fuzz Testing

1. The great advantage of fuzz testing is that the test design is extremely simple, and free of preconceptions about system behavior.
2. The systematical/random approach allows this method to find bugs that would often be missed by human eyes. Plus, when the tested system is totally closed (e.g., a SIP phone), fuzzing is one of the only means of reviewing its quality.
3. Bugs found using fuzz testing are frequently severe, exploitable bugs that could be used by a real attacker. This has become even truer as fuzz testing has become more widely known, because the same techniques and tools are now used by attackers to exploit deployed software. This is a major advantage over binary or source auditing, or even fuzzing's close cousin, fault injection, which often relies on artificial fault conditions that are difficult or impossible to exploit.

Limitations of Fuzz Testing

1. Fuzzers usually tend to find simple bugs; plus, the more a fuzzer is protocol-aware, the fewer weird errors it will find. This is why the exhaustive/random approach is still popular.
2. Another problem is that when you do some black-box testing, you usually attack a closed system, which increases the difficulty of evaluating the danger/impact of the found vulnerability (no debugging possibilities).
3. The main problem with fuzzing to find program faults is that it generally finds only very simple faults. The problem itself is exponential, and every fuzzer takes shortcuts to find something interesting in a timeframe that a human cares about. A primitive fuzzer may have poor code coverage; for example, if the input includes a checksum which is not properly updated to match other random changes, only the checksum validation code will be verified. Code coverage tools are often used to estimate how "well" a fuzzer works, but these are only guidelines to fuzzer quality. Every fuzzer can be expected to find a different set of bugs.[13,14]

Advantages of Manual Source Code Review

1. Requires no supporting technology
2. Can be applied to a variety of situations
3. Flexible
4. Promotes teamwork
5. Early in the SDLC

Limitations of Manual Source Code Review

1. Can be time-consuming
2. Supporting material not always available
3. Requires significant human thought and skill to be effective[15]

6.4.1 Static Analysis

Static program analysis is the analysis of computer software that is performed without actually executing programs. It is used predominantly to perform analysis on a version of the source code; it is also performed on object code. In contrast, dynamic analysis is performed by actually executing the software programs. Static analysis is performed by an automated software tool and should not be confused with human analysis or software security architectural reviews, which involve manual human code reviews, including program understanding and comprehension. When static analysis tools are used properly, they have a distinct advantage over human static analysis in that the analysis can be performed much more frequently and with security knowledge superior to that of many software developers. It thus allows for expert software security architects or engineers to be brought in only when absolutely necessary.

Static analysis (see Figure 6.3) is also known as static application security testing (SAST). It identifies vulnerabilities during the development or quality assurance (QA) phase of a project. SAST provides line-of-code-level detection that enables development teams to remediate vulnerabilities quickly.

The use of static analysis tools and your choice of an appropriate vendor for your environment is another technology factor that is key to success. Any technology that beneficially automates any portion of the software development process should be welcome, but this software has become

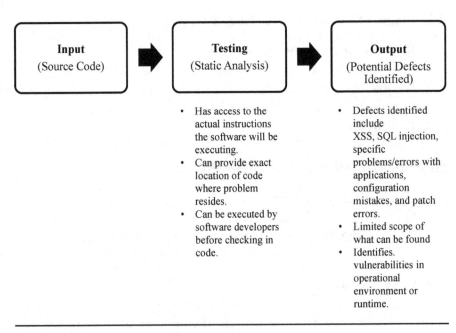

Figure 6.3   Static analysis flow diagram.

"shelfware" in many organizations because the right people and/or the right process was not used in selecting the tool or tools. Not all tools are created equal in this space: Some are better at some languages than others, whereas others have great front-end GRC (governance, risk management, and compliance) and metric analysis capabilities. In some cases you may have to use up to three different tools to be effective. Some of the popular SAST vendor products are Coverity,[16] HP Fortify Static Code Analyzer,[17] IBM Security AppScan Source,[18] klocwork,[19] Parasoft,[20] and Veracode.[21]

One of the challenges in using a static analysis tool is that false positives may be reported when analyzing an application that interacts with closed-source components or external systems, because without the source code it is impossible to trace the flow of data in the external system and hence ensure the integrity and security of the data. The use of static code analysis tools can also result in false negative results, when vulnerabilities exist but the tool does not report them. This might occur if a new vulnerability is discovered in an external component or if the analysis tool has no knowledge of the runtime environment and whether it is configured securely. A static code analysis tool will often produce false positive results where the tool reports a possible vulnerability that in fact is not. This often occurs because the tool cannot be sure of the integrity and security of data as it flows through the application from input to output.[22]

Michael Howard, in his Security & Privacy 2006 IEEE article titled "A Process for Performing Security Code Reviews,"[23] proposes the following heuristic as an aid to determining code review priority. The heuristic can be used as a guide for prioritizing static, dynamic, fuzzing, and manual code reviews.

- **Old code:** Older code may have more vulnerabilities than new code, because newer code often reflects a better understanding of security issues. All "legacy" code should be reviewed in depth.
- **Code that runs by default:** Attackers often go after installed code that runs by default. Such code should be reviewed earlier and more deeply than code that does not execute by default. Code running by default increases an application's attack surface.
- **Code that runs in elevated context:** Code that runs in elevated identities, e.g., root in *nix, for example, also requires earlier and deeper review, because code identity is another component of the attack surface.

- **Anonymously accessible code:** Code that anonymous users can access should be reviewed in greater depth than code that only valid users and administrators can access.
- **Code listening on a globally accessible network interface:** Code that listens by default on a network, especially uncontrolled networks such as the Internet, is open to substantial risk and must be reviewed in depth for security vulnerabilities.
- **Code written in C/C++/assembly language:** Because these languages have direct access to memory, buffer-manipulation vulnerabilities within the code can lead to buffer overflows, which often lead to malicious code execution. Code written in these languages should be analyzed in depth for buffer overflow vulnerabilities.
- **Code with a history of vulnerabilities:** Code that has shown a number of security vulnerabilities in the past should be suspect, unless it can be demonstrated that those vulnerabilities have been effectively removed.
- **Code that handles sensitive data:** Code that handles sensitive data should be analyzed to ensure that weaknesses in the code do not disclose such data to untrusted users.
- **Complex code:** Complex code has a higher bug probability, is more difficult to understand, and may be likely to have more security vulnerabilities.
- **Code that changes frequently:** Frequently changing code often results in new bugs being introduced. Not all of these bugs will be security vulnerabilities, but compared with a stable set of code that is updated only infrequently, code that is less stable will probably have more vulnerabilities.

In Michael Howard's 2004 Microsoft article titled "Mitigate Security Risks by Minimizing the Code You Expose to Untrusted Users,"[24] he also suggests a notional three-phase code analysis process that optimizes the use of static analysis tools:

Phase 1: Run all available code analysis tools.

- Multiple tools should be used to offset tool biases and minimize false positives and false negatives.
- Analysts should pay attention to every warning or error.

- Warnings from multiple tools may indicate that the code needs closer scrutiny (e.g., manual analysis). Code should be evaluated early, preferably with each build, and re-evaluated at every milestone.

Phase 2: Look for common vulnerability patterns.

- Analysts should make sure that code reviews cover the most common vulnerabilities and weaknesses, such as integer arithmetic issues, buffer overruns, SQL injection, and cross-site scripting (XSS).
- Sources for such common vulnerabilities and weaknesses include the Common Vulnerabilities and Exposures (CVE) and Common Weaknesses Enumeration (CWE) databases, maintained by the MITRE Corporation and accessible at: http://cve.mitre.org/cve/ and http://cwe.mitre.org.
- MITRE, in cooperation with the SANS Institute, also maintain a list of the "Top 25 Most Dangerous Programming Errors" (http://cwe.mitre.org/top25/index.html) that can lead to serious vulnerabilities.
- Static code analysis tool and manual techniques should, at a minimum, address the "Top 25."

Phase 3: Dig deep into risky code.

- Analysts should also use manual analysis (e.g., code inspection) to more thoroughly evaluate any risky code that has been identified based on the attack surface, or based on the heuristics as discussed previously.
- Such code review should start at the entry point for each module under review and should trace data flow through the system, evaluating the data, how it is used, and whether security objectives might be compromised.

Below is an example of an issue that can be found through static analysis. Injection vulnerabilities are at the top of the OWASP Top 10 2013 list.[25] These vulnerabilities occur when untrusted data is used directly for a query or as a result of construct commands without validation. There are different types of injection vulnerabilities, SQL, OS, and LDAP among them. SQL injection attacks are possible if user input is used directly to craft a SQL query.

Let's say that a user wants to review his account details. The application needs his user id or identifier to query account information from a back-end database. The application can pass this on through a URL parameter by doing something like this:

http://example.com/application/reviewaccount?account_id='1007'

In this case, the application is getting user account_id '1007' and will use this id to pull information from the database. Let's say the back-end query looks like this:

String insecureQuery = "SELECT * FROM accounts WHERE accountID=' " + request.getParameter("account_id") + " ' ";

If a malicious user changes the parameter value to ' or '1'='1, the following string insecure query will have the value

SELECT * FROM accounts WHERE accountID=' " ' or '1'='1';

'1'='1' will always be true, and thus this query can yield information about all accounts. This was not the intention of the developer, but by trusting user input to create a query, he or she has allowed a malicious user to execute arbitrary database commands.

Static analysis tools executed against code will identify that the query is built with user input and can result in SQL injection attacks.

6.4.2 Dynamic Analysis

Dynamic program analysis is the analysis of computer software that is performed by executing programs on a real or virtual processor in real time. The objective is to find security errors in a program while it is running, rather than by repeatedly examining the code offline. By debugging a program under all the scenarios for which it is designed, dynamic analysis eliminates the need to artificially create situations likely to produce errors. It has the distinct advantages of having the ability to identify vulnerabilities that might have been false negatives and to validate findings in the static code analysis.

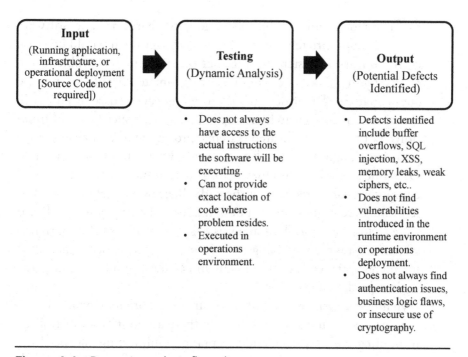

Figure 6.4   Dynamic analysis flow diagram.

Dynamic analysis (see Figure 6.4) is also known as dynamic application security testing (DAST). It identifies vulnerabilities within a production application. DAST tools are used to quickly assess a system's overall security and are used within both the SDL and SDLC. The same advantages and cautions about using static analysis tools apply to dynamic analysis tools. Some of the more popular DAST vendor products include HP Webinspect[26] and QAinspect,[27] IBM Security AppScan Enterprise,[28] Veracode,[29] and Whitehat Sentinel Source.[30]

The following explanation of how dynamic analysis is used throughout the SDLC is taken from the Peng and Wallace (1993) NIST Special Publication 500-209, *Software Error Analysis.*[31]

- Commonly used dynamic analysis techniques for the design phase include sizing and timing analysis, prototyping, and simulation. Sizing and timing analysis is useful in analyzing real-time programs with response-time requirements and constrained memory and execution-space requirements. This type of analysis is especially useful for determining that allocations for hardware and software are made appropriately for the design architecture; it would be quite costly to learn in system testing that the performance problems are caused by the basic system design. An automated simulation may be appropriate for larger designs. Prototyping can be used as an aid in examining the design architecture in general or a specific set of functions. For large, complicated systems, prototyping can prevent inappropriate designs from resulting in costly, wasted implementations.[32]

- Dynamic analysis techniques help to determine the functional and computational correctness of the code. Regression analysis is used to re-evaluate requirements and design issues whenever any significant code change is made. This analysis ensures awareness of the original system requirements. Sizing and timing analysis is performed during incremental code development and analysis results are compared against predicted values.[33]

- Dynamic analysis in the test phase involves different types of testing and test strategies. Traditionally there are four types of testing: unit, integration, system, and acceptance. Unit testing may be either structural or functional testing performed on software units, modules, or subroutines. Structural testing examines the logic of the units and may be used to support requirements for test coverage—that is, how much of the program has been executed. Functional testing evaluates how software requirements have been implemented. For functional testing, testers usually need no information about the design of the program, because test cases are based on the software requirements.[34]

- The most commonly used dynamic analysis techniques for the final phase of the SDLC are regression analysis and test, simulation, and test certification. When any changes to the product are made during this phase, regression analysis is performed to verify that the basic requirements and design assumptions affecting other areas of the program have not been violated. Simulation is used to test operator procedures and to isolate installation problems. Test certification, particularly in critical software systems, is used to verify that the required tests have been executed and that the delivered software product is identical to the product subjected to software verification and validation.[35]

Static analysis finds issues by analyzing source code. Dynamic analysis tools do not need source code but can still identify the problem. During our discussion of static analysis, we reviewed an SQL injection attack example. For that example, the tool would identify that account_id is passed as a URL parameter and would try to tamper the value of the parameter and evaluate the response from the application.

6.4.3 Fuzz Testing

Fuzz testing (see Figure 6.5), or fuzzing, is a black-box software testing technique that can be automated or semiautomated and provides invalid, unexpected, or random data to the inputs of a computer software program. In other words, it finds implementation bugs or security flaws by using malformed/semi-malformed data injection in an automated fashion. Inputs to the software program are then monitored for exception returns such as crashes, failing built-in code assertions, and potential memory leaks. Fuzzing has become a key element in testing for software or computer system security problems. Fuzz testing has a distinct advantage over

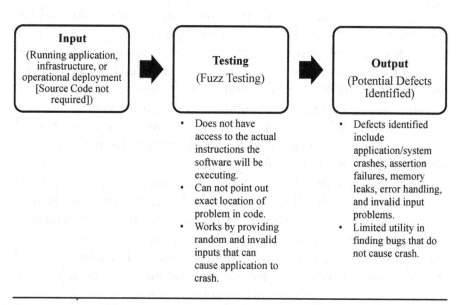

Figure 6.5   Fuzz testing flow diagram.

other tools in that the test design is extremely simple and free of preconceptions about system behavior.

Fuzzing is a key element of software security and must be embedded in the SDL. There are many vendors to choose from in this space, and some even develop their own tools. Two popular fuzzing tools are Codenomicon,[36] which is one of the most mature commercially available fuzzing tools on the market, and the Peach Fuzzing Tool,[37] which is one of the more popular open-source tools. Fuzzing is used for both security and quality assurance testing. Fuzzing has recently been recognized as both a key element and a major deficiency in many software development programs, so much so that it is now a U.S. Department of Defense (DoD) Information Assurance Certification and Accreditation Process (DIACAP) requirement.

Fuzzing is a form of attack simulation in which unexpected data is fed to the system through an open interface, and the behavior of the system is then monitored. If the system fails, for example, by crashing or by failing built-in code assertions, then there is a flaw in the software. Although all of the issues found by fuzzing tools are critical and exploitable, unlike static analysis tools, fuzzing can only find bugs that can be accessed through an open interface. Fuzzing tools must also be able to interoperate with the tested software so that they can access the deeper protocol layers and test the system more thoroughly by testing multiple layers.

While static analysis has the benefit of full test coverage and is a good method for improving the general software quality level, it cannot easily provide test results that solve for complex problems and, as discussed previously, it also results in a large number of false positives, both of which require further analysis by a human and consume valuable and limited resources. There are no false positives in fuzz testing, because every flaw discovered is a result of a simulated attack

Static analysis is performed on code that is not being executed, and it can only be performed offline. In contrast, fuzz testing must be executed against executable code, can be run against live software, and therefore can find vulnerabilities that may not be visible in the static code. Fuzz testing targets the problems attackers would also find and therefore is a good test for robustness while also streamlining the process by focusing only on the most critical interfaces that may be susceptible to attack. Because of its ability to test robustness, fuzz testing is typically used during the verification phase of the SDLC just before product release. As with static and dynamic analysis, fuzz testing can be used from the moment the first software components are ready and even after release—not just at some point in time during the SDLC process. This attribute, of course, can yield significant cost savings by finding and fixing vulnerabilities early in the SDLC.

Standard fuzz testing techniques are limited in their use of random mutation to create test cases, which will find only some of the software vulnerabilities. However, this testing still has value because these are the same vulnerabilities that attackers would find. It is important to remember that attackers use fuzzing tools as well, and it is a tell-tale sign of a weak software security development program if fuzzing tools by discoverers or attackers find flaws in products you have already released to your customers. More sophisticated fuzzing techniques are used to improve and optimize coverage by using protocol specifications to target protocol areas most susceptible to vulnerabilities and to reduce the number of test cases needed without compromising test coverage. Static code analysis is used to ensure that secure coding policies are being followed, but protocol fuzzing tools are used to gain an attacker's perspective to the threat and risk.

Another advantage of fuzz testing is that it can be used with black-box, gray-box, or white-box testing and does not require source code access. Like the dynamic analysis tools discussed in this chapter, this feature makes it a great tool for testing third-party software or software that has been outsourced for development. One drawback of fuzz testing, however, is that it is intrusive and may well crash the system, which will likely require initial testing to occur in a separate environment such as a testing lab or virtualized environment.

There are two main types of fuzz testing, "smart" and "dumb."

- In "smart" (generational) fuzzing, the fuzzer pushes data to the program in a logical way, usually by waiting for responses and possibly altering the stack. This method requires in-depth knowledge of the target and specialized tools, but less crash analysis is required and also less duplication of findings than with dumb fuzzing.[38,39]
- In "dumb" (mutational) fuzzing, the fuzzer systematically pushes data to the program without waiting for proper responses. This method is closely tied to denial-of-service attacks. This method requires no knowledge of the target and uses existing tools. However, more crash

analysis is required, and there is more duplication of findings than with "smart" fuzzing.[40,41]

To carry out a fuzz test, the following steps are followed for each file or field that feeds into the application:

1. Enter random data or spaces to some part of the input file.
2. Execute the application with that input file.
3. Evaluate results. What broke? What ran as normal? What was expected to happen?
4. Number each test case and report findings to project management.[42]

6.4.4 Manual Code Review

Manual security code reviews are typically done as a line-by-line inspection of the software to determine any security vulnerabilities in the software product. This will include a thorough review of programming source code of multitier and multicomponent enterprise software products. After the use of multiple automated tools, which help quickly analyze flaws and vulnerabilities, the code is reviewed manually. Every issue discovered is validated, and the code is inspected to overcome the limitations of the automated tools and techniques. Coding errors can be found using different approaches, but even when compared to sophisticated tools, manual code reviews have clearly proven their value in terms of precision and quality. Unfortunately, manual code reviews are also the most expensive to execute.

Manual code reviews by definition are human-driven, and although the highest value-add for their use is for architectural design reviews, these software security reviews are done with a holistic approach that includes people, policies, and processes. Assuming limited resources, manual code review is best performed on only the most critical components of an application. These reviews will also include manually reviewing the documentation, secure coding policies, security requirements, and architectural designs. There is also a mentoring aspect of manual reviews, in that the software security architects will be able to teach others on the development team about the art of testing, how to understand the security process, policy awareness, and the appropriate skills for designing or implementing a secure application. Even with seasoned and security-savvy development teams, software security architects should adopt a trust-but-verify model. This process is enhanced by the fact that the architects usually analyze documentation together with the stakeholders and appropriate development team members and also interview the designers or system owners for their input.

It should be noted that if good software engineering processes are adhered to, they can alleviate many of the concerns that are being assessed by the code review team. In most cases, static and dynamic analysis or fuzz testing is more efficient at catching implementation-level bugs than code review, but if some of the security vulnerabilities that manual code review finds are rare, it is the only way they will be found. Once a type of security vulnerability has been found through manual code review, it should be incorporated into automatic code review tools. As mentioned previously, efficient and effective software security requires a holistic approach and includes not just manual software reviews, but also mandatory software security training, security design reviews, threat modeling, fuzz testing, static and dynamic analysis, the identification of high-risk practices, and measurable criteria and requirements for each of the various phases in the software lifecycle, including servicing and support.

The following steps are typically used for manual software security reviews:

- The threat model that was used to identify the risk and tell the development team which code to look at first and with the most scrutiny will also help the team to understand existing security threats in relation to the software's functionality.
- The various automated tools described above are used to assess the code for semantic and language security vulnerabilities, and to optimize the search for the highest risk and the greatest effort to fix or mitigate.
- A line-by-line inspection of the software code is done manually to find logical errors, insecure use of cryptography, insecure system configurations, and other known issues specific to the platform.

Using a question-driven approach can help with the review activity. A list of standard questions can help you focus on common security vulnerabilities that are not unique to your software's architecture, This approach can be used in conjunction with techniques such as control flow and data flow analysis to optimize the ability to trace those paths through the code that are most likely to reveal security issues. Questions should address at least the most common coding vulnerabilities. Ask these questions while you are using control flow and dataflow analysis. Keep in mind that finding some vulnerabilities may require contextual knowledge of control and data flow, while others will be context-free and can be found using simple pattern matching. Some of the following techniques may be combined when doing a manual security review of the code:

- **Control flow analysis.** Control flow analysis is the mechanism used to step through logical conditions in the code. The process is as follows:

  1. Examine a function and determine each branch condition. These may include loops, switch statements, "if" statements, and "try/catch" blocks.
  2. Understand the conditions under which each block will execute.
  3. Move to the next function and repeat.

- **Data flow analysis.** Data flow analysis is the mechanism used to trace data from the points of input to the points of output. Because there can be many data flows in an application, use your code review objectives and the flagged areas from Step 2 to focus your work. The process is as follows:

  1. For each input location, determine how much you trust the source of input. When in doubt, you should give it no trust.
  2. Trace the flow of data to each possible output. Note any attempts at data validation.
  3. Move to the next input and continue.[43]

While performing data flow analysis, review the list of inputs and outputs, and then match this to the code that you need to review. You must pay particular attention to prioritizing any areas where the code crosses trust boundaries and where the code changes trust levels, just as you did during the threat modeling process. A set of common validation routines that your software can call as soon as it receives any untrusted data should be available which will give your software product a central validation area that can be updated as new information is discovered. As the data flow analysis is performed, give special attention to areas where the data is parsed and may go to multiple output locations, to ensure that the data is traced back to its source, and trust is assigned based on the weakest link.

There are other lists of questions that should be considered. Some of these are organized into sets of key areas based on the implementation mistakes that result in the most common software vulnerabilities relevant to the software product or solution being developed, also called hotspots. These questions are typically developed by the software security architect and revolve around the last top 10–20 CVE or OWASP "Top 10" lists described earlier in the book.

A review for security issues unique to the architecture should also be conducted as part of the manual security review process. This step is particularly important if the software product uses a custom security mechanism or has features to mitigate known security threats. During this step, the list of code review objectives is also examined for anything that has not yet been reviewed. Here, too, a question-driven approach such as the following list will be useful, as the final code review step to verify that the security features and requirements that are unique to your software architecture have been met.

- *Does your architecture include a custom security implementation?* A custom security implementation is a great place to look for security issues for these reasons:
  - o It has already been recognized that a security problem exists, which is why the custom security code was written in the first place.
  - o Unlike other areas of the product, a functional issue is very likely to result in security vulnerability.
- *Are there known threats that have been specifically mitigated?* Code that mitigates known threats needs to be carefully reviewed for problems that could be used to circumvent the mitigation.
- *Are there unique roles in the application?* The use of roles assumes that there are some users with lower privileges than others. Make sure that there are no problems in the code that could allow one role to assume the privileges of another.[44]

We would like to reiterate that it is not an either/or proposition between different types of security testing. For a product to be secure, it should go through all types of security testing—static analysis, dynamic analysis, manual code review, penetration testing, and fuzzing. Often, trade-offs are made during the development cycle due to time constraints or deadlines, and testing is skipped as a product is rushed to market. This might save some time and a product may be released a few weeks/months sooner. However, this is an expensive proposition from a ROI point of view. Further, security problems found after a product is released can cause a lot of damage to customers and the brand name of the company.

6.5 Key Success Factors

Success of this fourth phase of the SDL depends on review of policy compliance, security test case execution, completion of different types of security testing, and validation of privacy requirements. Table 6.1 lists key success factors for this phase.

Table 6.1 Key Success Factors

Key Success Factor	Description
1. Security test case execution	Coverage of all relevant test cases
2. Security testing	Completion of all types of security testing and remediation of problems found
3. Privacy validation and remediation	Effectiveness of privacy-related controls and remediation of any issues found
4. Policy compliance review	Updates for policy compliance as related to Phase 4

Success Factor 1: Security Test Case Execution

Refer to Section 6.2 for details on success criteria for security test execution plan.

Success Factor 2: Security Testing

It is critical to complete all types of security testing—manual code review, static analysis, dynamic analysis, penetration testing, and fuzzing. Issues found during each type of testing should be evaluated for risk and prioritized. Any security defect with medium or higher severity should be remediated before a product is released or deployed. Defects with low severity should not be ignored but should be put on a roadmap for remediation as soon as possible.

Success Factor 3: Privacy Validation and Remediation

Validation of privacy issues should be part of security test plans and security testing. However, it is a good idea to have a separate workstream to assess effectiveness of controls in the product as related to privacy. Any issues identified should be prioritized and remediated before the product is released or deployed.

Success Factor 4: Policy Compliance Review (Updates)

If any additional policies are identified or previously identified policies have been updated since analysis was performed in Phase 3, updates should be reviewed and changes to the product should be planned accordingly.

6.6 Deliverables

Table 6.2 lists deliverables for this phase of the SDL.

Security Test Execution Report

The execution report should provide status on security tests executed and frequency of tests. The report should also provide information on the number of re-tests performed to validate remediation of issues.

Table 6.2 Deliverables for Phase A4

Deliverable	Goal
Security test execution report	Review progress against identified security test cases
Updated policy compliance analysis	Analysis of adherence to company policies
Privacy compliance report	Validation that recommendations from privacy assessment have been implemented
Security testing reports	Findings from different types of security testing
Remediation report	Provide status on security posture of product

Updated Policy Compliance Analysis

Policy compliance analysis artifacts (see Chapters 4 and 5) should be updated based on any new requirements or policies that might have come up during this phase of the SDL.

Privacy Compliance Report

The privacy compliance report should provide progress against privacy requirements provided in earlier phases. Any outstanding requirement should be implemented as soon as possible. It is also prudent to assess any changes in laws/regulations to identify (and put on a roadmap) any new requirements.

Security Testing Reports

A findings summary should be prepared for each type of security testing: manual code review, static analysis, dynamic analysis, penetration testing, and fuzzing. The reports should provide the type and number of issues identified as well as any consistent theme that can be derived from the findings. For example, if there are far fewer XSS issues in one component of the application compared to another, it could be because developers in the former were better trained or implemented the framework more effectively. Such feedback should be looped back into earlier stages of the SDL during the next release cycle.

Remediation Report

A remediation report/dashboard should be prepared and updated regularly from this stage. The purpose of this report is to showcase the security posture and risk of the product at a technical level.

6.7 Metrics

The following metrics should be collected during this phase of the SDL (some of these may overlap metrics we discussed earlier).

- Percent compliance with company policies (updated)
  - Percent of compliance in Phase 3 versus Phase 4

- Number of lines of code tested effectively with static analysis tools
- Number of security defects found through static analysis tools
- Number of high-risk defects found through static analysis tools
- Defect density (security issues per 1000 lines of code)
- Number and types of security issues found through static analysis, dynamic analysis, manual code review, penetration testing, and fuzzing
  - Overlap of security issues found through different types of testing
  - Comparison of severity of findings from different types of testing
  - Mapping of findings to threats/risks identified earlier
- Number of security findings remediated
  - Severity of findings
  - Time spent (approximate) in hours to remediate findings
- Number, types, and severity of findings outstanding
- Percentage compliance with security test plan
- Number of security test cases executed
  - Number of findings from security test case execution
  - Number of re-tests executed

6.8 Chapter Summary

During our discussion of the design and development (A4) phase, we described the process for successful test case execution, the process of proper code review through the use of both automated tools and manual review, and the process for privacy validation and remediation to be conducted during this phase of the SDL. Perhaps the most important processes and procedures described in this chapter are those that provide the ability to effectively and efficiently test, tune, and remediate all known and discovered vulnerabilities, and to ensure that secure coding policies have been followed which provide the necessary security and privacy vulnerability protections before moving on to the product ship (A5) phase of the SDL.

References

1. Kaner, C. (2008, April). *A Tutorial in Exploratory Testing*, p. 36. Available at http://www.kaner.com/pdfs/QAIExploring.pdf.

2. Chmielewski, M., Clift, N., Fonrobert, S., and Ostwald, T. (2007, November). *"MSDN Magazine: Find and Fix Vulnerabilities Before Your Application Ships."* Available at http://msdn.microsoft.com/en-us/magazine/cc163312.aspx.

3. Microsoft Corporation (2012). *How To: Perform a Security Code Review for Managed Code (.NET Framework 2.0)*. Available at http://msdn.microsoft.com/en-us/library/ff649315.aspx.

4. Ibid.

5. Jackson, W. (2009, February). GCN—Technology, Tools and Tactics for Public Sector IT: "Static vs. Dynamic Code Analysis: Advantages and Disadvantages." Available at http://gcn.com/Articles/2009/02/09/Static-vs-dynamic-code-analysis. aspx?p=1.

6. Cornell, D. (2008, January). OWASP San Antonio Presentation: "Static Analysis Techniques for Testing Application Security." Available at http://www.denimgroup.com/media/pdfs/DenimGroup_ StaticAnalysisTechniquesForTestingApplicationSecurity_OWASPSan Antonio_20080131.pdf.

7. Jackson, W. (2009, February). GCN—Technology, Tools and Tactics for Public Sector IT: "Static vs. Dynamic Code Analysis: Advantages and Disadvantages." Available at http://gcn.com/Articles/2009/02/09/Static-vs-dynamic-code-analysis. aspx?p=1.

8. Cornell, D. (2008, January). OWASP San Antonio Presentation: "Static Analysis Techniques for Testing Application Security." Available at http://www.denimgroup.com/media/pdfs/DenimGroup_ StaticAnalysisTechniquesForTestingApplicationSecurity_OWASPSan Antonio_20080131.pdf.

9. Jackson, W. (2009, February). GCN—Technology, Tools and Tactics for Public Sector IT: "Static vs. Dynamic Code Analysis: Advantages and Disadvantages." Available at http://gcn.com/Articles/2009/02/09/Static-vs-dynamic-code-analysis. aspx?p=1.

10. Cornell, D. (2008, January). OWASP San Antonio Presentation: "Static Analysis Techniques for Testing Application Security." Available at http://www.denimgroup.com/media/pdfs/DenimGroup_ StaticAnalysisTechniquesForTestingApplicationSecurity_OWASPSan Antonio_20080131.pdf.

11. Jackson, W. (2009, February). GCN—Technology, Tools and Tactics for Public Sector IT: "Static vs. Dynamic Code Analysis: Advantages and Disadvantages." Available at http://gcn.com/Articles/2009/02/09/Static-vs-dynamic-code-analysis. aspx?p=1.

12. Cornell, D. (2008, January). OWASP San Antonio Presentation: "Static Analysis Techniques for Testing Application Security." Available at http://www.denimgroup.com/media/pdfs/DenimGroup_ StaticAnalysisTechniquesForTestingApplicationSecurity_OWASPSan Antonio_20080131.pdf.

13. The Open Web Application Security Project (OWASP) (2012). "Fuzzing." Available at https://www.owasp.org/index.php/Fuzzing.

14. R2Launch (2012). "Fuzz." Available at http://www.r2launch.nl/index.php/software-testing/fuzz.

15. The Open Web Application Security Project (OWASP) (2012). "Testing Guide Introduction." Available at https://www.owasp.org/index.php/Testing_Guide_Introduction#Manual_Inspections_.26_Reviews.

16. Coverity (2012). Coverity Static Analysis webpage. Retrieved from http://www.coverity.com/products/static-analysis.html.

17. HP (2012). HP Fortify Static Code Analyzer webpage. Retrieved from http://www.hpenterprisesecurity.com/products/hp-fortify-software-security-center/hp-fortify-static-code-analyzer.

18. IBM (2012). IBM Security AppScan Source webpage. Retrieved from http://www-01.ibm.com/software/rational/products/appscan/source.

19. Klocwork (2012). Klocwork webpage. Retrieved from http://www.klocwork.com/?utm_source=PPC-Google&utm_medium=text&utm_campaign=Search-Klocwork&_kk=klocwork&gclid=CMy0_q6svbICFUjhQgodOGwAFg.

20. Parasoft (2012). Static Analysis webpage. Retrieved from http://www.parasoft.com/jsp/capabilities/static_analysis.jsp?itemId=547.

21. Veracode (2012). Veracode webpage. Retrieved from http://www.veracode.com.

22. The Open Web Application Security Project (OWASP) (2012). "Static Code Analysis." Available at https://www.owasp.org/index.php/Static_Code_Analysis.

23. Howard, M. (2006, July–August). "A Process for Performing Security Code Reviews." *IEEE Security & Privacy*, pp. 74–79.

24. Howard, M. (2004, November). "Mitigate Security Risks by Minimizing the Code You Expose to Untrusted Users." Available at http://msdn.microsoft.com/msdnmag/issues/04/11/AttackSurface.

25. OWASP (2013). "Top 10 2013—Top 10." Retrieved from https://www.owasp.org/index.php/Top_10_2013-Top_10.

26. Hewlett-Packard (2012). Webinspect webpage. Retrieved from http://www.hpenterprisesecurity.com/products/hp-fortify-software-security-center/hp-webinspect.

27. Hewlett-Packard (2012). QAinspect webpage. Retrieved from http://www.hpenterprisesecurity.com/products/hp-fortify-software-security-center/hp-qainspect.

28. IBM (2012). IBM Security AppScan Enterprise webpage. Retrieved from http://www-01.ibm.com/software/awdtools/appscan/enterprise.

29. Veracode (2012). Veracode webpage. Retrieved from http://www.veracode.com.

30. White Security (2012). "How the WhiteHat Sentinel Services Fit in Software Development Lifecycle." Retrieved from (SDLC)https://www.whitehatsec.com/sentinel_services/SDLC.html.

31. Peng, W., and Wallace, D. (1993, March). NIST Special Publication 500-209, *Software Error Analysis*. Available at http://hissa.nist.gov/SWERROR.

32. Ibid.

33. Ibid.

34. Ibid.

35. Ibid.

36. Codenomicon (2012). Codenomicon website. Retrieved from http://www. codenomicon.com.
37. Peachfuzzer.com (2012). Peach Fuzzing Platform webpage. Retrieved from http://peachfuzzer.com/Tools.
38. Royal, M., and Pokorny, P. (2012, April). Cameron University IT 4444—Capstone: "Dumb Fuzzing in Practice." Available at http://www.cameron.edu/uploads/8d/e3/8de36a6c024c2be6dff3c34448711075/5.pdf.
39. Manion, A., and Orlando, M. (2011, May). ICSJWG Presentation: "Fuzz Testing for Dummies." Available at: http://www.us-cert.gov/control_systems/icsjwg/presentations/spring2011/ag_16b_ICSJWG_Spring_2011_Conf_Manion_Orlando.pdf.
40. Royal, M., and Pokorny, P. (2012, April). Cameron University IT 4444—Capstone: "Dumb Fuzzing in Practice." Available at http://www.cameron.edu/uploads/8d/e3/8de36a6c024c2be6dff3c34448711075/5.pdf.
41. Ibid.
42. Grembi, J. (2008). *Secure Software Development: A Security Programmer's Guide.* Course Technology, Boston.
43. Meier, J., et al. (2005, October). Microsoft Corporation—MSDN Library: *How To: Perform a Security Code Review for Managed Code (.NET Framework 2.0).* Available at http://msdn.microsoft.com/en-us/library/ff649315.aspx.
44. Ibid.

Chapter 7

Ship (A5): SDL Activities and Best Practices

Now that you have reached the last phase of the software development lifecycle, you need to ensure that the software is secure and that privacy issues have been addressed to a level at which the software is acceptable for release and ready to ship. Software security and privacy requirements should have come from initial phases and been refined throughout the cycle. In this chapter, we will take you through the last stage of policy compliance review, followed by the final vulnerability scan, pre-release penetration testing, open-source licensing review, and the final security and privacy reviews (see Figure 7.1).

As discussed in SDL Phases (A1)–(A4), SDL policy compliance covers all projects that have meaningful security and privacy risks and is analyzed in each phase and updated to cover new threats and practices. In the final policy compliance review, the SDL policy will be reviewed to ensure that the policy provides specific requirements based on different development criteria, such as product type, code type, and platform.

A vulnerability scan will look for any remaining vulnerabilities in your software and associated systems and report potential exposures. This process is usually automated, and it will typically be run by somebody in

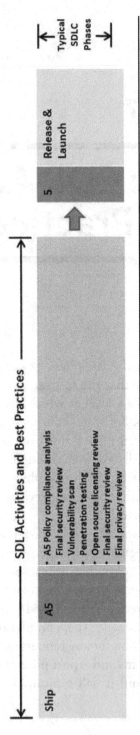

Figure 7.1 Ship (A5): SDL activities and best practices.

your own organization. In contrast, a penetration test actually exploits weaknesses in the architecture of your systems and requires various levels of expertise within your scope of the software and associated systems you are testing. A seasoned security individual or team that is part of a third party to provide an independent point of view, high-level or specialized external expertise, and "another set of eyes" typically conducts the testing.

During the final phase of the SDL security review of the software being assessed, all of the security activities performed during the process, including threat models, tools outputs, and performance against requirements defined early in the process will be assessed to determine whether the software product is ready for release and shipping. We will discuss the three options that can occur as part of this process.

It is essential to be in compliance with applicable open-source requirements to avoid costly and time-consuming litigation. The two primary areas that need to be of concern for those managing the SDL where open source software is used as part of the product or solution are license compliance and security.

The privacy requirements must be satisfied before the software can be released. Privacy requirement verification is typically verified concurrently with the final security review and in many cases is now considered part of the same process.

7.1 A5 Policy Compliance Analysis

As discussed for SDL Phases (A1)–(A4), SDL policy compliance covers all projects that have meaningful security and privacy risks and is analyzed in each phase and updated to cover new threats and practices. Specifically, activities and standards in the policy have been refreshed in each SDL phase, and have incorporated lessons learned from root-cause analysis of security incidents, adapted to the changing threat environment, and will have resulted in tools and technique improvements. During the subsequent phases, SDL policy compliance has been tracked and, if needed, exceptions have been issued for high-risk projects. From the beginning of the SDL process, the SDL policy has formally defined which projects qualify for SDL mandates and what the requirements are for compliance. This policy has become a significant part in the governance of the SDL process in that it:

- Standardizes the types of projects that fall under the SDL mandate and activities
- Defines the policy and processes that must happen at each phase of the SDL/SDLC for project compliance
- Sets the requirements for the quality gates that must be met before release

In the final policy compliance analysis, the policy will be reviewed to ensure that it provides specific requirements based on different development criteria, such as product type, code type, and platform.

7.2 Vulnerability Scan

Although there is no substitute for actual source-code review by a human, automated tools do have their advantages and can be used to save time and resources. They are particularly useful to conduct regression testing at this stage of the process, as a double check that any possible vulnerabilities have not inadvertently been re-introduced into the code and that all previously identified vulnerabilities have been mitigated throughout the process. It is also possible that other products with similar functionality have had publically disclosed vulnerabilities since the beginning of the SDL for a particular software product, and these can be checked during the final security review as well. Given that software products commonly include 500,000 lines or more of code, vulnerability scanners can be very useful as a cost-effective and time-limited final check of the SDL. These scanners can carry out complex and comprehensive data flow analysis to identify vulnerability points that might be missed in the course of manual human review. These products are a much quicker and more efficient way to analyze every possible path through a compiled code base to find the root-cause-level vulnerabilities than using the human approach. They are also good tools to "check the checker," that is, the software security architect who has conducted manual reviews throughout the process.

Vulnerability scanning tools explore applications and use databases of signatures to attempt to identify weaknesses. Vulnerability scans are not the same as penetration tests and should not be categorized as such; however, some of the same tools may be used in both processes. A vulnerability scan is actually an assessment, and as such will look for known vulnerabilities in the software and associated systems. It is automated, it can typically be run by a technician, and it will report potential exposures. Having your own development staff conduct the vulnerability scans will help them not only build up a baseline of what is normal for software security but also to understand it. In contrast, a penetration test actually exploits weaknesses in the architecture of your systems and requires various levels of expertise within your scope of the software and associated systems you are testing. Such testing is typically conducted by a seasoned software security professional such as a software security architect or seasoned software security engineer.

Vulnerability scanning is a necessary part of software security and the SDL. Given its automated nature and ease of performance, it should be run at various times through the SDL as a cost-effective, efficient, and minimally intrusive way to continually check your work. The results should be continually baselined to identify code or architectural changes that may have introduced new vulnerabilities during the process.

Although every effort must be taken to remediate all discovered vulnerabilities, there are some cases where the scanner may falsely identify vulnerability or exceptions are made. False positives are vulnerabilities where the scanner has identified the software as being vulnerable when, in fact, it is not. Of course, once this is proven, the false positive can be discounted. Exceptions are made because the remediation will prevent optimal software performance, restrict a critical function in the product, or even require a complete architecture redesign. The risk is deemed acceptable because compensating controls are in place or can be put in place with minimal effort to mitigate the risk. Exceptions may be permanent or they may have an expiration date attached. The typical vulnerability scan process is diagramed in Figure 7.2.

Static or dynamic source code vulnerability scanner tools, as discussed earlier in this book, can be used during this phase as appropriate. If the software is a Web application, you must use tools designed specifically for Web application vulnerability analysis. One mistake that should be avoided if you are using a Web application vulnerability scanner is not to scan for just the OWASP "Top 10" vulnerabilities, but rather scan for all software application vulnerabilities. As with static or other dynamic vulnerability scanners, if critical, high, or severe application vulnerabilities are identified by scanning, those vulnerabilities must be fixed before the

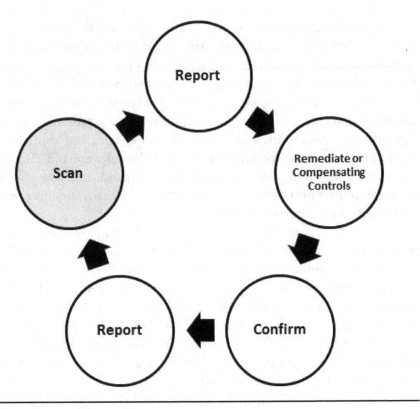

Figure 7.2   Typical vulnerability scan process.

application is released to the production environment or shipped. Some common Web application vulnerability scanners include:

- AppScan by IBM (http://www-01.ibm.com/software/awdtools/appscan)
- GFI Languard by GFI (http://www.gfi.com/network-security-vulnerability-scanner)
- Hailstorm by Cenzic (http://www.cenzic.com/index.html)
- McAfee Vulnerability Manager (MVM) by McAfee (http://www.mcafee.com/us/products/vulnerability-manager.aspx)
- Nessus by Tenable Network Security (www.nessus.org)
- Retina Web Security Scanner by eEye Digital Security (http://www.eeye.com/Products/Retina/Web-Security-Scanner.aspx)
- WebInspect by HP (http://www.hpenterprisesecurity.com/products/hp-fortify-software-security-center/hp-webinspect)

You should use as many vulnerability scanners as possible across the stack. Web application scanning alone will not be sufficient, as the software stack (operating system, Web servers, application servers) can also have vulnerabilities that need to be remediated. Vulnerability scanning should include external scans, internal scans and authenticated scans of the entire stack (especially in a cloud environment). External scans are primarily targeted at exploring security issues that can be found outside the firewall. Since a firewall often restricts ports, these scans may be of only limited utility at times; however, they can still be very valuable because findings from external scans are often also quite accessible to attackers. Internal scans are executed from inside firewalls and thus findings are not restricted to ports everyone can see from outside firewalls. Internal scans allow us to identify security issues that an attacker or malicious insider can exploit if he or she gets inside the network (and is not outside restricted by firewalls). Authenticated scans are most comprehensive in that they not only identify issues covered by external and internal scans but also identify missing patches and reduce false positives. Authenticated scans require software to log on to a system to scan it, however, and thus are most intrusive.

Earlier in the process, security architecture should have laid out configuration requirements for the software stack to harden the stack and remove attack surfaces. Configuration guidelines exist in various forms, including hardening standards for operating systems and other software on which the product will be deployed. For example, off-the-shelf operating systems will have many unnecessary services and configurations that increase the attack surface on the stack. Hardening guidelines can be instrumental in reducing risk from the default configuration.

In addition to vulnerability scanning, the security configuration should also be validated to ensure that the stack itself is hardened. An ideal solution is to create a "hardened image" of the stack itself and stamp it with security approval. Any variances from this image should raise a red flag when product is finally deployed in the operational environment.

7.3 Penetration Testing

Penetration testing is a white-box security analysis of a software system to simulate the actions of a hacker, with the objective of uncovering potential vulnerabilities resulting from coding errors, system configuration faults, or other operational deployment weaknesses. It is also used to validate whether code implementation follows the intended design, to validate implemented security functionality, and to uncover exploitable vulnerabilities. White-box testing requires knowledge of *how* the system is implemented in order to ensure the robustness of the software product and its associated systems against intended and unintended software behavior, including malicious attacks as well as regular software failures. The white-box test assessors must be skilled and seasoned security professionals who have the background and knowledge as to what makes software secure or insecure, how to think like an attacker, and how to use different testing tools and techniques to simulate the actions of a hacker. Penetration tests are typically performed in conjunction with automated and manual code reviews and require the analysis of data flow, control flow, information flow, coding practices, and exception and error handling within the software and its associated systems.

To successfully conduct a white-box security test of the code being developed and the systems with which it will be interacting, three basic requirements must be satisfied holistically, not independent of each other. The assessor(s)/tester(s) must:

1. Have access to and be able to comprehend and analyze available design documentation, source code, and other relevant development artifacts, and have the background and knowledge of what makes software secure
2. Be able to think like an attacker and have the ability to create tests that exploit software
3. Have knowledge and experience with the different tools and techniques available for white-box testing and the ability to think "outside the box" or unconventionally, as an adversary would use the same tools and techniques.

Independence is a key element and requirement for penetration testing, and that is why engaging a third-party external security firm to conduct a security review and/or penetration testing should always be considered. This provides the benefit of both an "outside set of eyes" and independence and should be mandatory for all projects that are considered to be a high business risk. An outside view and perspective will help identify the types of vulnerabilities that other processes are not preventing and make the current state of security maturity clear to all. The third party should be afforded access to the threat models and architectural diagrams created during the SDL to determine priorities, test, and attack the software as a hacker might. The level of scrutiny will always be predicated on the available budget, since these types of firms typically charge a premium for their services. Any security issues or vulnerabilities identified during penetration testing must be addressed and resolved before the project is approved for release and shipping.

To achieve the minimum requirements for penetration testing, the four-phase process shown in Figure 7.3 should be followed.

The penetration test report is the final deliverable of the penetration test. The main body of the report should focus on what data was compromised and how, provide the customer with the actual method of attack and exploit, along with the value of the data exploited. If needed or desired by the SDL and development teams, possible solutions can be included in the report as well. The detailed listing of the vulnerabilities

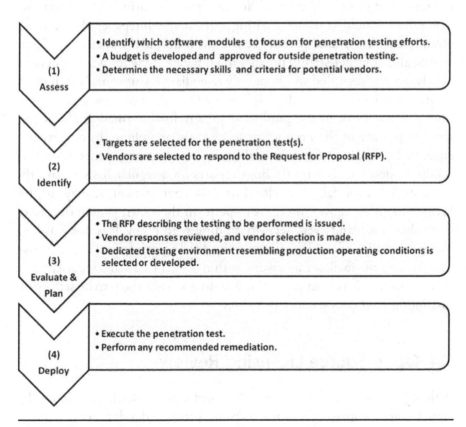

(1) Assess
- Identify which software modules to focus on for penetration testing efforts.
- A budget is developed and approved for outside penetration testing.
- Determine the necessary skills and criteria for potential vendors.

(2) Identify
- Targets are selected for the penetration test(s).
- Vendors are selected to respond to the Request for Proposal (RFP).

(3) Evaluate & Plan
- The RFP describing the testing to be performed is issued.
- Vendor responses reviewed, and vendor selection is made.
- Dedicated testing environment resembling production operating conditions is selected or developed.

(4) Deploy
- Execute the penetration test.
- Perform any recommended remediation.

Figure 7.3 The four-phase process of penetration testing.

that had attempted exploits and the false positives or vulnerabilities that were exploited but resulted in no data loss should be included in an appendix rather than the main body of the report, in order to keep the primary part of this report succinct and to the point.

The long list of possible exposures typically generated from a vulnerability scan should be in the vulnerability scan report or readout and not part of the final penetration report. As mentioned in the previous section, the purpose for each activity and its results are different.

Security has been in the limelight for all the wrong reasons of late, given that some very well known companies have been attacked, and some popular products have been in the news for having security holes. This has resulted in customers (whether for traditional software or SaaS/cloud service) asking that an enterprise demonstrate and prove its security posture for products/services they are purchasing. At this point in the release cycle, it is a good idea to get together with your sales and marketing team and create a framework for discussing security with customers. The group should consider creating a security whitepaper that can be given to customers (and potential customers) during the sales cycle. They should also consider setting up an annual review cycle for whitepapers as new issues are identified and hopefully remediated. Customers often need to demonstrate security and compliance within their own enterprise, and thus will reach out to the product company for information about the security posture of the product or service you are selling. In our experience, such requests often come in the form of requests for penetration test results or detailed security findings reports on a regular basis (quarterly or annually). Especially in a cloud or SaaS environment, it may not be feasible to either allow customers to perform their own penetration tests or to share each and every security finding with them. It is not feasible, however, to align the remediation service-level agreements of all your customers. In a nutshell, a framework within which to discuss security with your customers is very important if you do not want them to be setting or disrupting your own security priorities.

7.4 Open-Source Licensing Review

Although open-source software is free and it increases innovation, efficiency, and competitiveness for software product development, it must also be managed as an asset, the license obligations observed, and it must be as secure as internally developed software standards and requirements require. These sometimes unique and complex license and business risks can delay, and potentially prevent, software deployment or shipment if not properly managed. It is essential to be in compliance with applicable open-source requirements to avoid costly and time-consuming litigation. The two primary areas that need to be of concern for those managing an SDL in which open-source software is used as part of the product or solution are license compliance and security.

1. **Open-source software license compliance.** Noncompliance with open-source software licensing requirements can result in costly and time-consuming litigation, court time, copyright infringement, public press exposure, bad publicity, and negative risk to the noncompliant organization's reputation and business relationships. Mismanagement and noncompliance with open-source licenses may also result in difficulty or inability to provide software product support, delay of current release and ship dates, or the stoppage of orders currently scheduled to ship.

2. **Open-source software security.** SDL and development teams, as well as their executive sponsors, need to be aware of and understand vulnerabilities associated with open-source software code to be used in their own software product. As with the software being developed in-house, all vulnerabilities known to the open-source and software security community must be identified, assessed, and mitigated throughout the SDL process and include the same threat modeling, architectural security and privacy review, and risk assessment rigor and as the code being developed in-house.

To put this into perspective, a few examples of the consequences of not properly managing open-source software license or security are given below.

- **Diebold and PES.** Artifex Software, the company behind the open-source Ghostscript PDF processing software, filed a lawsuit against voting machine vendor Diebold and its subsidiary Premier Election Solutions. Artifex said that Diebold violated the General Public License (GPL) by incorporating Ghostscript into commercial electronic voting machine systems. Ghostscript, which was originally developed in the late 1980s, is distributed free under the GNU GPL. This license permits developers to study, modify, use, and redistribute the software but requires that derivatives be made available under the same terms. Companies that want to use Ghostscript in closed-source proprietary software projects can avoid the copyright requirement by purchasing a commercial license from Artifex. Among commercial Ghostscript users who have purchased licenses from Artifex are some of the biggest names in the printing and technology industries, including HP, IBM, Kodak, Siemens, SGI, and Xerox.[1]

- **Skype.** Skype was found guilty of violating the GNU GPL by a Munich, Germany, regional court. This decision has influenced the way companies approached GPL compliance since.[2]
- **Verizon.** Two software developers reached a settlement in a lawsuit against Verizon Communications in which they claimed the telecom giant's broadband service violated the terms of the widely used open-source agreement under which their product was licensed. The issue centered on claims that a subcontractor used an open-source program called BusyBox in Verizon's wireless routers. As part of the settlement, Verizon subcontractor Actiontec Electronics must pay an undisclosed sum to developers Erick Andersen and Rob Landley. It must also appoint an internal officer to ensure that it is in compliance with licenses governing the open-source software it uses.[3]
- **Google.** Google and other companies continue to receive bad publicity because they use the Android mobile platform, which was launched with known security vulnerabilities and continues to be a major target for hackers. Mobile malware tracked by McAfee exploded in 2012, growing almost 700 percent over the 2011 numbers. Close to 85 percent of this malware targets smart phones running Android. The big surprise in the huge increase is not that Android is being attacked: Google's smartphone platform has been a key focus for the bad guys for some time. The big surprise is that Google has not managed to stem the tide in any significant way. Security concerns about Android should not be news to Google, and Google should be putting security at the top of its list of priorities.[4]
- **Oracle.** Security experts accused Oracle of not paying attention to its flagship database software and underreporting the severity of a "fundamental" flaw. Even as Oracle fixed numerous flaws across

multiple products in their January 2013 Critical Patch Update, security experts criticized the company for the low number of database fixes and claimed that the company is downplaying the severity of a flaw in its flagship relational database. As Oracle expands its product portfolio and increases the total number of products patched through the quarterly CPU, there appears to be a "bottleneck" in Oracle's patching process. This CPU was the first time Oracle included the open-source MySQL database, which it acquired in 2010 as part of the Sun Microsystems acquisition.[5]

- **CNET Download.com.** CNET Download.com was caught adding spyware, adware, and other malware to thousands of software packages that it distributes, including their Nmap Security Scanner. They did this even though it clearly violated their own anti-adware policy. (They did remove the anti-adware/spyware promise from the page.) After widespread criticism of the practice, Download.com removed its rogue installer from Nmap and some other software, but the company still uses it widely and has announced plans to expand it. For these reasons, we suggest avoiding CNET Download.com entirely. It is safer to download apps from official sites or more ethical aggregators such as FileHippo, NiNite, or Softpedia.[6]

Using manual methods to find, select, monitor, and validate open-source code is time-consuming, inefficient, and an unnecessary drain on scarce development team resources. Automation through tools such as Black Duck Software (www.blackducksoftware.com) or Palamida (www.palameda.com) is essential to effectively and efficiently incorporate open-source software into SDLC development efforts to drive down development costs and manage the software and its security throughout the SDL. Black Duck Software's products and services allow organizations to analyze the composition of software source code and binary files, search for reusable code, manage open-source and third-party code approval, honor the legal obligations associated with mixed-origin code, and monitor related security vulnerabilities.[7-9] Palamida enables organizations to manage the growing complexity of multisource development environments by answering the question, "What's in your code?" Through detailed analysis of the code base, customers gain insight into their code inventory—a critical component of quality control, risk mitigation, and vulnerability assessment with the goal of eliminating legal and vulnerability concerns associated with its use.[10]

7.5 Final Security Review

During final security review of software being developed, all of the security activities performed, including threat modeling, tools output, and performance against requirements defined early in the process, are assessed again to determine whether the software product is ready for release and shipping. This process will result in one of three outcomes:

1. **The final security review is passed.** In this case, all final security review issues that have been identified have been corrected, the software is certified to have met all SDL requirements, and it is ready for release from a security perspective.

2. **The final security review is passed with exceptions.** In this case, not all issues that have been identified have been corrected, but an acceptable compromise has been made for one or more exceptions that the SDL and development team were not able to resolve. As exceptions, the unresolved issues will not be resolved in the current release and will be addressed and corrected in the next patch or release.

3. **The final security review is not passed and requires an escalation.** In this case, the SDL and development team cannot reach a compromise on a specific security vulnerability and its remediation, and so the software cannot be approved for release and shipment. There is typically a business justification identified earlier in the SDL process that prevents the identified issue from being compliant with an SDL security requirement. The SDL requirements that are blocking the release cannot be resolved by the two teams and must be escalated to higher management for a decision, which of course will take into account the risk and consequences identified if the software is released without meeting the requirement. The escalation to management should be a consolidated report composed by both the SDL and development teams that includes a description and rationale of the security risk.

The final security review must be scheduled carefully in order to maximize the time needed to fully analyze and remediate both known and any security issues that may be discovered during the final review, in ample time to account for the software product release and ship dates.

The final security review process should include the following:

- **Scheduling.** The product security review must be scheduled so that all required information from the SDL to complete this step has been acquired and is available, and enough time has been allowed to minimize any delay in the release date. The start date cannot be set until all security review activities defined and agreed to at the beginning of the SDL process have been completed, including in-depth security vulnerability reviews, threat modeling, and appropriate and relevant static, dynamic, and fuzz testing tool analysis.
- **Specific final security review tasks.**
  - The SDL and development team will meet to review and ensure that satisfactory responses have been made for all questions that have arisen and documented during the SDL process.
  - Threat models developed earlier in the process have been reviewed and updated as of the start date of the final security review, to ensure that all known and suspected threats identified through the process have been mitigated.
  - All security vulnerabilities have been reviewed against the criteria established for release early in the process, and at least the minimum security standard has been enforced throughout the SDL. Any security vulnerabilities that were rejected or deferred for the current release of the software product must be reviewed as well. It is important to note that if the SDL and development team is not constantly evaluating the severity of security vulnerabilities against the standard that is used during the SDL process, then a large number of security vulnerabilities may re-appear or be discovered during the final security review and result in unnecessary and possibly significant use of resources and time, thus delaying the release of the product.
  - The static, dynamic, and fuzz testing tools should be run before final security review so that results can be fully evaluated before a decision is made for final release. In some cases the tools may provide inaccurate or unacceptable results, in which case you may need to re-run the tools or find more acceptable alternatives to the ones used during the process.
  - You must review and ensure that all of the relevant internal security policies and external regulatory requirements have been

followed and that software being reviewed is in compliance with the requirements for each.

o If a specific SDL security requirement cannot be met and the overall security risk is tolerable, an exception must be requested, preferably well in advance of the final security review and as early as possible in the process.

The final product security review can be described as a four-step process as outlined below and represented graphically in Figure 7.4.

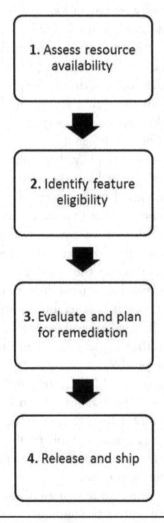

Figure 7.4   Four-step final security review process.

1. **Assess resource availability.** In this step, the resources that will be required and available in order to conduct the final security review are identified. The ability to enforce the quality gates required before the software can be released is also assessed. Minimum acceptable levels of security as it relates to quality are established through quality gates. Having the quality gates early in the SDLC process so that security risks are understood early in the SDL process helps ensure that vulnerabilities are identified and fixed early, which will avoid unnecessary work and delays later in the process. The SDL and development team must show compliance with the quality gates as part of the final security review. If security has truly been built into the SDLC process as a result of the SDL, the time required to complete the final security review will be minimal; if not, more time and resources will be required, which might delay the ability to release and ship on time.

2. **Identify feature eligibility.** During this step, security tasks that are eligible for work in the final security review are identified. Feature eligibility should have been done earlier in the SDL process, to avoid unfinished security work in the final security review. Scrutiny should have also been given to areas or sub-teams where vulnerabilities have not been reported yet during the SDL process but that historically have a history of vulnerabilities with high scores that could bring a surprise task to the teams during the final security review.

3. **Evaluate and plan for remediation.** During this step, the stakeholders responsible for the tasks identified in the previous step are notified, and scheduling for the final security review is set.

4. **Release and ship.** The product security review is completed after all SDL requirements, such as fuzzing, vulnerability scans, secure coding policies review, and other current security practices, as well as any exceptions to quality gates or vulnerabilities, have been formally reviewed and approved. Functional regression will have typically taken place during the final security review as well. Regression testing is used to discover new software vulnerabilities or regressions from what was already discovered, hence the term regression. These regressions can be a result of changes in the existing functional and nonfunctional areas of the software or the system after changes have been made. In short, regression testing assesses whether a change in one part of the software has resulted in a change in other parts of the software or system it interacts with.

7.6 Final Privacy Review

Typically, privacy requirements must be satisfied before the software can be released. Although the final security review must be completed before release, security exceptions as discussed previously highlights that not all security issues have to be satisfied before release. Privacy requirement verification is typically verified concurrently with the final security review and in many cases is now considered part of the same process. This requires that significant changes that occurred after the completion of the general privacy questionnaire, such as collecting different data types, substantively changing the language of a notice or the style of consent, or identification of new software behavior that negatively affects the protection of privacy are addressed. This entails reviewing the software for any relevant changes or open issues that were identified during previous privacy reviews or as part of the final security review. Specific privacy requirements for the final review should include the following.

- If the project has been determined to be a P1 project, then the SDL team and privacy lead must review the Microsoft SDL Privacy Questionnaire (Appendix C)[11] mentioned in the previous chapter or its equivalent to determine whether a privacy disclosure is required. If the privacy lead determines that a privacy disclosure is waived or covered, then there is no need to meet this requirement. The privacy lead will give final approval for release of the privacy disclosure statement.
- If the project has been determined to be a P2 project, then the privacy lead will determine if a privacy design review is being requested, provide a confirmation that the software architectural design is compliant with privacy standards applicable to this software product, or determine if an exception request is needed. The privacy lead typically works with the SDL and developer lead and legal advisor as appropriate to complete the privacy disclosure before public release of the product and ensure the privacy disclosure is posted appropriately for Web-centric products.
- If the project is a P3 project, then no changes affecting privacy requirements compliance have been identified, and no additional reviews or approvals are needed and the final privacy review is complete. If not, then the SDL team and privacy lead will provide a list of required changes.

In addition to the responsibilities, process, and procedures required for a response to software product security vulnerabilities discovered after release and shipment, a similar function to the product incident response team (PSIRT) is created for response to privacy issues discovered after release and shipment. This element will be discussed in the next chapter in relation to the post-release support activities.

7.7 Key Success Factors

Success of this fifth phase of the SDL depends on final review of policy compliance, comprehensive vulnerability scanning and penetration testing, and final security and privacy reviews. Table 7.1 lists key success factors for this phase, as discussed below.

Table 7.1 Key Success Factors

Key Success Factor	Description
1. Policy compliance analysis	Final review of security and compliance requirements during development process
2. Vulnerability scanning	Scanning software stack for identifying security issues
3. Penetration testing	Exploiting any/all security issues on software stack
4. Open-source licensing review	Final review of open-source software used in the stack
5. Final security review	Final review of compliance against all security requirements identified during SDL cycle
6. Final privacy review	Final review of compliance against all privacy requirements identified during SDL cycle
7. Customer engagement framework	Framework that defines process for sharing security-related information with customers

Success Factor 1: Policy Compliance Analysis

If any new security requirements have been identified (based on threats or updates to policies), they need to be vetted for feasibility of implementation so late in the development process. Some requirements may not make it into the product, while others might be important enough to delay the release date until the product does in fact incorporate them.

Success Factor 2: Vulnerability Scanning

Vulnerability scanning as well as security configuration validation provides one final opportunity to identify and remediate security issues across the software stack. Vulnerability scanning and security configuration validation should include assessment from different vantage points (external, internal, and authenticated). It should also cover all layers in the stack, from the operating system to applications.

Success Factor 3: Penetration Testing

Penetration testing provides an opportunity to determine what security flaws could be exploited and to what extent. Making sure there is no confusion between penetration testing and vulnerability scanning is important. Vulnerability scanning provides a list of security findings along with the potential impact if those findings can be exploited. Penetration testing, on the other hand, is *carte blanche* for security testers to exploit any/all security flaws and often in a cascading manner. Impact often depends on the skills, imagination, and experience of the penetration testers. Vulnerability scanning feeds into penetration testing, but it is just a starting point.

Success Factor 4: Open-Source Licensing Review

Final review of open-source software to be sure that all licensing requirements have been met is essential to mitigate legal liability. It also enables identification of technologies that need to feed into a different a type of security testing (vulnerability scanning and penetration testing).

Success Factor 5: Final Security Review

It is critical that a final security review be performed before this phase of the SDL ends. If all requirements are met, then security can say "Go" without any exceptions. If there are exceptions to security requirements, they need to be well documented and be time-bound. An example is a "conditional go," under which unmet requirements do not stop release but will be remediated by an agreed-upon date.

Success Factor 6: Final Privacy Review

Similar to Factor 5, this step allows final review of the product against privacy requirements that were laid out at the start of the cycle and that have been updated or refined since then. If any requirements are unmet, they should be documented as exceptions that are time-bound and require remediation by a definite date.

Success Factor 7: Customer Engagement Framework

As discussed earlier in the chapter, it is important that a framework be defined to engage customers in security-related discussions both during and after the sale process. This can limit ad-hoc requests and escalations from customers and give them confidence that your company has a handle on security.

7.8 Deliverables

Table 7.2 lists deliverables for this phase of the SDL.

Updated Policy Compliance Analysis

Policy compliance analysis artifacts (see Chapters 4, 5, and 6) should be updated based on any new requirements or policies that may have come up during this phase of the SDL.

Security Testing Reports

The findings summary as discussed in Chapter 6 should be updated to include vulnerability scanning (external, internal, and authenticated) as well as any new penetration testing that is performed during this phase. A customer-facing report should also be prepared to share with enterprise customers.

Table 7.2 Deliverables for Phase A5

Deliverable	Goal
Updated policy compliance analysis	Analysis of adherence to company policies
Security testing reports	Findings from different types of security testing in this phase of SDL
Remediation report	Provide status on security posture of product
Open-source licensing review report	Review of compliance with licensing requirements if open-source software is used
Final security and privacy review reports	Review of compliance with security and privacy requirements
Customer engagement framework	Detailed framework to engage customers during different stages of product life cycle

Remediation Report

In addition to updating security testing reports (or findings), the remediation report should also be updated to give a better idea of the security posture of the product going into release. Any findings that have not been remediated by now (and are not to be remediated before the release date), should be discussed and put on a roadmap.

Open-Source Licensing Review Report

A formal review report should be prepared of open-source software used in the software stack that outlines different licensing requirements (The MIT License, GNU General Public License, GNU Lesser General Public License, BSD License) and how they are being met. The security and privacy officers should review the report and sign off on it.

Final Security and Privacy Review Reports

After final review of compliance against security and privacy requirements, a formal sign-off by security and privacy officers should be required.

Customer Engagement Framework

A formally documented process to share security information with customers should be delivered as part of this phase. The process should
include types of information (and frequency) that should be shared with
customers, notification in case of security incidents, as well as security
findings and remediation SLAs.

7.9 Metrics

The following metrics should be collected during this phase of the SDL:

- Percent compliance with company policies (updated)
  - Percent of compliance in Phase 5 versus Phase 4
- Number, type, and severity of security issues found through vulner-
  ability scanning and penetration testing
  - Overlap of security issues found through different types of testing
  - Comparison of severity of findings from different types of testing
  - Mapping of findings to threats/risks identified earlier
- Number of security findings remediated (updated)
  - Severity of findings
  - Time spent (approximate) in hours to remediate findings
- Number, types, and severity of findings outstanding (updated)
- Percentage compliance with security and privacy requirements

7.10 Chapter Summary

In this chapter we have described the requirements for successful release
and ship of the software product after it has finished the SDLC and
associated SDL activities and best practices (see Figure 7.5). Now that
we have made it through SDL Phase A5 and the product has been
released, the next chapter will describe SDL Phase A6, which will outline the SDL post-release support activity (PRSA) phase of our SDL.
After a software product is released and shipped, the software security,
development, and privacy teams, with support from the corporate public relations, legal, and other groups must be available to respond to any
possible security vulnerabilities or privacy issues that warrant a response.

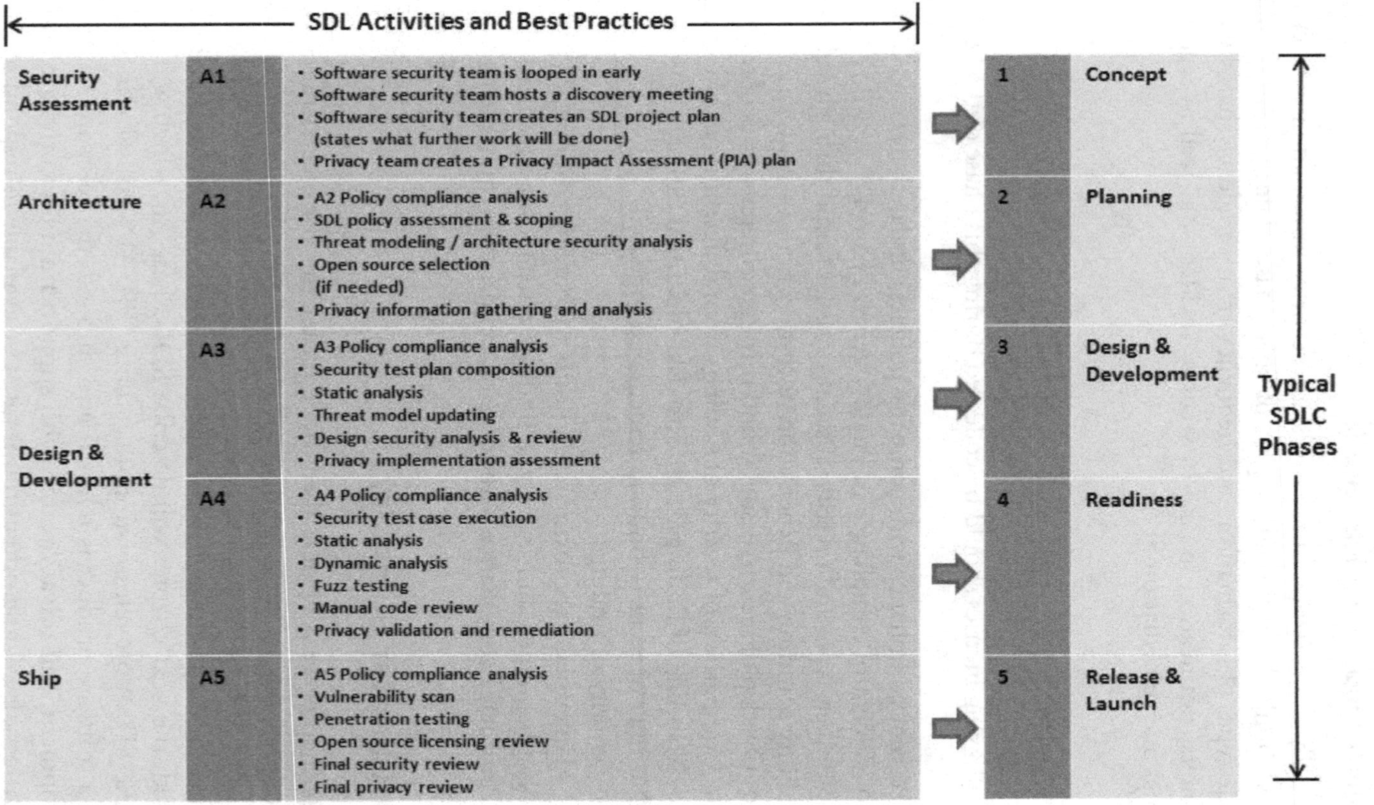

Figure 7.5 A1 to A5 SDL activities and best practices.

In addition, a response plan detailing appropriate processes and procedures must be developed that includes preparations for potential post-release issues. In addition to external vulnerability disclosure responses, this phase should include internal review for new product combinations or cloud deployment, post-release certifications, security architectural reviews, and tool-based assessments of current, legacy, and M&A products and solutions, as well as third-party reviews of released software products that may be required by customers, regulatory requirements, or industry standards.

References

1. Paul, R. (2008). "Diebold Faces GPL Infringement Lawsuit over Voting Machines: Artifex Software, the Company Behind Ghostscript, Has Filed a Lawsuit Against. . . ." *Arstechnica: Technology Lab/Information Technology,* November 4. Available at http://arstechnica.com/information-technology/2008/11/diebold-faces-gpl-infringement-lawsuit-over-voting-machines.
2. Broersma, M. (2007). "Skype Found Guilty of GPL Violations." IDG News Service, July 26. Available at http://www.pcworld.com/article/135120/article.html.
3. McDougall, P. (2008). "Verizon Settles Open Source Software Lawsuit: The Issue Centered on Claims That a Subcontractor Used an Open Source Program Called BusyBox in Verizon's Wireless Routers." *Information Week,* March 17. Available at http://www.informationweek.com/verizon-settles-open-source-software-law/206904096.
4. Koetsier, J. (2012). "Sorry, Google Fanboys: Android Security Suffers as Malware Explodes by 700%." *VentureBeat,* September 4. Available at http://venturebeat.com/2012/09/04/sorry-google-fanboys-android-security-sucks-hard-as-malware-explodes-by-700/#FKvUAhZrG8g5jywy.99.
5. Rashid, F. (2012). "Oracle Accused of Downplaying Database Flaws, Severity." *eWeek,* January 1. Available at http://www.eweek.com/c/a/Security/Oracle-Accused-of-Downplaying-Database-Flaws-Severity-155094.
6. Insecure.org (2013). "Download.com Caught Adding Malware to Nmap & Other Software." Available at http://insecure.org/news/download-com-fiasco.html.
7. Schwartz, E. (2007). "Open Source Lands in the Enterprise with Both Feet: Major Business Applications on Linux Turns OS into a Commodity." *Infoworld,* August 6. Available at http://www.infoworld.com/t/applications/open-source-lands-in-enterprise-both-feet-576.
8. Worthington, D. (2007). "Quacking Through Licensing Complexity: Black Duck's Open Source Licensing Solution Tackles GPLv3." *SDTimes,* August 6. Available at http://www.sdtimes.com/link/31007.

9. Boston Business Journal Staff (2007). "Battles over Open Source Carve Niche for Startup." *Boston Business Journal,* December 17. Available at http://www. bizjournals.com/boston/stories/2007/12/17/story13.html?page=all.
10. VentureBeatProfiles (2012). *Palamida.* Available at http://venturebeatprofiles. com/company/profile/palamida.
11. Microsoft Corporation (2012). "Appendix C: SDL Privacy Questionnaire." Available at http://msdn.microsoft.com/en-us/library/windows/desktop/cc307393. aspx.

Chapter 8

Post-Release Support (PRSA1–5)

Many of the functions and their associated activities and best practices described in this chapter (see Figure 8.1) are handled by groups other than the software security group that would have the principal oversight over SDL activities and best practices (A1–A5) described in the previous chapters. In this chapter we will describe them as activities that are the responsibility of the centralized software security group in an organization. We have found that this is a much more cost-effective and efficient way to manage these activities using existing resources. This is precisely the reason we highly recommend that the core software security group be composed of senior software security architects who have hard "dotted-line" relationships with the software security champions, who in turn have the same relationships with the software security evangelists. There should also be a strong relationship between the software security architects in the centralized software security group and the product managers of each Tier 1 software product, just as there is for the software security champions. It is also important that the software security group and function be in the right organization so they can be most successful.

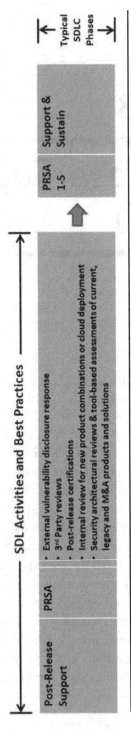

Figure 8.1 Post-release support (PRSA1-5): SDL activities and best practices.

8.1 Right-Sizing Your Software Security Group

First we will walk through each of the software security group relationships and the importance of putting everything into perspective in order to "right-size" the building of a successful software security program. Doing this means having

- The right organizational location
- The right people
- The right process

8.1.1 The Right Organizational Location

Although there have been great advances in software security technology over the last few years, we believe that people are still the most important element of a successful software security program that includes the implementation and management of the activities and best practices. In order to facilitate the best use of the people responsible for software security, they must be part of the right organization (see Figure 8.2). Having been in seven Chief Security Officer (CSO) and Chief Information Security Officer (CISO) roles, James Ransome, one of the co-authors of this book, has had software security reporting to him in several of his roles. Based on both his experience and communication with his peers in the industry, it is clear that the software security function ideally should fall within the engineering (software development) function and, in particular, within the quality function. The general consensus is that the application security role typically reports to the centralized information security role CSO/CISO position and should not be confused with the software security function. Typically, those who are in an application security role within an IT security organization are great at running tools but do not have the software development background necessary to fully interpret the results. To make this point clear, it is important to differentiate between software and application security. Perhaps the best way to clarity this distinction is with a quote from Gary McGraw:

> Software security is about building secure software: designing software to be secure; making sure making sure that software is secure; and educating software developers, architects, and users

about how to build security in. On the other hand, application security is about protecting software and the systems that software runs in a post facto way, only after development is complete.[1]

Another advantage of having the software security experts reporting to the engineering organization is that they are empowered by the fact that they are part of the same organization; are directly responsible for implementing the SDL policies and procedures and associated tools; and understand software development, its architecture, and the level of effort required to fix the same. Earlier in this book we described the importance of software security as an element of quality and organization, and the same relationship should exist within the engineering organization.

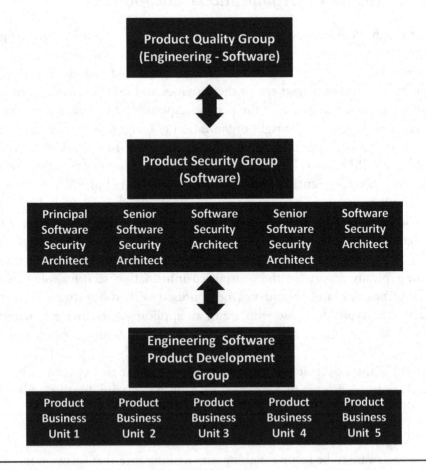

Figure 8.2 The right organizational location.

The authors believe that software security should be a group of its own within engineering/software development and should work very closely with the central security group; it may even have a "dotted-line" relationship to the CSO/CISO.

A few reasons for our preference for the software security group to report to the software quality group include the following.

1. Security vulnerabilities are, by definition, quality issues.
2. Security features are architectural functions with a very close relationship to product management.
3. Based on (1) and (2) above, security is both a feature and a quality function.
4. Quality is best served when it is integral to the development process (engineering) and includes security.

8.1.2 The Right People

In Chapter 2 we discussed the talent required to make the SDL model we describe in this book a success. This will include a minimum of one principal software security architect, a mix of senior and general software security architects, and, ideally, one software security architect in the software product security group per software product security group in the organization. This relationship is represented in Figure 8.3. This talent pool provides the ability to scale in that there will also ideally be one software security champion (SSC) per Tier 1 software product within each engineering software product development group. Another element of the talent is the software security evangelists (SSEs) for organizations that are large enough to have extra candidates for the software security champions' (SSCs) role, who can be candidates for SSEs until there is a slot for them as a SSC. SSEs have two roles, as a SSC in training and as an evangelist for the overall software product security program promulgated policy, enforcing policy, and evangelizing the overall SDL process.

8.1.3 The Right Process

The right process is the core SDL activities and best practices described in this book so far and summarized in Figure 8.4. In addition to the

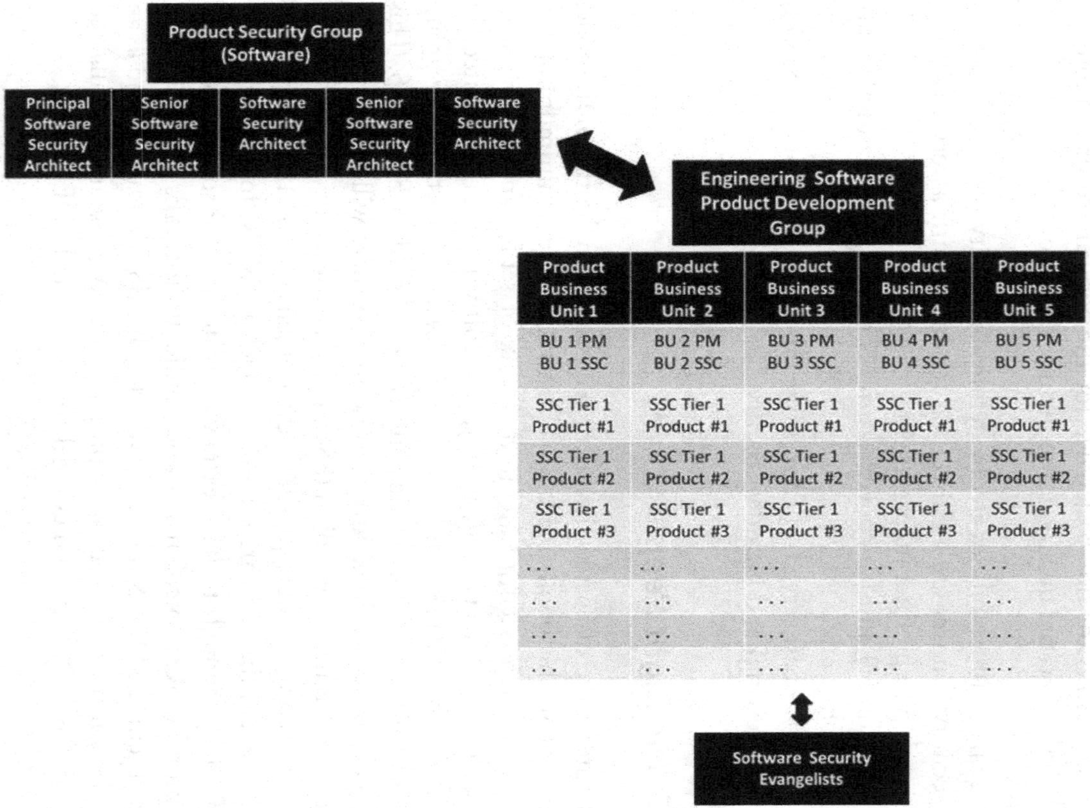

Product Security Group (Software)

Principal Software Security Architect	Senior Software Security Architect	Software Security Architect	Senior Software Security Architect	Software Security Architect

Engineering Software Product Development Group

Product Business Unit 1	Product Business Unit 2	Product Business Unit 3	Product Business Unit 4	Product Business Unit 5
BU 1 PM / BU 1 SSC	BU 2 PM / BU 2 SSC	BU 3 PM / BU 3 SSC	BU 4 PM / BU 4 SSC	BU 5 PM / BU 5 SSC
SSC Tier 1 Product #1	SSC Tier 1 Product #1	SSC Tier 1 Product #1	SSC Tier 1 Product #1	SSC Tier 1 Product #1
SSC Tier 1 Product #2	SSC Tier 1 Product #2	SSC Tier 1 Product #2	SSC Tier 1 Product #2	SSC Tier 1 Product #2
SSC Tier 1 Product #3	SSC Tier 1 Product #3	SSC Tier 1 Product #3	SSC Tier 1 Product #3	SSC Tier 1 Product #3
…	…	…	…	…
…	…	…	…	…
…	…	…	…	…

Software Security Evangelists

Figure 8.3 The right people.

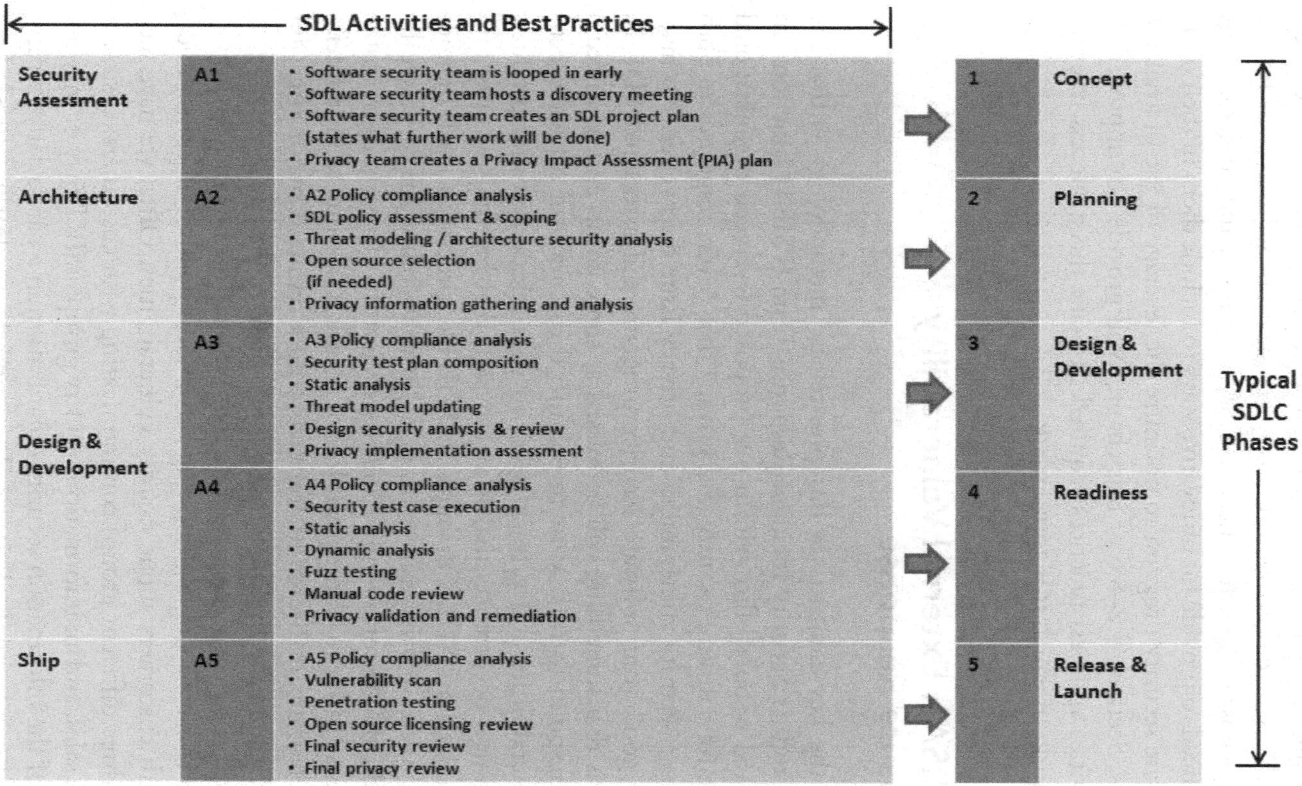

Figure 8.4 SDL A1–A5 activities and best practices.

		SDL Activities and Best Practices		Typical SDLC Phases
Security Assessment	A1	• Software security team is looped in early • Software security team hosts a discovery meeting • Software security team creates an SDL project plan (states what further work will be done) • Privacy team creates a Privacy Impact Assessment (PIA) plan	1	Concept
Architecture	A2	• A2 Policy compliance analysis • SDL policy assessment & scoping • Threat modeling / architecture security analysis • Open source selection (if needed) • Privacy information gathering and analysis	2	Planning
Design & Development	A3	• A3 Policy compliance analysis • Security test plan composition • Static analysis • Threat model updating • Design security analysis & review • Privacy implementation assessment	3	Design & Development
	A4	• A4 Policy compliance analysis • Security test case execution • Static analysis • Dynamic analysis • Fuzz testing • Manual code review • Privacy validation and remediation	4	Readiness
Ship	A5	• A5 Policy compliance analysis • Vulnerability scan • Penetration testing • Open source licensing review • Final security review • Final privacy review	5	Release & Launch

core activities and best practices, we have added the activities and best practices highlighted in Figure 8.1. Given the continued pressure to do more with less, we don't believe most organizations will have the luxury of having most of the elements of PRSAs 1–5 as separate organizations but will need to provide for innovative ways to include them in their overall software security program to optimize the leverage of use of available resources. Sections 8.2–8.6 of this chapter will provide our approach to the activities and best practices required to make this a success in every organization in which it is appropriate.

8.2 PRSA1: External Vulnerability Disclosure Response

One of the key elements of our post-release methodology is that the typical Product Security Incident Response Team (PSIRT) function can be a shared responsibility within our proposed leveraged organizational structure for software security and privacy that covers responses to both post-release security vulnerability and privacy issue discoveries. No matter how good your software security program and associated SDL is, the fact is that something will be missed at some point, and you need a plan to respond to this. Most important, if discovery of software security vulnerabilities and privacy issues in post-release software products is a common occurrence, that is a clear sign that building security into the organization's SDLC through an SDL-like process is weak or nonexistent. Such weakness can result in negative visibility due to publically disclosed exploitation of vulnerabilities or security flaws inherent to the post-release software, subsequent loss of market share due to brand defamation, lawsuits or breach of contracts, and a resultant major target for further exploitation by adversarial opportunists.

Based on our experiences, we cannot emphasize enough how important it is to have a single group that acts a focal point of all communications with customers about security vulnerabilities. Often we have seen at least three different groups communicating with customers: customer support, sales, and an information security group. PSIRT may or may not be part of the information security organization in a particular company, though this is certainly desirable. To summarize, a clearly defined chain of communications with customers is of critical importance to prevent disclosure of unintended information and to avoid panic and putting entire accounts at stake.

8.2.1 Post-Release PSIRT Response

In relation to software security, a Product Security Incident Response Team (PSIRT) is responsible for responding to software product security incidents involving external discoveries of post-release software product security vulnerabilities. As part of this role, the team manages the investigation of publicly discovered security vulnerabilities of their company's software products and the systems they interact with. The external discoverers might be independent security researchers, consultants, industry organizations, other vendors, or benevolent or possibly even nefarious hackers who identify possible security issues with software products for which the PSIRT is responsible. Issues identified are prioritized based on the potential severity of the vulnerability, typically using the CVSS scoring system described earlier in the book as well as other environmental factors. The resolution of a reported incident may require upgrades to products that are under active support from the PSIRT's parent company.

Shortly after its identification and during the investigation of a claim of vulnerability, the PSIRT should work collaboratively with the discoverer to confirm the nature of the vulnerability, gather required technical information, and ascertain appropriate remedial action.

When the initial investigation is complete, the results are delivered to the discoverer along with a plan for resolution and public disclosure. If the incident reporter disagrees with the conclusion, the PSIRT should attempt to address those concerns.

The discoverer(s) will be asked to maintain strict confidentiality until complete resolutions are available for customers and have been published by the PSIRT on the company's website through the appropriate coordinated public disclosure typically called a security bulletin (SB). During the investigation and pre-reporting process, the PSIRT coordinates communications with the discoverer, including status and documentation updates on the investigation of the incident. Further information may also be required from the discoverer to validate the claim and the methods used to exploit the vulnerability. Discoverers will also be notified that if they disclose the vulnerability before publication by the PSIRT, then the discoverers will not be given credit in the public disclosure by the company and the case will be treated as a "zero day," no-notice discovery that has been reported publically by an external source. In the case of a zero-day discovery, the PSIRT and development teams work together to remediate the vulnerability as soon as possible, according to the severity of the Common Vulnerability Scoring System (CVSS) (http://nvd.nist.gov/cvss.cfm) scoring for the particular vulnerability. In the case of a zero-day, highly scored vulnerability, the company PR team will work closely with the PSIRT to manage potential negative press and customer reaction.

During the investigation of a reported vulnerability, the PSIRT coordinates and manages all sensitive information on a highly confidential basis. Internal distribution is limited to those individuals who have a legitimate need to know and can actively assist in resolution of the vulnerability.

The PSIRT will also work with third-party coordination centers such as the CERT Coordination Center (CERT/CC) (http://www.cert.org/certcc.html), and others to manage a coordinated industry disclosure for reported vulnerabilities affecting the software products they are responsible for. In some cases, multiple vendors will be affected and will be involved in the coordinated response with centers such as CERT. If a coordination center is involved, then, depending on the circumstances, the PSIRT may contact the center on the behalf of the discoverers, or assist them in doing it themselves.

If a third-party component of the product is affected, this will complicate the remediation process because the PSIRT will be dependent on a third party for remediation. A further complication is that the PSIRT will have to coordinate and in many cases notify the vendor directly to ensure coordination with the third-party coordination center and likely direct involvement with the discoverer. Even though a third-party component has been used, the assumption is that the owner of the primary software product is ultimately responsible for all components of the software, whether they own them or not.

As mentioned above, PSIRTs generally use the CVSS to assess the severity of a vulnerability as part of their standard process for evaluating reported potential vulnerabilities in their products and determining which vulnerabilities warrant external and internal reporting.

The CVSS model uses three distinct measurements or scores that include base, temporal, and environmental calculations, and the sum of all three scores should be considered the final CVSS score. This score represents a single moment in time; it is tailored to a specific environment and is used to prioritize responses to a particular externally discovered vulnerability. In addition, most PSIRTs will consider modifying the final score to account for factors that are not properly captured in the CVSS score. PSIRTs typically use the following CVSS guidelines when determining the severity of a particular vulnerability and the need to report it:

- High (H)—Critical—CVSS base score of 7.0–10.0
- Medium (M)—CVSS base score of 4.0–6.9
- Low (L)—CVSS base score of 0.1–3.9[2]

If there is a security issue involving a third-party software component in the product the PSIRT is responsible for, then, depending on the situation, and whether the third party has a CVSS score, the PSIRT may use the CVSS score provided by the component creator and/or may adjust the score to reflect the impact on the overall software product.

Public disclosure, including the relevant base and temporal CVSS scores and a CVE ID[3] report, is typically made for an external post-release discovery event when one or more of the following have occurred:

- The incident response process has been completed and has determined that enough software patches or other remediations exist to address the vulnerability. Public disclosure of code fixes can be issued to address high-severity vulnerabilities.
- Active exploitation of a vulnerability that could lead to increased risk for the PSIRT company's customers has been observed that requires a published security vulnerability announcement. The announcement may or may not include a complete set of patches or other remediation steps. When possible, compensating controls are included in the public announcement to provide interim protection that will limit exposure until the permanent fix is announced.
- A zero-day announcement or other potential for increased public awareness of a vulnerability affecting the PSIRT company's product is probable that could lead to increased risk for customers. In these cases, the PSIRT has worked closely with the company PR team to help assess public indicators and warnings such as Twitter feeds and blogs that this exposure is imminent and will have prepared for a statement ahead of time. Again, this accelerated public vulnerability announcement will not include a complete

set of patches or other remediation steps, but, ideally, interim compensating controls to limit exposure can be identified.

A typical step-by-step PSIRT case-handling process will include the following steps.

1. Notification of vulnerability as assessed by an individual discoverer or organization is received.
2. The responsible software product development group is identified, together with resources required for assessment of the discoverers' vulnerability claim.
3. If the claim is credible, an impact assessment is made and a timeline for a fix is determined. The level of effort needed and priority to develop a fix is balanced against the likelihood of public disclosure of the severity and risk of the vulnerability. In some cases, external resources may be required due to other critical tasks the development team is carrying out. If the claim is not credible, additional information is requested from the discoverer to ensure the threat was properly re-created in the testing environment. If it is not credible after the testing environment has been confirmed, then the discoverer is notified of the company's findings. If the discoverer goes public claiming the vulnerability is credible even though the company has determined it is not, then the PSIRT typically works with the company's PR team to publish the results of the company's finding as a counter to the discoverer.
4. The timeframe for remediation, the resources needed to fix a confirmed vulnerability, and the reporting format (e.g., security bulletin, knowledge base article, or other form of public notification) are committed to.
5. After patch or other remediation methods have been identified, all customers are notified simultaneously on the date of the availability of the fix through the reporting format determined in Step 4.

8.2.1.1 ISO 29147 and ISO 30111

Two International Standards Organization (ISO) standards expected to be released by the end of the year 2013 relate to the proper functioning of a vendor PSIRT:

- ISO Standard on Vulnerability Disclosure (29147)
- ISO Standard on Vulnerability Handling Processes (30111)

The following information is derived from a presentation of Katie Moussouris at the 2013 Carnegie Mellon CERT Vendor Meeting in San Francisco.[4]

ISO 29147 provides guidance on how vendors should deal with vulnerability reports from external finders and the recommended process for interfacing between vendors and the external discoverers or finders. These discoverers can be either benevolent or adversarial in nature. In order for vendor to optimize their ability to respond to externally discovered vulnerabilities in their products they should, as a minimum:

- Have a clear way to receive vulnerability reports
- Acknowledge receipt of vulnerability reports within 7 calendar days
- Coordinate with finders
- Issue advisories that contain useful information, as a minimum:
  - Some unique identifier
  - Affected products
  - Impact/severity of damage if vulnerability is exploited
  - How to eliminate or mitigate the issue (guidance or patching instructions)
  - Consider giving finders credit in the advisory if the finder wishes to be publicly acknowledged

ISO 30111 provides guidance on how vendors should investigate, triage, and resolve all potential vulnerabilities, whether reported by external finders or via the vendor's internal testing. In order for vendors to optimize their ability to respond to discovered vulnerabilities in their products, they should, as a minimum:

- Have a process and organizational structure to support vulnerability investigation and remediation
- Perform root-cause analysis
- Weigh various remediation options to adjust for real-world risk factors and balance speed with thoroughness
- Try to coordinate with other vendors if appropriate, such as in cases involving multi-vendor or supply-chain issues

A detailed five-step process recommended for handling and processing vulnerability reports is

1. Vulnerability report received
2. Verification
3. Resolution development
4. Release
5. Post release

The overall process is similar for either an external finder or a vulnerability discovered as a result of internal testing, but the risks may be different. If an external finder is involved, ISO 29147 should be followed and it is important to

- Understand the communication expectations
- Take into consideration the finder's intentions and publication plans during the resolution-development phase
- Release the remediation via an advisory, as outlined in the processes defined in ISO 29147

8.2.2 Post-Release Privacy Response

In addition to post-release security issues that may be discovered and disclosed, potential privacy issues may also be discovered. In our experience, privacy-related issues do not get as much attention as security vulnerabilities, nor is a group charted specifically to deal with such issues. A software development company may have a chief privacy officer (CPO) or equivalent, such as a specialized counsel on retainer, but most do not have a staff and are likely limited to one privacy support expert at best. This necessitates a close alignment and working relationship between the PSIRT function and the centralized software security group and the privacy function of the company, whether the latter is in- or out-sourced. Post-release privacy response should be built into the PSIRT process just as security should be built into the SDLC. Given the potential legal nature of privacy issues or privacy control vulnerability exploitations, the privacy advisor should script basic talking points, response procedures, and legal escalation requirements for the response team to use to respond to any potential privacy issues discovered post-release. Some basic guidelines follow:

- Privacy experts should be directly involved in all incidents that fall into the P1 and P2 categories described earlier in this book.
- Additional development, quality assurance, and security resources appropriate for potential post-release privacy issue discovery issues should be identified during the SDL process to be participate in post-release privacy incident response issues.
- Software develop organizations should develop their own privacy response plan or modify the Microsoft SDL Privacy Escalation Response Framework (Appendix K)[5] for their own use. This should include risk assessment, detailed diagnosis, short-term and long-term action planning, and implementation of action plans. As with the PSIRT responses outlined above, the response might include creating a patch or other risk-remediation procedures, replying to media inquiries, and reaching out to the external discoverer.

8.2.3 Optimizing Post-Release Third-Party Response

Collaboration between different teams and stakeholders provides the best possible chance of success in post-release response. The collective of software security champions, software security evangelists, and an ongoing formal software security programmatic relationship with the software development product managers and quality team to support and collaborate with the centralized software security team as proposed in this book provides several distinct advantages over solely dedicated teams to handle post-release PSIRT and privacy support:

- Direct PSIRT and privacy response ownership is achieved by imbedding these functions into the engineering and development groups directly responsible for fixing the product directly affected by the discovered vulnerability or privacy issue.
- Direct knowledge of the code, architecture, and overall software product design and functionality with a direct influence on the remediation process will result in increased efficiency, control, and response over an external organizational entity without direct knowledge of the product. Essentially, this removes the middleman and streamlines the process.
- This process provides for better return on investment for both the PSIRT and the privacy response function through the leverage

of resources, and direct knowledge of the software product at the source through the direct involvement and ownership by the development teams.

- Direct empowerment of the development teams and project managers, their more direct ownership of the remediation process, and a centralized software security group embedded in the engineering/ software development group provide single-organizational responsibility for the response.
- Software security champions and software security evangelists operate locally with the software product manager and appropriate product development resources to directly drive the assessment and remediation (if needed) of the claimed vulnerability by an external discoverer.
- All the above result in faster time to execution and response and, most important, help speed up the mitigation of negative press exposure and customer risk. We believe there is an advantage to our proposed organizational infrastructure in providing a cost-effective, minimal resource, and an efficient way to respond to this type of incident while reducing the burden on resources dedicated to the development of the software itself.

8.3 PRSA2: Third-Party Reviews

Over the last few years, customers of software vendor have increasingly requested independent audits to verify the security and quality of software applications they have either purchased or are evaluating for purchase. Software vulnerabilities have increasingly been tied to high-profile data breaches over the last few years and have resulted in more customers requiring independent and visible proof that the software they purchase is secure. This, of course, has helped put pressure on companies that develop software to ensure that the secure software development processes are built into the SDLC to avoid the very costly discovery of vulnerabilities that are caught post-release—often a sign of an immature, ineffective, or nonexistent software security program. Because of the preponderance of post-release code having security vulnerabilities and privacy issues that should have been caught during development, third-party assessment of post-release or near-release code has become the norm in the industry, whether the company producing the software has a reputation for producing secure code or not. In some cases it is demanded by the prospective or current customer, and in other cases it is conducted pro-actively by the company producing the code.

Even for companies that have outstanding software security programs, software applications can alternate in and out of compliance with poli-cies or regulatory requirements over long periods of time for a variety of reasons. For example, a new functionality or use case in a new version of the application may introduce new vulnerabilities or planes of attack, causing the application to drop out of compliance. Additionally, these requirements may change over time. Many companies use third-party code reviews to help identify these situations rather than spend the lim-ited resources of their internal teams.

Third-party testing should include testing the entire stack, not just your product. That means performing testing as outlined in earlier chap-ters as well as continuous post-release testing. At a minimum, post-release testing should include annual penetration testing (application and soft-ware stack). Any new code released after initial release should follow the SDL requirements outlined in previous chapters.

The biggest challenge is to do this in a timely and cost-effective man-ner while also protecting the source code and other intellectual property during the process. Some of the choices for third-party testing include the following.

1. *Hand over source code to a third party for inspection.* This is not a real option for those who want to protect the most precious intellectual property that a software development organization possesses—their source code.
2. *Contract manual penetration testing services that can also do deep-dive code and software architectural design reviews for each new release.* To avoid the risk of source code leaving the control of the company that is developing it, contractors must be required to work onsite in a controlled environment, under special nondisclosure agreements and under specific guidelines. These typically include a source-code protection policy and IP protection guidelines. An alternative to this approach is to employ a company that only uses tools that require the exposure of binary code only. In this case, the contractor inspects the application at the same level as it is attacked, the binaries, and can ensure that all threats are detected. This type of testing can be done onsite or remotely as a service.

3. *Purchase, install, and train development teams to use on-premise tools and function as lower-level software security architects as an extension of the software security group to conduct the "people side" of the software security architectural review.* Then invite auditors into your organization to document your processes. Many mature software security organizations have done this. A mature software security program such as that described in this book will help scale and reduce the need for additional headcount to do this work. Building this into your SDL/SDLC process is a cost-effective, efficient, and manageable way to do this.

4. *Require third-party suppliers of code in your application to do the same.* In today's software development environments, a majority of software development organizations make use of code developed elsewhere, either Commercial Off-The-Shelf (COTS) or open-source software. Just as with internally developed software, a third party should prepare an attestation report per the software application owner's requirements, which may include an attack surface review, review of cryptography, architecture risk analysis, technology-specific security testing, binary analysis if source code is unavailable, source code analysis if it is, and fuzz testing in addition to a general pen testing routine.

8.4 PRSA3: Post-Release Certifications

There are numerous security-focused certifications that a software development team may face after the release of the product that are added on as a requirement rather than during the development process for a variety of reasons. These reasons may include use of the software in industry or government sectors that were not planned for during design and development, new uses for the software, and new government, country, regional, business or industry sector, or regulatory requirements that did not exist prior to the release of the product. Post-release certification requirements that did not exist prior to the release of the product are a forgivable offense, but missing any that are currently required and were missed early in the SDL are not. Avoiding noncompliance to certifications required for the use of the software that is being developed requires either an internal resource in the company dedicated to following software use certifications and other requirements, including privacy requirements, or an individual or organization that specializes in this area of experience. This becomes particularly challenging as the number of these types of certifications and requirements increases rapidly around the globe. Following is a short list of examples of security or privacy certifications or standards that could become necessary for a software product to comply with post-release requirements due to market or use-case changes:

- The Federal Information Security Management Act (FISMA)[6]
- Federal Information Standard 140-2 (FIPS 14-2)—Security Requirements for Cryptographic Modules[7]
- The U.S. Department of Defense Information Assurance Certification and Accreditation Process (DIACAP)[8,9]
- The Health Insurance Portability and Accountability Act of 1996 (HIPAA) (privacy and security rules)[10]
- Safe Harbor (privacy)[11]
- The Federal Service for Technical and Export Control (FSTEK of Russia) Certification (Privacy and Security)[12,13]

8.5 PRSA4: Internal Review for New Product Combinations or Cloud Deployments

In our profession, we continue to encounter the misconception that once software has been through a SDL, you can re-use the software code any way you want. This presumption is false because any architectural changes that have occurred after release of a software product will likely introduce new attack vectors in the previously secure code. For this reason, software code must be put through the SDL process again when there is a new use of the software or an architectural change to the code post-release. Any new code must also be vetted through the various types of security testing outlined in earlier chapters.

8.6 PRSA5: Security Architectural Reviews and Tool-Based Assessments of Current, Legacy, and M&A Products and Solutions

8.6.1 Legacy Code

Although they may have once been viewed as an unnecessary cost burden, the best activities and best practices we have outlined in our SDL are a consequence of the discovery that security was not always a key element of the software development process and sometimes led to security vulnerabilities and risk mitigation costs that rivaled the initial cost of the software to be developed. The acceptance of legacy code is based on an assumption of what is expected to happen, in that the software must be proven to be functionally correct and operationally viable. However, when it comes to software security, the unexpected is what typically causes the vulnerabilities. Not only are these security vulnerabilities financially unacceptable, they are also unacceptable from an operational, functional, and overall risk perspective. This is particularly true when the software supports embedded critical systems and applications such as those found in national and regional infrastructures, transportation, defense, medicine, and finance. In these applications, the liabilities, costs, mission, and business impacts associated with unexpected security software and system vulnerabilities are considered unacceptable. Unless the architecture of legacy software is correctly assessed and analyzed from a security perspective, the impact of changes cannot be predicted, nor can changes be applied effectively. This is why the same testing and review rigor that is followed during the SDL must be followed during legacy code reviews: as a means of mitigating the unexpected. If done with the proper process and rigor, this will go far in ensuring secure code implementation that is consistent between legacy and new code.

A legacy software application is one that continues to be used because of the cost of replacing or redesigning it and often despite its poor competitiveness and compatibility with newer equivalents. The most significant issue in this regard is that the organization has likely been depending on this legacy software application for some time, and it pre-dates software development security activities such as those described in our SDL and the mandates that currently drive these practices. Further, a considerable amount of money and resources may be required to eliminate this security "technical debt." Technical debt is the difference between what was delivered and what should have been delivered. The importance of working with legacy code and technical debt is critical for most companies that develop software.[14]

Legacy code with technical debt can also exist because even though the product should be have been put in "end of life" status, one or more customers do not or cannot upgrade to a newer version of the software, and that customer happens to be a critical customer who considers this product essential to its business. This "critical customer" status often leads to legacy code and products staying in service so the relationship with the customer(s) still using the product is not jeopardized.

It is not always necessary to pay your technical debt, as it is your financial debt. There may be parts of the code that should be fixed but the software product still works as advertised; optimizing the code and removing known technical debt may not yield a worthwhile return on investment. You may also decide to just take the code out of the program because it no longer serves a purpose. In cases like these, you may never need to pay off that technical debt.

Most important to this discussion is that the technical debt in legacy software may contain security vulnerabilities. Over the course of a project, it is tempting for an organization to become lax regarding software quality and security. Most commonly, this results when teams are expected to complete too much functionality in a given time frame, or quality and security are simply not considered high-priority characteristics for the software.[15] In these situations, there may be security vulnerabilities in the legacy code that exist as a result of the technical debt. From a software product security perspective, the key task when looking at legacy code is to balance the return on investment of addressing the security technical debt against the risk of leaving it in. Two primary decisions must be considered:

1. How much new code presumably scrubbed by the SDL are you writing to replace the existing old code? At what rate will the volume of old code be replaced, and what security risk is there for whatever remains?
2. Reviewing old code is a slow and tedious process. Serious return on investment decisions must be made. You must reserve resources for this work to reduce the technical security debt for current resources. The level of effort for this work will depend on whether the SDL existed at the time the code was developed. If there was no SDL at the time the legacy code was being developed, the level of effort will be high.

This is the basic process for assessing the security of legacy software applications:

- Assess the business criticality of the application. The software application has likely been successfully relied on for years, and this may be the first time it has been looked at from a security perspective. In fact, it is highly probable that this is the first time it has been examined with this level of scrutiny. If any security vulnerabilities or flaws are discovered, even though there may be only one or two, they will likely require a large-scale effort and significant resources to mitigate. It is important to identify business criticality in order to balance the business risk versus the security risk and return on investment in these cases.
- Identify someone who is very familiar with the code. Since the legacy code is "old" code, it most likely has not been updated recently and there may be few if any people in the organization who understand the software anymore. Further, it may have been developed on top of an old language base, and/or poorly documented or commented. If this is the case, then the next step will be to conduct a software security assessment very similar to what is done during the SDL process. If the original developers, documentation, and history exist for the legacy software, and some security was built into the software, then the security assessment process can be shortened to focus just on assessing the gaps in current knowledge.
- Other basic questions should also be asked, such as:
  - Has this application previously been exploited because of a known security vulnerability or flaw?
  - Has it been fixed? If not, what can be done about it now?
  - Have there been any changes in the software architecture, function, or use that may have added new security vulnerabilities or new planes of attack?
- Assess the security of the software using the key software security assessment techniques of the SDL.
- Create a proposal that will tell the business how to remediate the security vulnerabilities or flaws in the software (cost + time) or how quickly they should think about replacing it (cost). If it is determined that the software is to be replaced, there will be risks in the interim, so you need to make sure you know where the security vulnerabilities and flaws are and develop a plan to mitigate and limit any damage that may result from an adversarial attack or exploitation of the software until the legacy code is replaced.

- If the cost of remediation is considered unacceptable by the business and there are no customer, industry, or regulatory requirements that require that security vulnerability or flaws be fixed, then the senior management for the business unit developing the software and possibly the head of the software engineering development organization and legal counsel will be required to sign off on accepting the risk for continued use of the legacy software.

8.6.2 Mergers and Acquisitions (M&As)

To be competitive, most companies want to develop new products and access new markets and will seek alternatives such as a merger and acquisition (M&A) when they cannot do this with their current resources. M&As occur for many reasons but are typically driven by the desire to improve competitiveness, profitability, or other value to the company and its products. In the software world, this is typically a function that you need in your solution set or in the product itself. The talent that may come with acquisition will be a bonus if the primary focus of the M&A is the software of the target company. The activities of an M&A start when the initial discussions for the M&A begin and continue through the due-diligence phase and on to the integration of the target company and/or the acquired technology into the parent company. The level of effort and scope of work in the process will depend on the size and complexity of the effort. It should be noted that M&As do not always include all of the resources of the target company. They may include the code for one software product, or multiple technologies or products that are attractive and of value to the acquiring company.

The due-diligence phase of an M&A is critical, and security plays a vital role in helping make it successful. If software is included as part of the M&A, a security architectural review and use of automated tools will be required. This may be done either through the use of the potential acquirer's software security staff or through a third party, depending on the restrictions that are imposed as part of the assessment and whether source code can be reviewed. Due to the proprietary nature of source code, most target companies with not allow a review of their source code during the M&A assessment process. Thus an automated tool will be needed that can conduct comprehensive code review via static binary analysis. This is done by scanning compiled or "byte" code at the binary level rather than reviewing source code and typically includes static, dynamic, and manual techniques.

Perhaps the best checklist for conducting a M&A software security assessment can be found in Table 1, "Software Assurance (SwA) Concern Categories," and Table 2, "Questions for GOTS (Proprietary & Open Source) and Custom Software," in the Carnegie Mellon *US CERT Software Supply Chain Risk Management & Due-Diligence, Software Assurance Pocket Guide Series: Acquisition & Outsourcing, Volume II, Version 1.2,*[16] which can be accessed at https://buildsecurityin.us-cert.gov/sites/default/files/ DueDiligenceMWV12_01AM090909.pdf. Another similar and useful resource is the Carnegie Mellon Software Engineering Institute Working Paper, "Adapting the SQUARE Method for Security Requirements Engineering to Acquisition,"[17] which can be accessed at www.cert.org/.../ SQUARE_for_Acquisition_Working_Paper_v2.pdf. SQUARE stands for Systems Quality Requirements Engineering. This particular paper describes the SQUARE for acquisition (A-SQUARE) process for security require-ments engineering and is adapted for different acquisition situations.

Some key items that a software security assessor should keep in mind during an M&A software security review include the following.

1. The intent of the M&A software security review is not to focus on getting rid of elements of the target software, but rather to assess any business risk that could result from any security risks identified.
2. Highlight anything that may shift the nature of the deal or nega-tively affect the integration.
3. Look for anything that may be a possible deal breaker.

8.7 Key Success Factors

External Vulnerability Disclosure Response Process

In this post-release phase of the SDL cycle, it is critical to have a well-defined and documented external vulnerability disclosure response process. Stakeholders should be clearly identified and a responsibil-ity assignment or responsibility assignment matrix (Responsible, Accountable, Consulted, and Informed [RACI] matrix) should be created. Most important, only one team should have responsibility to interface with customers to discuss vulnerabilities and remediation. All other teams and stakeholders should work with that team and assure that there are no other channels of communication or any information leaked selectively to customers. It is often the case that large accounts or enterprise customers are given preferential treatment and are privy to information that small and medium-size businesses is not. This is not a good security practice. Vulnerability information should be disclosed to everyone or no one. Selective disclosure is not a good idea, plays favorites with customers, and in some cases may be illegal and/or counter what constitutes fair and equitable treatment of all customers.

It is also important to define and formalize the internal vulnerability-handling process as part of overall vulnerability management and reme-diation programs. In addition to security teams and external researches, employees or internal customers of the products/services will often iden-tify security problems and communicate them to the product or opera-tions team. There needs to be a well-defined process to make sure all relevant security vulnerabilities are captured and put through the reme-diation queue.

Post-Release Certifications

Relevant certifications needed after the product is released (or deployed in the cloud) should have been identified in one of the earlier phases of the SDL cycle. Requirements for certifications should have been included in security and privacy requirements. This will prevent any retrofitting or findings during compliance audits for certifications. Certifications often do require annual audits or surveillance audits. The security team should work with the security compliance team to ensure that all relevant con-trols requirements are met.

Third-Party Security Reviews

As we have discussed, third-party reviews are often critical to demonstrate "security" to end users and customers. A preferred list of vendors should be created by the software team, and these vendors should be vetted for their skills as well as ability to handle sensitive information. Since these vendors will be handling sensitive security information, it is important to note if they use full disk encryption, communicate securely, dispose of any customer data as soon as testing ends, and so on. Any time there is a need for security testing, one of these vendors should be selected for the testing. Security testing of the entire software stack and product portfolio should be performed at least annually.

SDL Cycle for Any Architectural Changes or Code Re-uses

Any architectural or code changes or code/component re-uses should trigger SDL activities (though not all may be needed, depending on the significance of the changes).

Security Strategy and Process for Legacy Code, M&A, and EOL Products

Legacy code most likely will never be updated or modified. In addition, a legacy software stack will also never be patched or upgraded. Software running on old Apache Web server will have severe dependencies on it as well as the operating system and thus will not be upgraded without the application itself being changed. Any security issues identified in legacy code will take a long time to remediate (if at all). The best way to deal with legacy code is to move away from it as soon as you can. Alternatives include defining a security process for managing security vulnerabilities in legacy code, monitoring legacy code closely (at least annually), and quarantining products running legacy code so that they pose minimal risk to the environment.

M&A security assessment strategy is one of the key success factors in the post-release phase. As mentioned earlier, you may not have access to source code, so assessment strategies need to take this into account—that is, you may need to use binaries rather than source code. In the end, M&A security assessment should provide input into the overall quality of the software being acquired. If this assessment is not thought through carefully or done correctly, the software security group or the information security group may end up dealing with repercussions for a long time to come. A weakness in acquired software may weaken the software posture of other products deployed in the environment.

In addition to a strategy for treating legacy code and products and M&A, it is important to define end-of-line plans for the current version of the product/release. An end-of-line road map can guide security strategy from this point on.

8.8 Deliverables

Key deliverables for this phase are listed in Table 8.1.

External Vulnerability Disclosure Response Process

This deliverable should clearly identify stakeholders in the process and create a RACI for their role in it. In addition, communication cadence with customers should be formalized and published so that everyone in the company is aware of it and can invoke it if needed. Most important, the process should be followed every time a security comes from external channels or needs to be disclosed to customers.

Post-Release Certifications

Post-release certifications may include multiple deliverables or certifications based on target markets, regulatory needs, and customer requests. Any one of these factors may drive a certification strategy. Certification should be renewed if drivers for these certifications are still present.

Table 8.1 Key Deliverables

Deliverable	Description
External vulnerability disclosure response process	Process to define evaluation and communication of security vulnerabilities
Post-release certifications	Certifications from external parties to demonstrate security posture of products/services
Third-party security reviews	Security assessments performed by groups other than internal testing teams
Security strategy and process for legacy code, M&A, and EOL plans	Strategy to mitigate security risk from legacy code and M&As

Third-Party Security Reviews

This deliverable consists of multiple security assessments from independent third parties. At least two reports based on assessments should be created: one for internal consumption and one for external use. External reports should not list details of security vulnerabilities or expose critical information. Reports for internal consumption should be as detailed as possible and provide short- as well as long-term remediation recommendations.

Security Strategy for Legacy Code, M&A, and EOL Plans

There are three different deliverables under this umbrella: security strategy for legacy code and products, security strategy for M&As, and end-of-life plans. Each of these should be vetted with relevant stakeholders and implemented in practice once they have been signed off by everyone.

8.9 Metrics

The following metrics should be captured as part of this phase of the SDL:

- Time in hours to respond to externally disclosed security vulnerabilities
- Monthly FTE (full-time employee) hours required for external disclosure process
- Number of security findings (ranked by severity) after product has been released
- Number of customer-reported security issues per month
- Number of customer-reported security issues not identified during any SDL activities

8.10 Chapter Summary

This chapter concludes the step-by-step overview of our SDL and covers what we believe to be a unique, practical, timely, and operationally relevant approach to post-release security and privacy support. This approach not only brings the tasks and organizational responsibilities back into the SDL but also keeps the centralized software security group and engineering software development teams empowered to own their own security process for products they are directly responsible for. Most important, we covered the organizational structure, people, and process required to do this both effectively and efficiently while maximizing the return on investment for security and privacy support in the post-release environment. In the next chapter, we will take everything we have discussed so far and make it relevant to the various software development methodologies, whether Waterfall, Agile, a blend, or something in between. We have included deliverables and metrics (Chapters 3 through 8), which can be used by organizations to manage, optimize, and measure the effectiveness of their software security programs. In Chapter 9, we bring it all together to apply elements of the SDL framework as solutions to real-world problems.

References

1. McGraw, G. (2006). *Software Security: Building Security In.* Addison Wesley/Pearson Education, Boston, p. 20.
2. Mell, P., Scarfone, K., and Romanosky, S. (2013). *CVSS: A Complete Guide to the Common Vulnerability Scoring System Version 2.* Retrieved from http://www.first.org/cvss/cvss-guide.html.
3. Mitre (2013). *CVE—Common Vulnerabilities and Exposures—The Standard for Information Security Vulnerability Names.* Retrieved from http://cve.mitre.org/index.html.
4. Moussouris, K. (2013). "A Tale of Two Standards: Vulnerability Disclosure (29147) and Vulnerability Handling Processes (30111)." PowerPoint presentation given at the 2013 CERT Vendor Meeting, San Francisco, February 25.
5. Microsft Corporation (2013). "Appendix K: SDL Privacy Escalation Response Framework (Sample)." Retrieved from http://msdn.microsoft.com/en-us/library/windows/desktop/cc307401.aspx.
6. U.S. Department of Homeland Security (2013). *Federal Information Security Management Act (FISMA).* Retrieved from http://www.dhs.gov/federal-information-security-management-act-fisma.
7. National Institute of Standards and Technology (2001). *Federal Information Standard 140-2 (FIPS 14-2)—Security Requirements for Cryptographic Modules.* Retrieved from http://csrc.nist.gov/publications/fips/fips140-2/fips1402.pdf.
8. U.S. Department of Defense (2013). *Department of Defense Information Assurance Certification and Accreditation Process (DIACAP).* Retrieved from http://www.prim.osd.mil/Documents/DIACAP_Slick_Sheet.pdf.
9. U.S. Department of Defense (2003). *Department of Defense Instruction Number 8500.2, February 6, 2003—Information Assurance (IA) Implementation.* Retrieved from http://www.dtic.mil/whs/directives/corres/pdf/850002p.pdf.
10. U.S. Government Printing Office (1996). *Health Insurance Portability and*

Accountability Act of 1996 (HIPAA), Public Law 104-191, 104th Congress. Retrieved from http://www.gpo.gov/fdsys/pkg/PLAW-104publ191/html/PLAW-104publ191.htm.

11. Export.gov (2013). *U.S.-EU & U.S.-Swiss Safe Harbor Frameworks*. Retrieved from http://export.gov/safeharbor.

12. Government of the Russian Federation (2013). *Federal Service for Technical and Export Control of the Russian Federation*. Retrieved from http://government.ru/eng/power/96.

13. Technology Risk Consulting (2010). Russian Federal Technical and Export Control Order of February 5, 2010 No. 58—*Regulations on the Methods and Means of Securing the Personal Data Information Systems*. Retrieved from http://technology-risk.com/lawproject/FSTEK58.html.

14. Mar, K., and James, M. (2010). *CollabNet Whitepaper: Technical Debt and Design Death*. Retrieved from http://www.danube.com/system/files/CollabNet_WP_Technical_Debt_041910.pdf.

15. Ibid.

16. United States Government—US CERT (2009). *Software Supply Chain Risk Management & Due-Diligence, Software Assurance Pocket Guide Series: Acquisition & Outsourcing, Volume II Version 1.2*, June 16, 2009. Retrieved from https://buildsecurityin.us-cert.gov/swa/downloads/DueDiligenceMWV12_01AM090909.pdf.

17. Mead, N. (2010). *Carnegie Mellon Software Engineering Institute Working Paper: Adapting the SQUARE Method for Security Requirements Engineering to Acquisition*. Retrieved from www.cert.org/.../SQUARE_for_Acquisition_Working_Paper_v2.pdf.

Chapter 9

Applying the SDL Framework to the Real World

By Brook Schoenfield

In this chapter, we would like to introduce you to Brook Schoenfield. He is a true thought leader and a well-respected software and enterprise security architect. Because of Brook's extensive experience as a software security architect, we have asked him to write this chapter. We believe this topic to be the most difficult and critical part of the SDL and requires a seasoned software security architect's point of view to lend credibility to the solutions proposed. Brook has been a co-worker and great friend of ours for several years and has experienced the same challenges that we have in building, mentoring, managing, and providing technical leadership to both large and small software and enterprise security programs. The following chapter is the result of many years of experience by Brook of what works, what doesn't work, and most important, what should work to secure software during development. The model presented in this chapter is also the result of many months of brain storming between James and Brook. As part of our introduction to Brook, we are including an overview of his background below.

Brook S. E. Schoenfield is McAfee's Principal Architect, Product Security. He provides technical leadership for all aspects of product security across McAfee's broad product portfolio. Previously, he was Autodesk Inc.'s Enterprise Security Architect, leading technical IT security strategy. As Cisco Systems' Senior Security Architect, he was the technical lead for SaaS product security for the enterprise. Mr. Schoenfield has been a speaker at conferences including RSA, Software Professionals, SANS What Works Summits, and many others, presenting in his areas of expertise: SaaS security, software security, information security risk, Web security, service-oriented architectures, and identity management. He has been published by SANS Institute, Cisco, and IEEE.

9.0 Introduction

Software security depends on a series of properly executed tasks. There is no "silver bullet" task whose execution will deliver "good enough" software security. Security must be designed in from very early in the development lifecycle. And each activity for finding defects is complementary to the others. Leave out one of the activities and the others compensate only so much for what's been missed. The differences between software projects dictates which tasks will deliver the most security return for investment; some activities will be irrelevant for some systems. While the application of some SDL security tasks depends on each project's particular attributes, there are other SDL tasks that lie at the heart of secure development. These tasks are core to developing software that can be relied on and that is also self-protective. This set of core activities applies to every software project that must maintain a security posture, whatever that posture may be. These tasks are applied to every project.

Regardless of the development methodology employed, there will be high-level system architecture tasks, software architecture considerations, and software design issues. These constitute those tasks that must be done before much production code has been written (though one may choose to skip some of these when experimenting). After there is code to test, there is the test plan to execute, which must include the functional tests as well as testing from the attacker's point of view. In between these process markers, i.e., design time and testing, code will be written. Code production is the heart of software development. In some methodologies, there may be some design work that occurs just before writing, or even as code is developed. Whatever the approach, there are table-stake tasks that lie at the very heart of secure development: correctness for security, peer review, and static analysis (if available).

None of these tasks, by itself, constitutes a silver bullet activity that will deliver secure software. Each task complements the others. Creating a secure and securable architecture, with flows that can be understood and with controllable trust boundaries, enables the software's features to be written into an environment that supports security. A thoughtful security architecture should require those features that will foster secure deployment and usage. Once the architecture supports the required security features, these can be designed from the start rather than attempting to bolt security on after the fact.

Since secure coding is still very much an art, with local language and runtime variations adding to complexity, a strong, real-world SDL operates by "trust but verify." Trust your developers to write secure code. But check that code with multiple, independent, and complementary assurance methods: peer review, static analysis, functional testing, and dynamic analysis of the input paths.

In short, prepare for security, think about how to implement required features, build these, then test the code to make sure that the security features work as intended and that no vulnerabilities have been introduced while coding.

We believe that, ultimately, software security is a problem that people must solve; technology is merely an extension of the human mind. Relationships, as we will see, are the key to a successful SDL. Obviously, humans design, write, and test code. Humans must do each of these things with security in mind in order for the finished product to have all the attributes that comprise "secure software." Since execution of each of the SDL tasks requires intelligent, highly skilled, creative people, it is the people who execute the SDL who are the most important ingredient. As we explore each portion of the secure development lifecycle, we will take note of the approaches that strengthen relationships and provide people with motivation to produce secure software.

Figure 9.1 illustrates the flow of activities through the SDL:

Architect => Design => Code => Test

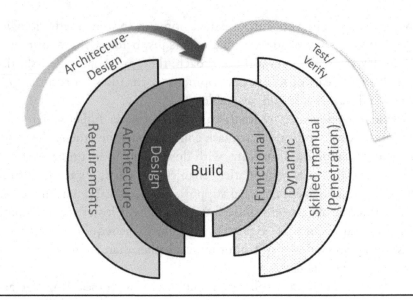

Figure 9.1   The real-world software development lifecycle.

Ultimately, the SDL flow in Figure 9.1 reduces to a simple SDL paradigm: Architecture feeds design, which is then built, i.e., "coded." The coded design must be put through a series of validations, "test." This chapter details exactly which activities fit into each of the high-level buckets illustrated by Figure 9.1, and how those activities are used within either Waterfall or Agile development. As we examine the SDL from the implementation view, we will ask key questions to determine precisely which activities must be engaged to what type of software project. In order to apply the secure development lifecycle activities appropriately, it's important to understand that not every activity is required for every project. Applying every security task to every project, from entirely new concepts ("greenfield") and/or complete redesign to a minimal set of user interface changes is wasteful and expensive. Requiring that every project go through Web vulnerability scanning, even those that have no Web server, is just plain silly. Not only will effort be expended with little security reward, but development teams are likely to resist the SDL as meaningless "administrivia," ergo, work with no benefit, empty bureaucracy.

In the past, choosing the appropriate set of tasks out of the complete SDL menu has been performed by skilled security professionals, often the security architects or security engineers. As the security architect came to understand the system, she or he was able to prescribe the correct activities to deliver secure software. Knowing that there is a Web server that will be deployed only within a segregated network and that will be used only by a few trusted administrative staff, the architect might choose to forego a detailed Web vulnerability scan in favor of network and application access restrictions. The required security posture defense in depth can be achieved through applying multiple controls, each complementing the other. Like a painter with a palette of technical controls, the architect builds the security posture out of his or her palette.

Some organizations don't have much flexibility in the security controls that can be deployed: They can only deploy a few; a complete "palette" of solutions isn't possible. Or the organization may not have the project analysis skills that are required to appropriately assign SDL tasks to projects. Or there may be too few analysts to scale to a large or diverse software development portfolio. In these and similar situations, one tendency has been to employ a "one size fits all" approach. This approach applies every SDL task to every project, regardless of project size, the amount of intended software change, or change of the included components. In our experience, this approach is fraught with pitfalls: resistance, misapplication, missed schedules, or teams simply ignoring security tasks altogether. Integrating security into software projects is not a "one size fits all" problem. Not only will there be wasted, even useless effort, but the engineers tasked with carrying out the tasks will lose faith in the SDL. This can lead to apathy, even gaming the system to get around what appears to developers to be a valueless bureaucracy.

Instead, we propose a straightforward approach that builds on years of successful security analysis of hundreds of software projects at many diverse organizations. This extensive experience has been distilled into a set of key questions and the task flows that follow from the answers. Successful application of the SDL activities can be accomplished by asking these few important questions either at project initiation, or before each high-level phase of development. Each defining question must be answered before the SDL phase in which its associated tasks are to be completed.

This is not to suggest that executing these tasks is trivial. As has been pointed out by Microsoft threat modelers, threat modeling can be performed by anyone with an inquisitive mind. Still, in current practice, it usually takes an experienced architect who understands the project's architecture, the intended deployment model, the development languages, and runtime. The architect must also have a strong grasp of the sort of threat agents who are active against this sort of software. Indeed, she or he must understand the relevant attack methods in order to build a realistic threat model. Static analysis tools require considerable expertise, as do most forms of dynamic testing, from Web vulnerability scanning to input fuzzing. The existing tools are nontrivial to learn and run effectively. Code review requires an understanding of general security correctness, the flow and structure of the particular code under review, as well as how the intended function *should* be implemented. Your most junior engineer is probably not the best resource to apply to any of these tasks—at least, not without significant support from experienced practitioners.

If one can build the right set of questions into the SDL, choosing the correct set of high-level tasks turns out to be fairly straightforward. This is true even if executing those tasks is nontrivial. There are dependencies, process flows of tasks that follow logically out of the answers. Once the task flow is engaged, the appropriate activities will take place in a more or less linear fashion.

Making the SDL relevant and obviously appropriate opens the door for meaningful interactions among the different stakeholders of the SDL. As has been noted, asking intelligent, busy people to do things about which they cannot perceive value does not enhance confidence in the security team. Conversely, a transparent process that is inherently obvious has the opposite effect. Empowering SDL participants to answer basic questions about which activities are appropriate for their current project is inherently trust-building. It remains true that execution of many of these tasks requires deep technical (and often interpersonal) expertise.

The current state of the art does not simplify many SDL tasks enough to allow these to be executed by "just anyone," even when every member of the development team holds a modicum of technical skill. For most organizations in which we have participated, architecture assessment or vulnerability scanning remain expert domains. Because of this state of affairs, *relationships* become even more important. Achieving secure software requires many people to pull together toward shared goals—which, obviously, means that non-security participants must understand that security is a "shared goal." Hence, we advocate as much transparency as possible coupled to an SDL implementation that stresses people and relationships as much as technology. The key determining questions are one step toward achieving a "people" focus of the SDL in the real world.

The key determining questions will be presented later in the chapter, in context. First we will examine the heart of every SDL; those activities that are not dependent on amount of change or type of interface. Without these core tasks, the SDL lacks its most essential ingredients to produce code that is written correctly for security and that contains as few defects as possible: writing secure code, reviewing the code, and then running the code through static analysis.

As we examine the SDL tasks as they are applied to real-world projects, this chapter will detail the supporting parts of a software security program that will foster and grow the required skills to execute the tasks well.

9.1 Build Software Securely

At the heart of secure software development, there are three core activities. Figure 9.2 delineates the three core activities and their relationship within both Agile and Waterfall development. Every programmer must attempt to write safe, defensive, self-protective code. There is no secure path around the need for coders to understand what must be done *in the language in which they are working*. Different languages and different execution environments demand different emphases. In fact, issues in one language may not be worth considering in another; one only has to look at the differences between C/C++ and Java to understand this fact. The C/C++ language allows the mishandling of memory; in fact it's very easy to do something insecure. In contrast, the Java programming language takes care of all memory handling; programmers need not worry about the allocation and the de-allocation of memory at all.

Even experts at writing correct, secure code make mistakes. And the current reality is that there are very few coders who are experts in security, much less the security issues of a particular language and runtime. In addition, it should be remembered that writing software code is as much an art as it is engineering. While there are correct implementations and incorrect implementations (engineering), a great deal of creativity is involved in expressing that correctness. There may be several algorithmic approaches to a particular problem. There will be many possible expressions of whatever algorithm has been chosen. And this does not take into account innovation: The programmer may encounter computer problems that have not yet been attempted; she or he will have to create an entirely

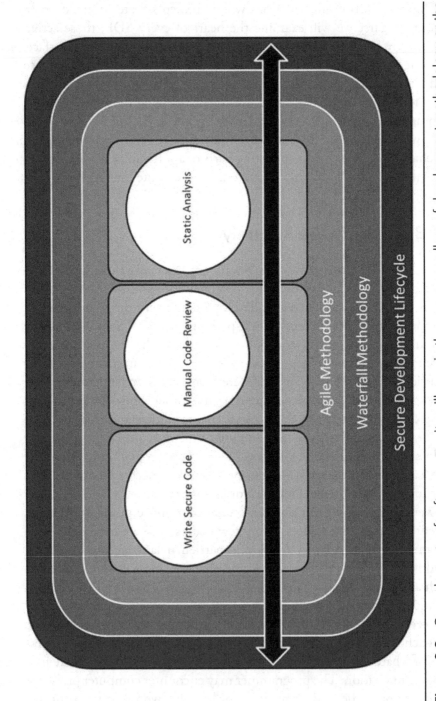

Figure 9.2 Core elements of software security will remain the same regardless of development methodology or the SDL that you use.

new algorithm or significantly modify a standard. And, even with naming conventions and other coding standards, programming languages are, in essence, expressive. That may be one of the motivators for becoming a programmer: creativity at one's job. But with creativity and innovation come mistakes. Mistakes are the price we pay for innovation. Not every idea works; perhaps most fail? One very successful approach is to learn about a problem by trying to solve it. Such an iterative approach is often used when building software, but iterative discovery guarantees a certain level of failure and error. We would posit that defects and vulnerabilities are a direct result of innovation (although, of course, innovation and creativity are not the only causes of vulnerabilities).

The software security practitioner is faced with a trade-off between curtailing innovation and perhaps job satisfaction and delivering code whose security can be assured. This is where the assurance steps provide appropriate help. We recommend that at the heart of whatever development process is used, include manual code review and static analysis. That is, give the creative coder considerable help to deliver correct code.

Figure 9.3 visually reinforces the central coding flow: Produce secure code which is then statically analyzed and manually code-reviewed. This is the essential "secure" version of "build" in software construction terms, i.e., the "heart" of a secure development lifecycle. These core tasks lie at the center of secure software, regardless of the development process being used.

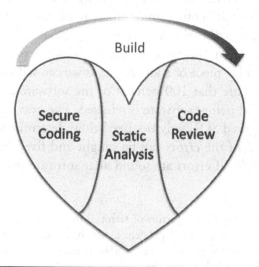

Figure 9.3   The heart of an SDL.

9.1.1 Produce Secure Code

Every program has (at least) two purposes: the one for which it was written and another for which it wasn't.[1]

If software engineers, those who write software, could produce correct, error-free code, there would be far less of a software security problem.* And with only correct software there is no need for all the non-design related tasks of the SDL. At the risk of stating the obvious, writing correct code has always been difficult, even without security considerations. Since the dawn of the software industry, when software engineers adopted the term "bug," meaning "software error," engineers have struggled to produce code that is correct, both logically and without runtime error. Inferring from the vast experience of all the software that has been written, we can conclude that writing error-free code is very, very difficult. It's not impossible, but it remains an expensive ideal rather than a norm.

Realizing the error-prone nature of producing code, software engineers have attempted to find a metric that shows how dependable and error-free any particular piece of code might be. One measure is the number of defects, "bugs," per line of code written. It is generally accepted that production software contains approximately 1 error per 1000 lines of code. This is a very general statistic. It is possible to produce software that has far fewer errors; one need look only at critical space mission or military software, which often must adhere to much stricter defect limits. And, of course, poorly written software may have orders of magnitude more errors than 1 in 1000. Generally, however, there are errors in any moderately complex piece of code. As far as we can tell today, there is no way for us to ensure that 100 percent of the software or security errors will be eliminated before software is released. The best approach is to go through the required SDL activities (see below, determining questions) to ensure that most of the errors can be caught and fixed before a product is deployed or sold. If errors are found after software release, one should

---

* There would still logical errors, errors of architecture and design omission and commission. Logical errors are not dependent upon correct code. It is quite possible to insecurely specify, and then code that mistake correctly to the specification. That is, it is possible to correctly follow the incorrect specification and introduce a logical vulnerability.

essentially follow a foreshortened SDL cycle to get the errors remediated, tested, and released.

Testing shows the presence, not the absence of bugs.[2]

Out of the population of extant errors, some proportion will have effects that can be manipulated to the advantage of an attacker; that is, these errors will be security "vulnerabilities." We focus here on vulnerabilities.

There is reasonable certainty that developers will produce incorrect code at least some of the time and some of those errors will be subject to malicious manipulation, ergo, there will be vulnerabilities in the code. This is not a reason to abandon efforts to write correct code. The advantages of correctness at the outset far outweigh the expenditure; it is an established fact that achieving correctness as early as possible in the development cycle is by far cheaper and easier. The earliest point will be when the code is written.

There are several complementary activities that, when put together, will contribute to fewer security defects as code is being written: developer training, safe libraries, and proven implementations generalized for reuse.

Obviously, developers must know what is expected of them, where to pay attention to security, and what the correct behavior is that must be programmed. Any and all training approaches have benefit, although some approaches have less effectiveness than may be obvious.

Developers should understand, at a very high level, that some defects have profound effects within the software they write. Functional specifications describe how the software will be used. Among these specifications will be those security attributes and features that users and the owners of the software require. Generally, that which has been specified gets built. That is not to say that errors don't creep in; they do. But since the properties are a part of the requirements, developers have an organic exposure to systems such as authentication and authorization, and to the API functions and classes that implement communications protections, such as TLS/SSL. If specified, the developer will generally attempt to build the functionality.

The security industry has primarily been interested in vulnerability (something that can be exploited), that is, in security weakness. Vulnerabilities are defects that when manipulated cause side effects that can be used to advantage; vulnerabilities are bugs. Since security practitioners ultimately must assess risk, a part of which is vulnerability, it is a natural focus of the occupation. Unfortunately, developers do not focus on vulnerability. They must focus on correctness. Is the algorithm written correctly? Does this code implement the specification exactly? Will this logical series produce the correct paths? Is this code clear enough to be maintained by someone who has never seen it before? Will this code reject invalid input? Can this code fail and the program recover after that failure? These are the sorts of questions that dominate developer thinking. Vulnerability is generally a side effect of error, often not an error by itself.

Tracking back from vulnerability to defect or code error is one of the big misses in information security as of this writing. Security people talk about vulnerability. Developers want to know where the bug is and how to fix it: Developers typically ask, "What is the correct behavior that must be implemented?"

It's useful for coders to understand that bugs can make a program vulnerable. However, training should focus on what is correct, self-defensive behavior. US-CERT's Key Practices for Mitigating the Most Egregious Exploitable Software Weaknesses[3] are a refreshing start, focusing on correct, secure programming. The focus of this publication is not vulnerability side effects or attack patterns, but rather, on the system properties and algorithms that will prevent issues. For instance, for cross-site scripting (XSS, also represented as XXS) errors, which are endemic to today's Web applications, Key Practices recommends complementary programming solutions that together will prevent XSS. The following quote recommends a specific algorithm which would then be "correct" and also prevents one variation of the vulnerability, XSS.*

> When the set of acceptable objects, such as filenames or URLs, is limited or known, create a mapping from a set of fixed input values (such as numeric IDs) to the actual filenames or URLs, and reject all other inputs.[4]

Training that focuses on correct behavior is a key to fewer security vulnerabilities. A secure coding training program might begin with the necessary high-level attributes of a secured system. There are any number

---

* The algorithm quoted is not intended to be an XSS "fix-all"; it is chosen for specificity, not for its completeness.

of security design principle collections. The Open Web Application Security Project (OWASP) provides a distillation of several of the most well known sets of principles:

- Apply defense in depth (complete mediation).
- Use a positive security model (fail-safe defaults, minimize attack surface).
- Fail securely.
- Run with least privilege.
- Avoid security by obscurity (open design).
- Keep security simple (verifiable, economy of mechanism).
- Detect intrusions (compromise recording).
- Don't trust infrastructure.
- Don't trust services.
- Establish secure defaults[5]

Even if developers thoroughly understand these principles without further training, as they design and implement, security correctness will be one of the key attributes that will emerge as programs take shape.

Training must be readily available and easily consumable. Generally, week-long courses are very difficult to schedule broadly due to lost productivity and lost opportunity costs. While an immersive approach certainly has benefits, any material that is not quickly applicable to tasks at hand may be rapidly lost. Instead, shorter segments that can be taken in small doses and then practiced on the job will likely deliver better results. One pattern that we've found very effective is to establish a baseline understanding and skill level with:

- High-level application vulnerability introduction
- Secure design and coding principles
- Three to five required, easily understandable short courses (30 minutes maximum), demonstrating correct fixes for common vulnerabilities applicable to the developer's platform and language.

Once the baseline training has been established, provide additional training on common fixes. Training in these commonly encountered patterns must be easily consumable. Developers tend to be very jealous of their time. Alongside highly focused, shorter pieces, also provide more in-depth training on software security. In this manner, developers may follow their own interests. If they have to fix a particular error, they may choose to take the short, focused training. Or, if they catch the "security fire," they may want to pursue such deeper topics as encryption implementations or access control systems. Any training program should remind engineering staff that security skills are marketable and a premium skill.

Training by itself is less effective without opportunities to use the learned skills. Practice definitely makes perfect. This is a strong reason to give developers time between training sessions to apply the new skills. A natural rhythm of training then practice should be established:

- 30–60 minutes of secure coding training
- Several weeks of practical application

Those who become experts can assist those with less skill. Further, these experts become senior code reviewers, capable not only of finding defects during manual code review, but also disseminating the correct approaches and algorithms.

Alongside a robust secure coding training program, thoroughly debugged implementations can be created. These libraries should be designed to generalize solutions across many implementations. They should provide easily implementable Application Programming Interfaces (APIs) to the correct implementations contained within the library. These correct libraries may then be included in each software project with the knowledge that security has been well implemented. And, if an error is found in the library, it can be fixed in only one place rather than in many disparate implementations.

The OWASP Enterprise Security API[6] is an example of a vetted implementation that solves various security problems within a Web application. For instance, to prevent XSS, there are functions that will validate all input against a whitelist before passing on the input for use within the application:

> *All input must be validated against a strict whitelist pattern using the Validator.* methods before used.*[7]

Whether correct APIs are built internally or acquired, these should be a key technology to ensure that code is correctly secure. Creating and using vetted libraries ensures that correct implementations are used and reused. This will also avoid the problem of implementation errors creeping into each coder's individual realization.

Another solution that may be of help is *pairs programming*. Kent Beck defines pairs programming as follows:

> *Pairs of programmers program together. Pairs don't just make test cases run. They also evolve the design of the system. Changes aren't restricted to any particular area. Pairs add value to the analysis, design, implementation, and testing of the system. They add that value wherever the system needs it.*[8]

In this manner, both design and implementation are improved by the collective skill of the pair of programmers.

Writing secure, correct code is a product of several approaches taken together. Training complements practice. Practice creates expertise that can be applied to vetted implementations, which can be reused to minimize implementation errors. Collaborative approaches build team expertise while catching errors during the writing process. However, secure writing is not enough; correctness must be verified.

9.1.2 Manual Code Review

Due to the expressive nature of computer languages and the infinite variety of logical problems tackled in programs, it is important to employ independent, skilled reviewers who can provide a safety net for the coder, and a check on correctness. Manual code review is particularly good at finding errors in the logic of the code. If the reviewer understands what the code will be doing but has not been involved in writing the code, he or she can often spot errors, especially logical errors. The reviewer can certainly check to see that coding standards have been adhered to. If the reviewer has security expertise, she or he may also spot security defects as well. Since there is a dearth of secure coding experts, it may be necessary to focus on logical and stylistic elements. However, if every developer is trained in basic defensive programming, particularly with respect to inputs, manual code review can at least find the egregious input validation errors that plague so much of the code produced today. In any event, code review is not panacea. While it is possible to get expert manual code reviewers who can literally rewrite your code to be not only secure but also be efficient, elegant, and maintainable, these are very expensive. And there are very few such "code gurus" from which to draw. Making use of these experts may be very valuable for critical code, but it is infeasible for most projects in most organizations. What is feasible is to complement several different approaches, some targeted assurance, some broad, both manual and automated. A methodology that maximizes the complementary nature of approaches has proven to find the broadest level of defects while also being scalable.

To maximize manual code review, for the large amount of grunt, well-understood, typical code that must surround the critical pieces and the proprietary business logic modules, it's probably sufficient for most organizations to use peer review. Manual peer code review is when one or more of the coder's peers reviews code before commit for build. Members of the same development team will likely be familiar with what was intended by the code, the environment in which the code will run, and the general architecture of the project. It should therefore not be too difficult for them to understand and comment constructively. For code that is not too complex, such as routines that call a broadly understood API, a single reviewer may be sufficient. For more complex code, multiple reviewers may be employed. In fact, one of the soft benefits from a strong peer review program is the trust that members of the team develop in each other. Further, reviewers will become backups to the coder so that no single person becomes indispensable. On one team, the coders came to trust each other so much that they would often ask for three or four reviewers on their code; the resulting code was much more correct and efficient than it had been previous to this team code review. If the team is sufficiently skilled by themselves, peer review may be adequate for even critical or highly sensitive algorithms.

Typically, however, especially at fast-moving organizations where there may be movement between teams or even periods of turnover, peer review will be insufficient for critical code. The worst situation is where a junior programmer shows her or his code to another junior programmer who looks at it and replies, "Your code looks just like mine. Pass." Inexperienced coders are not going to find many sophisticated errors. Still, one of the more interesting code review processes we've seen involved a junior reviewer explaining code to a very senior developer.* While this

---

* Instituted by Joe Hildebrand, CTO of Jabber, Inc.

may be a more time-consuming approach, the training and development benefits are obvious. A code review becomes an opportunity to mentor and instruct.

We recommend that critical algorithms, complex functions, security modules, and cryptography implementations be manually reviewed by someone who has the skill to assess correctness and who understands the types of vulnerabilities that can be introduced. This will typically be someone very senior on the team or who can be made available to the team. It should be someone who is familiar with the intended functionality; usually, it's someone who has implemented the same or similar functions successfully in the past.

9.1.3 Static Analysis

Static code analysis is the process of running an automated tool that reads either the source or the compiled object code after it has been written. The tool has preprogrammed patterns and errors for which it searches in the body of the code. Since, as has already been noted, computer languages are expressive; this is what's known in computer world science as a "nontrivial" problem. That is, static analysis must understand not only the legality and semantics of a language (duplicating what the compiler does), but must also understand typical constructs and those constructs' mistakes and misuses. Further, the static analysis must create a graph of all the possible interactions, "calls" within the code, in order to arrive at vulnerable interactions. One limited and simplified way to describe modern static analysis is that the compiler finds what is illegal or disallowed in the language. A static analyzer builds on legality by finding that which is "ill-advised." Again, this is a gross oversimplification of the capabilities bundled within an industrial-strength static analyzer.

With respect to the SDL, how a static analysis takes place is not particularly important. More important is the sorts of errors that static analysis finds, and the sorts of errors that will be overlooked. For languages where direct memory manipulation, allocation, and de-allocation are required, static analysis has proven excellent at identifying code where memory is susceptible to misuse. For instance, common stack-based overflows in C/C++ occur when the size of data to be copied into a stack-based buffer is not checked before the copy or the length of the copy is not limited to the size of the buffer. This is considered a classic security vulnerability. If that buffer can be accessed from a point outside the program (that is, through an input path), the overflow can be used to execute code of the attacker's choosing.

Most static analysis tools will readily identify failure to check size of the copy as a memory-handling error. Some tools may even be able to establish seriousness by identifying an input path that leads to the copy. This is particularly true for static analysis which builds an execution graph of the software before error analysis.* Or, conversely, the analyzer may find that there is no such input path, thus downgrading the seriousness of the issue. In the latter case, dynamic analysis will never find the issue, as there is no input leading to the buffer copy. In the former case, dynamic analysis may or may not find the issue, depending on the inputs attempted.

Because static analyzers can view all the code, not just the code that can be reached through inputs, we place static analysis at the point where the code is still close to the developer. Several of the industrial-strength static analyzers build a code graph of every path through the code. Building such a graph gives the analyzer a holistic view not only of paths through the code, but of relations between modules, use of APIs, data exposure and hiding, and other subtle programming patterns. With the true graph, the analyzer can assign seriousness to issues with far more information about relations between pieces of the code when it finds an error. And, of course, since the static analyzer has the source code, it can point precisely in the code where a potential error lies. This saves significant amounts of time for developers fixing defects.

The downside of the holistic but not executing view is that errors that may have less potential to get exercised may be reported alongside and equivalent to those that absolutely are exposed. These unexposed errors, in fact, may not be particularly significant even when they are exposed, due to runtime considerations. That is, not all potential buffer overflows have equal impact. The classic example is a buffer overflow that requires very high privileges in order to exploit. Attackers who have escalated privilege to the required level have no need to exercise an additional

---

* The advantage of the call graph is that every possible path through the code can be examined. The disadvantage of a call graph is that many of the possible paths enumerated in the graph may never be executed. There are limited approaches for static analysis to determine which paths are critical and actually exposed to an attack surface. The analyzer takes a "best guess" approach.

attack that executes the attacker's arbitrary code. On most modern operating systems, at that privilege level, an attacker can execute whatever he or she wants without a further exploit. In other words, such a buffer overflow has no potential attack value. Such an overflow is entirely theoretical. Still, because the static analyzer is not executing the program and has no notion of user privileges, the analyzer cannot distinguish between a high-privilege arbitrary code execution and a low-privilege one. It will take developer analysis to qualify such a reported defect.

> *The Embarrassment of Riches problem means that a modern commercial static analysis tool generally finds more bugs than the user has resources, or willingness, to fix.*[9]

One practical solution to the "embarrassment of riches" problem is to start with a well-understood, high-confidence analysis. "High confidence" means: "Report only those defects for which there is very high confidence that there is in fact an exploitable defect that must be fixed." This means turning down the "aggressiveness" or similar configuration to a low setting. Configure only those checks that the manufacturer of the static analyzer believes will deliver 90 percent or better confidence in the results—that is, 10 percent or less false positives. Obviously, this means that some defects will flow through. We offer the adage that any reduction in attack surface is a significant win for security. It is extremely hard to achieve 100 percent; even 80 percent may be difficult in the first few releases of a program. A reduction in attack surface or vulnerability of even 20 percent in the early stages of a program to build secure software (an SDL program) is quite significant.

> *Political resistance to static analysis bugs is sometimes warranted, sometimes mere laziness, but sometimes deeper and cultural: Avoiding the kinds of bugs that static analysis finds is largely a matter of discipline, which is sometimes unpopular among programmers. Fixing these bugs, and verifying that your organization has done so, will require adaptability and judgment. Attempts to design simple rules and metrics for this are, in my opinion, at best premature, and perhaps impossible.*[10]

Starting with lower targets that will deliver high-confidence results will be accepted much faster, as engineering teams quickly gain confidence in the tools' results. We suggest a soft target of engineers trusting the static analyzer similarly to the way they trust their compilation tools. Starting small and focusing on high confidence is likely to gain that sort of trust. And once that trust is gained, teams can begin experimenting with more checks, broader defect analysis, and more aggressive scans. Still, in our experience, engineering team confidence and trust is critical to the success of the static analysis program.

In other words, it is typically a mistake to simply turn on the default or "everything but the kitchen sink" analysis when first getting a start. Teams will be bombarded with unmanageable defect totals (sometimes in the tens of thousands from a single analysis). Defect tracking systems will be overwhelmed. Such numbers are likely to generate "political resistance" to adoption. Engineers will lose confidence that the tool can deliver usable and reliable results.

Instead, we advise starting small, clean, and manageable. Build on successes. Template successful builds, configurations, and test suites that teams can adopt easily and quickly. Have successful teams assist those that may be struggling. Let the teams that have reduced their defect counts evangelize to those that are just getting started or are new to analysis. We have successfully used precisely this approach several times in different organizations.

One key is to place static analysis in the correct development "spot." Like the compiler, through which the code must pass successfully in order to generate object code, the code must pass through static analysis and likewise be free from incorrect uses and identified vulnerabilities before it can be built (that is, linked into a library, executable, or other fully linked and executable object). Static analysis can be thought of as a part of the check-in and build process; static analysis is the mandatory step for qualifying code as buildable.

If the analysis tool supports developer use during development, let engineers have this additional check for the code they produce. Programmers will learn and trust the tool. They will also learn about security and secure coding; security mistakes will be pointed out during code creation. Still, we believe that while this use delivers obvious benefits, the code should still be analyzed again when committed for build into the product or release. Give coders every advantage. Give them every possibility for delivering correct code. And verify correctness at some formal gate through which the code must pass. If the code is clean, there is little lost from putting it through static analysis—commercial analyzers are generally quite fast once they are properly configured and tuned. However, if there are vulnerabilities, this is the bottom line. These "must not pass" into executable objects that then have the potential for getting into production uses. "Trust, but verify." We recommend empowering coders to verify their work while also verifying implementations before these can be fully committed for potential release.

At the heart of every development lifecycle, there are three processes that interlock and complement each other to deliver secure code. Developers need to be trained and have the discipline to try and write correct, error-free, vulnerability-free code. This practice and discipline will require training, practice, and a space in which developers can make mistakes, try new things, learn, and be relatively free during the learning process. It takes astute management to work with high-functioning, creative people who are learning their craft while practicing it at the same time. After the code is written, the next core step of the secure build process is manual code review. Like secure programming, manual code review is also a discipline and a practice. Code review is also an opportunity for learning and mastery; manual code review is the other side of writing correct code. Great code reviewers become great coders. Great coders become great code reviewers. The two processes work hand in hand to deliver cleaner code and more sophisticated programmers. Finally, at the heart of the development process, checking and complementing the code review, is static analysis. Complementing the human element, static analysis is an automated procedure that looks holistically across multiple dimensions at the same time. Whether Waterfall or Agile, secure coding, code review, and static analysis should lie at the heart of any secure development lifecycle.

9.2 Determining the Right Activities for Each Project

9.2.1 The Seven Determining Questions

Recurring often, continually, and across every organization with which we've worked, is a sense from developers and engineering teams that adding security will be yet another impediment to delivery. It's important to note that many if not most software organizations reward at least in part upon the delivery of features on time, and under budget. Typically, the focus on timely delivery is well embedded at the point when a software security practice is started or improved. It is only natural that teams will want to know how, in their already busy schedules, they will manage to accomplish a series of what appear to be additional tasks.

Obviously, one can argue that developers should have been integrating security into development practices already. Interestingly, many times, teams have responded that they are, in fact, doing just that: producing "secure" software. "Secure" here is an operative term; "security" has no precise meaning and is highly overloaded.

Digging a little deeper, we will be told that the authentication mechanism for the software has been well thought through and is built and tested. Or, perhaps, all communications going over the network can be placed within an encrypted tunnel (usually, TLS). Rarely, previous to the instantiation of a strong SDL program, do teams respond in a holistic manner, acknowledging the range of tasks that must receive attention, from design through testing. And that is precisely the problem that working with the SDL is supposed to address: holistic, built-in security, soup to nuts, end to end.

Because security is often presented as a matrix of tasks, teams may see the large number of tasks and become overwhelmed as a result. Time and again, we have heard team leads and development managers ask, "What do I have to do?" Since the answer to that question really should depend on the type of project at hand, the security architect may answer, "Well, that depends." This answer is not very satisfying to people who have made a practice out of timely and orderly software delivery: product managers, project managers, technical leads, and development managers.

Then, the security person will be asked, "What is the minimum set of activities that my project will have?" Requesting a minimum task set is certainly a relevant and worthy question. The answer, "Well, that depends," is once again not at all satisfying. We realized that having the security architect as the sole arbiter of what must be done too often makes a mystery of the entire process. Planning becomes more difficult. Yet again, security is seen as a hindrance and an obstacle, not as one of the required deliverables that must be a part of production software.

After much trial and error over many years, on divergent development groups operating within multiple enterprise organizations, we have crystallized a set of questions that can be easily answered by project managers, architects, technical and engineering leads, and/or product managers. These people typically have the understanding to assess the amount of planned architecture and design change, whether there will be additions of sensitive data and third-party code, the types of interfaces to be added or changed, and the expected deployment models. Each of these dimensions influences which security activities must be executed in order to generate the correct set of security features and requirements. Some of these dimensions determine what types of security testing will be required. Together, the answers to these questions will map the required SDL security task flows to individual project circumstances.

We do not recommend a "do it all" approach. Threat modeling additions that make no substantive change to a previously and thoroughly analyzed security architecture delivers no additional security value. Plus, requiring this step when it has no value will not engender trust of security's process judgment. Engineers often spot valueless activities (they tend to be smart, creative people!). Nobody likes to waste time on useless bureaucracy. Most engineers will quickly realize that requiring dynamic Web testing when there is no Web server has no value. Rather, let teams exercise their skills by allowing them to answer fundamental questions that sensibly add activities only when these are applicable.

These questions can be asked up front, at the beginning of the development lifecycle, or at appropriate stages along the way. Timing is critical. Answering each question after the appropriate time for the associated activities in the SDL has past will cause delays; required security tasks will be missed. As long as each question is asked before its results are needed, your security results will be similar. Architecture questions can be asked before any architecture is started, design before designing, testing answers need to be gathered for the testing plan, and so on throughout the lifecycle. However, asking these seven determining questions at the very beginning allows those responsible for budgeting and resource allocation to gather critical information about what will need to be accomplished during development.

1. What changes are proposed? (The following answers are mutually exclusive; choose only one.)
   a. The architecture will be entirely new or is a major redesign.
   b. The architecture is expected to change.
   c. Security features or functions will be added to the design.
   d. Neither changing the architecture nor adding security features to the design will be necessary (i.e., none of the above).
2. Will any third-party software be added? Yes/no

3. Will any customer data (personally identifying information [PII]) be added? Yes/no
4. Will this organization or any of its partners host any of the systems? Yes/no
5. Is a Web server included? Yes/no
6. Will there be any other inputs to the program? (i.e., non-Web input, configuration file, network listeners, command line interfaces, etc.) Yes/no
7. Is this a major release?

Very early in the process, even as the concept begins to take shape, it's important to ask, "What's new?" That is, find out how much change is intended by this project, through this effort. The question is meant to be asked at the architecture level; there are four possible answers:

1. Everything is new. This is a "greenfield" project or a major redesign.
2. The architecture will change significantly.
3. Security features will be added to the architecture or design.
4. None of the above.

What changes are proposed?

When everything will be new, there are certain pre-architectural activities that can help determine the set of requirements and features that will meet the security challenges for the intended use and deployment of the software. Figure 9.4 illustrates the task flow for projects that are completely new, involve major redesign, or where the system has never had any security review. Having a complete set of requirements has proven to deliver more inclusive and effective architectures, by far. Among the complete set of requirements must be security. The goal is to "build security in," not to bolt it on later. If the required features are not included in the architecture requirements, they most likely will not get built. This forces deployment teams to make up for missing security features by building

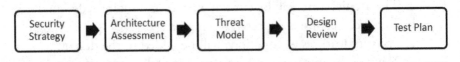

Figure 9.4 Architecture task flow when a project is new or a redesign.

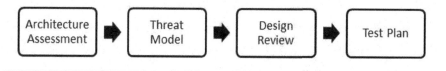

Figure 9.5 Architecture task flow when there will be changes to the architecture.

the required protections into the encompassing runtime or infrastructure, often as a "one-off," nonstandard implementation.

When everything or almost everything will be new and there is no existing, legacy architecture or design for which architects must account, there is an opportunity to thoroughly consider not only current threats and their attacks, but the likely attacks of the future against which the software must protect itself. This kind of early, strategic thinking is rare in the world of software re-use. It's a great advantage to take the time and think about what the security system will need holistically. Software security strategy is best done before making decisions that cause the secure design course to be ruled out entirely or made much more difficult to implement.

If the architecture is changing, then the process should start at architecture assessment and threat modeling. Figure 9.5 describes the task flow. The changes must be examined in light of the existing architecture so that any additional security requirements can be smoked out. The assumption is that the existing architecture has been assessed and threat-modeled to ensure that appropriate security requirements have been built into the design. In cases where there never has been an architecture assessment and threat model, the architecture should be treated the same as a greenfield project.

Even if there are no additions or changes to the existing architecture, adding any feature with security implications indicates the necessity for design work. The design makes the architecture buildable. Programmers work from the design. So it's important that any security requirement or feature be designed correctly and completely. Security expertise is critical; the purpose of the design review is to ensure that the appropriate security expertise is applied to the design. Figure 9.6 shows the flow of these two design-related SDL tasks.

Like any other feature or function, every security function must be thoroughly tested for correctness in the test plan. Creating the test plan is part of the design work. The test plan is an artifact of the design.

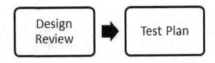

Figure 9.6   Design task flow when designing security features.

The answers to the question, "What's new?" are a pick-list choice. There should be one and only one choice. The answers are not mutually exclusive. Rather, the second choice, "architecture changes," is a subset of the first; "greenfield" implies that the architecture will change. The answer, "security features," is independent of the first two. "Security features" is meant to catch changes for which the project's design must be considered. If the architecture is changing, it can be presumed that the design will change as well.

The answers to the remainder of the questions are "yes/no" or binary.

Will any third-party software be added?

Adding third-party software presents two challenges.

1. The additional software may have security vulnerabilities that then become incorporated into the finished product. Typically, for commercially created software, the development team does not have the source code to the software. An organization will be entirely dependent on the third party to fix vulnerabilities. Or, if the software is open source, there may be legal and monetary considerations if the development team chooses to fix security defects. According to many licenses, that fix must be contributed back to the open-source community for everyone to use. That may not be commercially viable.

2. Added to the conundrum surrounding whether to fix a third party's defects are the licensing issues attached to the software that will be added. Different open-source and freely available licenses vary widely in restricting what a commercial organization can or cannot do with software that incorporates this functionality. Your ability to sell your product might be constrained. Or proprietary intellectual property may have to be exposed. Because of these considerations, we believe it is essential that decisions to use third-party software include consultation with an expert familiar with software licensing

(usually someone in the legal department). The software licensing expert will review the licensing details thoroughly.

Answering "yes" to this question adds a legal licensing review to the required tasks. It may also require the need to monitor for security patches of the third-party software for as long as it's included.

The third-party SDL set of tasks and the linear flow of these tasks are illustrated In Figure 9.7.

Figure 9.7   Third-party and open-source task flow.

Will any customer data (personally identifying information) be added?

If your software will face privacy challenges and regulations, it's imperative to find out if personally identifying information (PII) will be handled by the application under development. Depending on the organization, security may be tasked with protecting customers' information and meeting each legal jurisdiction's privacy regulations. Privacy duties may also reside in a dedicated team, or as part of legal, or some other part of the organization. Whatever team is responsible, these will need to be brought in for a data protection review. Hence the question, "Are you adding customer data?" This is a much easier question to answer without specialized privacy knowledge.

We phrased this question as "customer data" because, depending on the jurisdiction, the definition of PII varies widely. And those organizations that will be subject to regulations in multiple jurisdictions must ascertain how they will meet regulations that may in fact conflict. Generally, legal privacy expertise is required for these determinations. Most development teams will not have the expertise to understand the various regulations and laws that define PII and to which an application may be subject. However, we have found that it's very easy for teams to understand whether the application is handling customer data or not. Depending on your development team expertise, you may want to let determination about whether or not there are privacy issues be answered by the appropriate personnel with privacy expertise. Simply flagging customer data ensures that, at the very least, the right team will be engaged for privacy issues.

Well-designed and well-implemented security protects data; that is one purpose of information security. However, it should be noted that security of customer data is not the only dimension of appropriate (and legally compliant) privacy. Privacy also may encompass policies, presentations, consent, limitations to geographic transportation and storage of data, and other dimensions that have little to do with the security design and implementation. Thus, security does not equal privacy. On the other hand, the ability to comply with some privacy laws and expectations certainly demands sufficient security. And, of course, many dimensions of digital security are independent of the privacy domain.

Will this organization or any of its partners host any of the systems?

The deployment model and execution environment of a system influence not only what security features and controls will be required, but, at a higher level of abstraction, the security lens through which these controls and features will be filtered. Not every control is required in every system. How to choose?

Software that is intended to be deployed by others outside the organization, for instance, by customers, must have sufficient capabilities to fulfill the customer's security posture from within the customer's environment. The security goal is to empower the customer while at the same time not reducing the customer environment's security posture.

On the other hand, software that will be hosted from within the perceived borders of an organization has fundamentally different security responsibilities. We use the term "perceived borders" because customers, media, and public influencers often don't make a fine discrimination between a "partner" and the organization. In the face of a successful attack, the largest or most well known entity or brand will get tagged with responsibility for the failure, regardless of any tangle of arms-length relationships. In light of this aspect of perception, we suggest taking a broad view of responsibility. Of course, each organization will have to define its acceptable boundaries for incident responsibility.

A system to be hosted by a known and controlled infrastructure inherits the security posture of that infrastructure. Thus, systems that will be deployed by the organization can make assumptions that are not possible with systems that will be deployed by those outside the organization, beyond organizational boundaries, on third-party premises. Assumptions can be made about which security functions are built into the infrastructure on which the system will be deployed. Indeed, the other side of that coin is that a locally deployed system also can be prepared for weaknesses within a known infrastructure. That is, an organizationally hosted system inherits the security posture of the infrastructure on which it is deployed. Figure 9.8 represents the set of tasks associated with deployment to a hosted infrastructure.

A hosted system also must meet all local policies and standards. This makes configuration, hardening, and tuning much more specific. For software to be deployed by others, it's important to design for unknown security requirements. In the case of hosted software, the requirements are typically apparent; these requirements can be anticipated, planned into the design, and pre-built.

In order to understand what security will need to be prepared and what weaknesses will need to be mitigated, it is important to ask "Organizationally hosted?" during requirements gathering and architecture. If those responsible for security requirements (typically, the security architects) are not familiar with the infrastructure into which the system will be deployed, an assessment of the infrastructure must take place. Likewise, policies and standards must be thoroughly understood in order to apply them to the system being built.

Typically, for a running security architecture practice, there will be experts in the existing infrastructure and policy experts. For hosted

Figure 9.8   Task flow for hosted systems.

systems, these subject-matter experts can be engaged to help refine the analysis so the requirements precisely fit the infrastructure into which the system is to be deployed. In this way, the hosted systems will meet organizational policies. On the other hand, if it is a new infrastructure, there is a due diligence responsibility to examine every security factor that is applicable. Insist that the new infrastructure be studied as a part of the systems under analysis.

Failure to look at the infrastructure, instead focusing solely on the systems being built, opens the possibility that an attacker could walk right through that infrastructure despite a designer's best efforts to build a sound defense in depth. Security architecture must, by dint of its due diligence responsibilities, always be front to back, side to side, bottom to top, thoroughly analyzing all components that support or interact. Every system that connects opens the distinct possibility that the interconnected system's security posture will in some way affect the security posture of the system to which it connects. This is a fundamental law of doing architectural analysis for security. Failure to be thorough is a failure in the security analysis. That analysis must include the infrastructure into which systems will be deployed if that infrastructure is under the control of the organization's policies. Thus, always ask, "Will any part of this system be hosted by this organization or its partners?"

Is a Web server included?

As of the writing of this book, security testing of Web servers utilizes a specialized set of tools and skills. For this reason, we have found it useful to identify the need for Web server testing so that the appropriate testing is engaged. Generally, every input into the software must be thoroughly tested. Specialized tools are run against custom Web application code. These tools take expertise not only in understanding Web attacks and their variations, but also each particular tool, what it does well, and its limitations. So we include a separate path within the overall testing plan that identifies the presence of the Web server so that the Web inputs get the needed specialized attention. This kind of testing is called dynamic testing. While there is certainly overlap among most of the various dynamic testing tools, we recommend that tools specific to Web applications be applied. Importantly, many attackers specialize in Web vulnerabilities. And, of course, if the system will be exposed to the public Internet, it will be attacked constantly and must prepare itself to defend against these common variations. However, even if the system will normally be deployed on a more trusted network, we believe that strong Web server dynamic testing is important. Sophisticated attackers sometimes manage to breach their way onto these trusted networks. A weak Web server can be a target in and of itself, or a server can present a hop-off point to more valuable targets. Therefore, it is good practice to identify all Web servers in order to benefit from this specialized testing.

Will there be any other inputs to the program?

Beyond Web server inputs, there are myriad other inputs that may be built into a system: command-line interfaces, configuration files, network inputs, native forms, scripting engines, and so forth. Each of these is an attack surface. Each input has the potential for a logic mistake that goes around access controls such as authentication and authorization. Logic mistakes may allow the misuse of the program to do unintended things, such as sell a product for a reduced or nonexistent price. Additionally, in programming languages where the programmer manipulates computer memory directly, poor input handling may allow serious abuse of the program or even the operating system. Memory-related errors often allow privilege escalation on the system or permit code of the attacker's choice to run. Inputs are an important attack point in any program, often the prime attack surface.

Before the test plan is written, all the inputs to the system should be enumerated. Each of the enumerated inputs should be tested to determine that the correct input values are handled properly. Further, tests must be run to prove that variations of incorrect input do not cause the system to fail or, worse, act as a vector of attack beyond the boundaries of the software (as in a buffer overflow allowing privilege escalation and code of the attacker's choice). A common tool as of this writing is a fuzz tester. These tools simulate the many variations that attackers may run against the software. Once a fuzzer is prepared for a particular input, it will automatically run through a set of variations that attempt improper inputs. The fuzzer will stop when the program begins to misbehave or crashes. In this way, unsafe input handling, even improper memory handling, can be smoked out. We recommend that every input that has been changed during this development cycle be fuzzed.

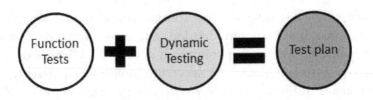

Figure 9.9   Test plan ingredients.

There is some overlap between what fuzzers cover and Web vulnerability analysis tools. If testing time is short, we recommend that Web vulnerability tools be run against the Web server, and all other inputs be fuzzed. However, it's not a bad idea to overlap the vulnerability scan by fuzzing the Web server's inputs as well. Since Web scanning tools look for known exploit patterns and fuzzers check generally bad input, employing both types of dynamic analysis provides better coverage than using either alone.

The test plan will likely include both testing of intended security functions and dynamic tests to ensure that no vulnerabilities have crept through manual review and static analysis, as indicated in Figure 9.9.

Is this a major release?

The seventh and last question is about the importance of this project or release in relationship to the software as a whole. Are the additions to the software in this development cycle going to be considered a major addition and/or revision? If there are going to be significant architectural changes, possibly accompanied by major feature additions or maintenance revisions of currently running code, there is a likelihood of introducing subtle logical changes, perhaps even errors, into the code base. Some of the most subtle bugs occur due to unintended side effects affecting other pieces of the code. Indeed, it is very hard to test thoroughly for interactions; this is particularly true when adding new features whose side effects interact with legacy code in unanticipated ways.

In addition, consumers of software tend to expect more from larger revisions. A major release will tend to get more scrutiny and perhaps wider distribution than a minor update.

For these reasons, it may be worthwhile considering a more thorough and holistic look at the security properties and vulnerabilities of a major release when the release is considered "code complete."

This can be accomplished through an independent attack and penetration. "Independent" in this context means independent from building the software and testing it. Since penetration testing requires significant skill, experts should be employed. It should also be remembered that no two testers deliver the same results; each penetration test is more or less unique to the tester and to the software under examination. Therefore, it is good practice to have a major release penetration test performed by someone with significant skills in the deployment model, execution stack, and even language in which the software is written. Failure to match tester to software type will likely deliver suboptimal results. You want a tester who understands how to attack the kind of software you're producing.

Through the application of a highly skilled attacker against your software, you can discover the sorts of vulnerabilities that sophisticated attackers will likely find and exploit. Subtle and sophisticated errors can be uncovered and fixed before the software goes live. Plus, you will have a much clearer picture of any residual risks in this release.

In this way, you can deliver both to your organization and to the consumers of the software assurance that the software is indeed self-protective as well as correct. We have found that for highly competitive markets and/or widely distributed software; a provable penetration test can be a competitive advantage, demonstrating not only the security of the software but also the commitment of the software maker to customers' safety.

Answering these seven determining questions can control security task flow for both Waterfall and Agile processes. Placement of the appropriate activities into each flow of development differs. These differences will be described below.

The answer to each of the seven questions answers "What is the minimum set of activities my project must perform?" However, it should never be suggested to teams that they can't supplement the minimum set with other activities if these might provide additional security value. For instance, if there's time, even threat modeling an existing architecture and design may uncover something useful. Attack patterns change over time; yesterday's popular attack may be superseded by another, easier or more successful approach.

Ask "What's new?" to assess the scope of proposed change. There are additional activities that flow from each answer. And these earlier, more architectural activities will lead to the later design, build, and test tasks. Tables 9.1 and 9.2 describe the selection of activities.

Table 9.1 Architecture and Design Activities Indicated by SDL Determining Questions

Question	Step 1	Step 2
Greenfield or redesign?	Determine the required security posture and the intended security strategy with the stakeholders. Generate the high-level security requirements.	Perform "architecture change" steps flow (see Figure 9.4).
Architecture change?	Review the architecture for security and create a threat model for architecture. Produce architecture requirements.	Perform "adding security features" flow (see Figure 9.5).
Will any security features be added?	The design must be reviewed to ensure correctness and eliminate logical vulnerabilities.	Add functional tests for each security feature to the test plan.
Are you adding customer data (personally identifiable information [PII])?	Conduct a privacy review.	
Are any systems to be hosted by the organization or its partners?	Review infrastructure security.	Perform a third-party vulnerability test on the software in the infrastructure before release.

Table 9.2 Coding Imperatives and Testing Activities from SDL Determining Questions

Question	Step 1	Step 2
Are you adding any third-party software?	Perform a legal licensing review.	Post-release, monitor for vulnerabilities that are discovered in the third-party software.
Is this a Waterfall build cycle or a cycle of Sprints in Scrum/Agile?	Code securely. Perform manual code review. Run static analysis.	Fix defects as discovered.
Is there a Web server?	Perform Web dynamic vulnerability testing.	Fix defects.
Is there a need to enumerate other inputs?	Fuzz all non-Web inputs.	Fix defects.
Is this a major release?	Consider an independent vulnerability assessment and pen test.	

Table 9.1 lists the activities that apply regardless of whether you are using a Waterfall or an Agile methodology. These have been previously described in the respective sections.

For a Waterfall development methodology, the following tasks will flow in a linear fashion: design, then build, then test. For an Agile methodology, the following tasks will be iterated through in each development cycle ("Sprint" in Scrum). Rather than a single period of design which must be completed before development may begin, each short cycle will design for the increments that have been selected for build. The cycle will complete when those features have been tested and are ready for release, i.e., "code complete." Hence, in Agile development, there are short, focused design periods, followed by coding, and then testing. However, it is not uncommon to redesign as more is known about any particular increment. And testing may begin whenever there is code to test. For this reason, the table contains the security tasks for each development cycle, to be executed as needed by the Agile team during Sprints. All three activities may be occurring in parallel during a Sprint. Table 9.2 shows those activities that fall within the "build" portion of either a Waterfall or Agile process and their associated determining questions.

We will examine these task flows more fully in Section 9.3.

It's important to assess the security impact of legacy code and projects that have not been through a formal SDL. When a mature SDL hasn't been in place for previous development (that is, before the current round of changes), a due diligence responsibility will be to decide whether there is a need to assess previous work. In the case of a brand-new SDL, it may be assumed that no review has taken place; but it's always a good practice to ask rather than assume. The determining questions are phrased, "Are you adding. . . ?" because this process assumes that in prior development cycles security has been attended as per the SDL. Therefore, the seven questions focus on what is being changed rather than any inherited legacy. When implementing or changing your SDL, one of the tasks will be to assess how much change will be required to your legacy code and projects as you apply your new SDL to your current development. What is your security technology debt? How many design misses exist, and how much vulnerable code are you carrying forward in the current development cycle?

One approach to SDL legacy technology debt is to ask, "How fast are my applications changing?" In periods of rapid change, it may make sense to carry the debt until it is replaced.

Concomitantly, in situations where legacy code will be carried forward for the foreseeable future, it may make sense to whittle away at vulnerabilities and exposures. One successful approach devotes a day each month to "bug bashes." Developers take a day off from producing new code and instead fix older defects. Such a "bash" can be done as a party, a relief from the rigors of code production. In this way, "tech debt" is whittled away and removed from production code bit by bit.

Bug bashes usually don't treat design issues. Architecture and design features to bolster an existing product's security will have to be considered against other feature requests. If sales are being missed due to the lack of security features, then the value of these features should be obvious. Often, however, the customer's security people interact with the software producer's security people in a separate dialog. Security people understand each other. Also, the customer's security folks want to gain some assurance that the vendor's security people are involved in the software's security as it's designed and built. Product management must be included in these customer security conversations. Product managers need to understand that the customer's security team often has a "no" vote, or may be expending extra resources on exceptions in order to deploy the software. When product managers and security architects align, security features can be taken in their rightful place as customer-enhancing rather than as a "nonfunctional" set of requirements.

Any security requirements that come out of an assessment of legacy software need to be added to the backlog of feature requests. These should be prioritized through risk rating. The risk rating can then be taken into consideration alongside customer needs. Likely, a security subject-matter expert should be included in this dialog.

Ultimately, treatment of technological debt is a risk decision. If the treatment is more expensive than the loss, it may not make sense to treat the risk. Various factors will have to be weighed, including the opportunity cost lost when not building new technology. We have seen situations where as many as 75,000 defects have been listed for large code bases. The known set of automated tools as of this writing is not sophisticated enough to provide absolute assurance that every discovered finding is in fact a defect. Simply determining which of 75,000 findings are actually defects is a significant chore. The execution of this chore, not to mention fixing the defects that are qualified, should be carefully considered. It's important to remember that, as Brad Arkin, CSO for Adobe, told one of the authors, "Vulnerabilities are not exploits." Indeed, defects are not necessarily vulnerable. A risk-based approach will focus on exploitable vulnerabilities when the vulnerabilities are exposed by the intended deployment model. Raw defect numbers, by themselves, are meaningless.

9.3 Architecture and Design

Systems Architecture is a generic discipline to handle objects (existing or to be created) called "systems," in a way that supports reasoning about the structural properties of these objects. . . . Systems Architecture is a response to the conceptual and practical difficulties of the description and the design of complex systems. Systems Architecture helps to describe consistently and design efficiently complex systems.[11]

Why include architecture in the SDL at all? There is a dictum in information security: "Build security in, don't bolt it on." Architecture is the structure, flow, and data of a system. Decisions made about the architecture can radically influence the security posture of the system. Failure to add an authentication mechanism may at best mean adding it after the architecture is set. The worst case is that there is a requirement for authentication, but no authentication mechanism can be added to the architecture: Authentication has been designed out.

Over and over, we have seen systems that assumed they were running on a highly restricted network. Assuming the network will provide appropriate restriction, the application is then designed to pass sensitive information between components without any protections in the architecture. Flows may not be protected because it is assumed that only the components in the target system would be deployed to that protected network. In a world of heterogeneous networks, advanced persistent threat attacks, and huge cloud-based server farm environments, the likelihood that any application will get its own highly restricted network is exceedingly small. The vast majority of networks are shared; there are very few highly trusted networks deployed. The assumption that the network will protect all the components of the system and all the intercomponent flows is a major architectural error. And yet, we see it repeatedly. The result will be a choice between exposing components and flows on the shared network or attempting to manage complex firewall rules in the shared environment. Also, the firewall capabilities may not provide the deep application protections that are required.

Security architecture has particular characteristics:

- Security architecture has its own methods. These methods might be the basis for a discrete security methodology.
- Security architecture has its own discrete view and viewpoints.
- Security architecture addresses non-normative flows through systems and among applications.
- Security architecture introduces its own normative flows through systems and among applications.
- Security architecture introduces unique, single-purpose components into the design.
- Security architecture calls for its own unique set of skill requirements in the IT architect.[12]

The vast majority of architectural design choices will have at least some security implications. Some of those choices will have profound security effects that suggest very particular patterns of security control. Hence, the security dictum, "Build it in." Building security in is illustrated by Figure 9.10.

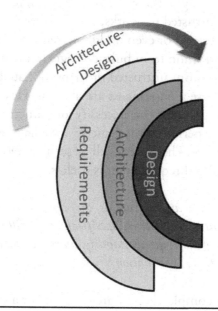

Figure 9.10 Strategize for requirements: architect, threat model, and design review.

Generally, the architecture flow starts with requirements gathering. From those requirements, an architecture that meets the requirements is proposed and then refined iteratively. This is true for an entirely new system as well as for changing an existing system. Other influencing factors, of course, are what can be built currently, what currently exists, and general architectural goals and strategies into the future. Current capabilities have a profound influence on proposed solutions. This is true for security capabilities just as much as database, network, server types, and the people and processes that support these. In fact, maximizing current capabilities might be one of the requirements. Using an existing authentication mechanism might be one of the security requirements of the system.

We strongly suggest that security be included during the requirements-gathering phase. As we have noted, part of a holistic security picture for a system will be the security features that get built into it. A Web system that gives access to financial information will likely have requirements for authentication to make sure that the information is given only to the holder of the information. Such a system is likely to have an authorization mechanism as well, so that the right access is given to the appropriate user. Indeed, such a Web system will also have other, less obvious security requirements: hardening of the systems so they can resist the omnipresent level of attack on untrusted networks, careful layering such that compromise of front-end systems or even middle systems does not provide access to the data, authentication from business logic to the data store such that inappropriate access from untrusted or inappropriate applications is not granted. Some of these requirements are obvious. However, we have seen many systems that ignored the necessity of gathering specific security requirements, to the peril of project success. We have even seen a security requirement stated as: "The system will be secure." Obviously, this sort of nonspecific, generalized requirement is useless.

> *Enterprise security architecture is the component of the overall enterprise architecture designed specifically to fulfill . . . the overall objective . . . to preserve the availability, integrity, and confidentiality of an organization's information.*[13]

In the case of a completely new architecture (or a complete redesign), security should be engaged early to strategize how the proposed system can meet future as well as present expectations, change, and growth. The security architect must have a strong grounding in the current types of threat agents and their attack methods whose targets are similar to the system under consideration. In these strategy sessions, the security architect should also have a good feel for emerging trends in threats and attack methods. What new threat agents are just beginning to become active? Of these new threats, what will be their likely attack methods? As the threat agents' organization and sophistication grow, how might they expand attack patterns? With these sorts of questions, the architecture can be designed not only for the intended use cases of the present, but also for the foreseeable future. Typically, enterprise-level architects consider similar questions regarding the growth of the organization, growth in user populations, growth in data, and expansion of capabilities. The same sort of consideration should be given to security needs of the future just as much as for the present.

Out of any architecture assessment will come requirements that the architecture must meet. Typically, early requirements are of a more general nature: Users will be authenticated, systems will need to be hardened, Payment Card Industry (PCI) certification (at the appropriate level) will need to be met, and so forth. The details will then be baked into the emerging architecture.

As architecting the system proceeds in earnest, the security requirements will begin to take on specificity. A particular authentication system will be chosen: For a major server farm, for instance, a system may be chosen which can handle millions of authentications per minute, can handle millions of user identities, can interface with the appropriate runtime and execution environments, and so forth. Or, if the authentication system will be very modest, perhaps there is an integral library, or another module which will suffice. Using the former implies tremendous growth and heavy user traffic, perhaps even heterogeneous systems. When using the latter authentication system, the smaller library may preclude major server farm growth. In considering the intended use (say, an authentication system for a customer-deployable appliance), a relatively constrained mechanism may be warranted. In any event, a particular choice will be made based on the requirements of the system in the intended deployment and with respect to the expected growth. The architecture will grow more specific and particular. The output of the security architecture process is specific components providing particular services and communicating using known protocols.

For systems within an existing architecture, any change to that architecture may have security implications, so the security of each architectural change should be considered. For instance, the addition of a third-party partner to whom finance data may flow will engender the addition of mechanisms to protect that finance data in transit. Further, protections will need to be put into place such that only the intended partner will be able to interact. In other words, the security needs of an existing architecture will change in the face of new components, or new communication flows, or new data types. Changes to any part of the architecture must be considered in light of the whole architecture, of all the existing security services. This work is very similar if not identical to the design work when building an entirely new architecture. Hence, we specify architectural assessment of the security of the system after the security strategy for the system has been considered or when any architectural changes are being made to an existing system. This set of SDL task flows presumes that the existing architecture has been through a holistic, thorough security assessment as required for an entirely new system. If there has been no previous security assessment, then the existing architecture should be treated as entirely new.

Once the architecture and all its ancillary components, including the deployment model and any infrastructure involved, is thoroughly understood, a threat model should be built. A threat model involves setting trust boundaries and identifying attack surfaces. Every attack method is not germane to every system. Importantly:

- Deployment models open or close attack surfaces.
- Execution environments provide services and attack surfaces of their own, which are inherited by the system.
- Existing infrastructure will bequeath security postures and weaknesses to the systems deployed on it.
- Different languages and runtime models deliver unique strengths and weaknesses.

Some components will be more exposed, and thus untrusted, while other components may need to be shielded, or lie at the heart of a trust boundary.

Consider the interaction between a user interface and a piece of software that must become part of an operating system (e.g., a kernel driver). The user software will be an obvious point of attack. The attacker might be after the user's data or communications. Or the attacker's goal may be control of the operating system through the user interface to the kernel driver. A kernel driver that is poorly protected can be an avenue for privilege escalation. A kernel driver becomes a part of the most trusted heart of the operating system. The user interface component should protect itself, but also the kernel driver. However, recognizing that protections fail, the kernel driver must protect itself as well. The driver must also protect the operating system, and not add any vulnerability to the kernel, the highest-privilege core of the operating system.

It should be obvious that there is a natural trust boundary between the user interface module and the kernel driver. It should also be obvious that any threat model built for this simple system should consider not only the user interface, the obvious attack surface, but also the interchange or flow between user software and kernel. The user software may choose to trust the kernel driver. However, under no circumstances should the kernel driver accept communications from any module except the user interface as intended. Also, that user interface must be highly self-protective against attempts to use it as a way to get to the kernel. From this very simple threat model, you can see emerging security requirements that must be built into the architecture and design:

- User interface input validation
- Intermodule authentication
- Kernel input validation from the user interface (in case the authentication or the user interface's input validation fails)

Depending on the operating system, there may be a slew of requirements concerning load order, execution permissions, installation mechanisms, configuration file permissions, configuration file validations, etc.

We do not believe that threat modeling is sufficient by itself.* The threat model requires the output from the architecture analysis: complete

---

* Threat modeling systems such as Microsoft's STRIDE make assumptions that we do not. STRIDE assumes that the modelers will already be intimately familiar with the target system's architecture, as any mature, heterogeneous development team is likely to be. For highly shared security architects, however, this will likely not be the case. Further, STRIDE's aim is to empower non-security-trained development teams to make a start. Hence, STRIDE is purposely simplified. We applaud STRIDE and similar methodologies. If your situation matches the intended purpose of STRIDE, we encourage you to employ it.

understanding of all the components, flows, and data. An architecture analysis identifies security feature requirements (that is, to fulfill the security needs of the potential users). Without this information, the threat model may be incomplete. With the architecture structure and the security requirements in hand, a threat model can be built to understand the attack surfaces that will be presented by the system. Since, as noted previously, every attack is not credible against every system, the threat model considers likely attack scenarios based on analysis of the preferred attack methods promulgated against similar systems.

It is always true that any requirements output from the threat model will create new test plan items. These new test cases ensure that the security requirements have been built correctly. Thus, if the threat model produces requirements, the test plan will receive new test cases. Security test cases are dependent on architecture analysis and threat modeling.

Generally speaking, if there is no architectural change, then architectural analysis and threat modeling can be bypassed. (This assumes that the existing architecture went through security assessment and threat modeling.)

The design of the system must implement all the requirements given from the architecture. If an architecture is the structure, flow, and data, then the design is the expected implementation of that structure. The design must have enough specificity that it can actually be coded.

Given adequate, clear, and detailed enough requirements or user stories (Scrum), skilled software designers generally have no trouble translating architecture and its requirements into a software design. This can be done before coding in a Waterfall process, or for each incremental build cycle in an Agile process. In either process case, it's important to pay particular attention to the security features and requirements. These must be absolutely correct or the implementation may open up vulnerabilities or, worse, create a new, unprotected attack surface. The logic has got to be watertight for critical security functions such as encryption routines or authorization schemes. Users of the system will be depending on these features to protect their resources.

We place a security design review at a point when designers believe that the design is very nearly completed. A security design review should be performed by a security assessor who understands the architecture and functionality well; usually, the review is best done by someone who has experience designing and even implementing security features. We further suggest that the reviewer be independent of the design team. Peer review is a powerful tool for validating design correctness and completeness. Another set of eyes can often spot errors which those closer to the design may have missed. If any security features or requirements are to be built in the current cycle, perform a security review.

As has been noted, every portion of the intended design must engender a thorough functional test plan. This is true of security just as well as any other part of the design. If Transport Layer Security (TLS) is to be added as an option to the network protocol stack, the test plan must include a test with and without TLS, each case having a pass condition. Security in the design always means security in the test plan.

How does an organization train people so that they can perform these difficult, architectural tasks? Software security expert Gary McGraw says:

For many years I have struggled with how to teach people . . . security design. The only technique that really works is apprenticeship. Short of that, a deep understanding of security design principles can help.[14]

McGraw's statement implies that, in order to build a qualified team, each organization will either have to invest in sufficiently capable and experienced practitioners who can also mentor and teach what they do, or hire consultants who can provide appropriate mentorship. Neither of these is likely to be cheap. As of this writing, there is a dearth of skilled security architects, much less the subset of those who can and want to impart what they know to others. The architecture and design skills necessary to an SDL program are probably going to require time to build, time to find key leaders, and then time for those leaders to build a skilled practice from among the available and interested people at hand. In one such long-running mentorship, even highly motivated junior people have taken as long as two or three years before they could work entirely independently and start to lead in their own right. This is a significant time investment.* In the same blog entry quoted above, McGraw cites Salzer and Schroeder's seminal 1975 paper, "The Protection of Information in Computer Systems,"[15] as a starting point for a set of principles from

---

* Please note that not every person who begins training will have the aptitude and motivation to finish. Our experience is that between one-third and one-half of those starting will not become security architects.

which to architect. These may also be used as a training and mentorship basis. McGraw's principles are

1. Secure the weakest link.
2. Defend in depth.
3. Fail securely.
4. Grant least privilege.
5. Separate privileges.
6. Economize mechanisms.
7. Do not share mechanisms.
8. Be reluctant to trust.
9. Assume your secrets are not safe.
10. Mediate completely.
11. Make security usable.
12. Promote privacy.
13. Use your resources.[16]

An in-depth discussion of these principles is beyond the scope of this work. Security practitioners will likely already be familiar with most if not all of them. We cite them as an example of how to seed an architecture practice. From whatever principles you choose to adopt, architecture patterns will emerge. For instance, hold in your mind "Be reluctant to trust" and "Assume your secrets are not safe" while we consider a classic problem. When an assessor encounters configuration files on permanent storage the first time, it may be surprising to consider these an attack vector, that the routines to read and parse the files are an attack surface. One is tempted to ask, "Aren't these private to the program?" Not necessarily. One must consider what protections are applied to keep attackers from using the files as a vector to deliver an exploit and payload. There are two security controls at a minimum:

1. Carefully set permissions on configuration files such that only the intended application may read and write the files.
2. Rigorously validate all inputted data read from a configuration file before using the input data for any purpose in a program. This, of course, suggests fuzz testing these inputs to assure the input validation.

Once encountered, or perhaps after a few encounters, these two patterns become a standard that assessors will begin to catch every time as they threat model. These patterns start to seem "cut and dried."* If configuration files are used consistently across a portfolio, a standard can be written from the pattern. Principles lead to patterns, which then can be standardized.

Each of these dicta engenders certain patterns and suggests certain types of controls that will apply to those patterns. These patterns can then be applied across relevant systems. As architects gain experience, they will likely write standards whose patterns apply to all systems of a particular class.

In order to catch subtle variations, the best tool we have used is peer review. If there is any doubt or uncertainty on the part of the assessor, institute a system of peer review of the assessment or threat model.

Using basic security principles as a starting point, coupled to strong mentorship, a security architecture and design expertise can be built over time. The other ingredient that you will need is a methodology for calculating risk.

Generally, in our experience, information security risk[†] is not well understood. Threats become risks; vulnerabilities are equated to risk in isolation. Often, the very worst impact on any system, under any possible set of circumstances, is assumed. This is done rather than carefully investigating just how a particular vulnerability might be exposed to which type of threat. And if exercised, what might be the likely impact of the exploit? We have seen very durable server farm installations that took great care to limit the impact of many common Web vulnerabilities such that the risk of allowing these vulnerabilities to be deployed was quite limited. Each part (term) of a risk calculation must be taken into account; in practice, we find that, unfortunately, a holistic approach is not taken when calculating risk.

A successful software security practice will spend time training risk assessment techniques and then building or adopting a methodology that

---

* Overly standardizing has its own danger: Assessors can begin to miss subtleties that lie outside the standards. For the foreseeable future, assessment and threat modeling will continue to be an art that requires human intelligence to do thoroughly. Beware the temptation to attempt to standardize everything, and thus, attempt to take the expert out of the process. While this may be a seductive vision, it will likely lead to misses which lead to vulnerabilities.

† Information security risk calculation is beyond the scope of this chapter. Please see the Open Group's adoption of the FAIR methodology.

is lightweight enough to be performed quickly and often, but thorough enough that decision makers have adequate risk information.

9.4 Testing

Designing and writing software is a creative, innovative art, which also involves a fair amount of personal discipline. The tension between creativity and discipline is especially true when trying to produce vulnerability-free code whose security implementations are correct. Mistakes are inevitable.

It is key that the SDL security testing approach be thorough; testing is the linchpin of the defense in depth of your SDL. Test approaches must overlap. Since no one test approach can deliver all the required assurance, using approaches that overlap each other helps to ensure completeness, good coverage both of the code as well as all the types of vulnerabilities that can creep in. Figure 9.11 describes the high-level types of testing approaches contained in the SDL. In our experience, test methodologies are also flawed and available tools are far from perfect. It's important not to put all one's security assurance "eggs" into one basket.

Based on a broad level of use cases across many different types of projects utilizing many of the commercial and free tools available, most of

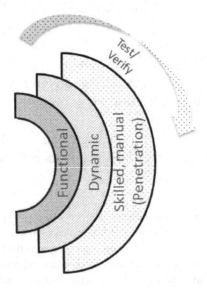

Figure 9.11 Complete test suite.

the comprehensive commercial tools are nontrivial to learn, configure, and use. Because testing personnel become proficient in a subset of available tools, there can be a tendency to rely on each tester's tool expertise as opposed to building a holistic program. We have seen one team using a hand-tailored approach (attack and penetration), while the next team runs a couple of language- and platform-specific freeware tools, next to a team who are only running static analysis, or only a dynamic tool. Each of these approaches is incomplete; each is likely to miss important issues. Following are our suggestions for applying the right tool to the right set of problems, at a minimum.

As noted previously, we believe that static analysis belongs within the heart of your SDL. We use it as a part of the developers' code writing process rather than as a part of the formal test plan. Please see the first section for more information about the use of static analysis in the SDL.

9.4.1 Functional Testing

Each aspect of the security features and controls must be tested to ensure that they work correctly, as designed. This may be obvious, but it is important to include this aspect of the security test plan in any SDL. We have seen project teams and quality personnel claim that since the security feature was not specifically included in the test plan, testing was not required and hence was not performed. As irresponsible as this response may seem to security professionals, some people only execute what is in the plan, while others creatively try to cover what is needed. When building an SDL task list, clarity is useful for everyone; every step must be specified.

The functional test suite is a direct descendant of the architecture and design. Each security requirement must be thoroughly proved to have been designed and then built. Each feature, security or otherwise, must be thoroughly tested to prove that it works as designed. Describing a set of functional tests is beyond the scope of this chapter. However, we will suggest that using several approaches builds a reliable proof.

- Does it work as expected?
- Test the corner and edge cases to prove that these are handled appropriately and do not disturb the expected functionality.
- Test abuse cases; for inputs, these will be fuzzing tests.

Basically, the tests must check the precise behavior as specified. That is, turn the specification into a test case: When a user attempts to load a protected page, is there an authentication challenge? When correct login information is input, is the challenge satisfied? When invalid credentials are offered, is authentication denied?

Corner cases are the most difficult. These might be tests of default behavior or behavior that is not explicitly specified. In our authentication case, if a page does not choose protection, is the default for the Web server followed? If the default is configurable, try both binary defaults: No page is protected versus all pages are protected.

Other corner cases for this example might be to test invalid user and garbage IDs against the authentication, or to try to replay session tokens. Session tokens typically have a time-out. What happens if the clock on the browser is different than the clock at the server? Is the token still valid, or does it expire en route? Each of these behaviors might happen to a typical user, but won't be usual.

Finally, and most especially for security features, many features will be attacked. In other words, whatever can be abused is likely to be abused. An attacker will pound on a login page, attempting brute-force discovery of legal passwords. Not only should a test plan include testing of any lock-out feature, the test plan should also be able to uncover any weaknesses in the ability to handle multiple, rapid logins without failing or crashing the application or the authentication service.

In our experience, most experienced quality people will understand "as designed" testing, as well as corner cases. Abuse cases, however, may be a new concept that will need support, training, perhaps mentorship.

9.4.2 Dynamic Testing

> *Dynamic testing refers to executing the source code and seeing how it performs with specific inputs. All validation activities come in this category where execution of the program is essential.*[17]

Dynamic tests are tests run against the executing program. In the security view, dynamic testing is generally performed from the perspective of the attacker. In the purest sense of the term, any test which is run against the executing program is "dynamic." This includes vulnerability scans, custom code vulnerability scans (usually called application scanning), fuzz testing, and any form of attack and penetration testing. We will examine the place of attack and penetration testing within an SDL in the next section. Due to the skill required and the typical expense, we have reserved attack and penetration testing as a special case. However, we encourage any organization that can afford attack and penetration testing at scale to do as much of this as possible. In real-world tests, skilled attack and penetration testers always exceed the results of Web vulnerability scanners and typical fuzzing of inputs. For most organizations, the expense of the skilled practitioners and the fact that they can't be scaled across multiple organizations and multiple projects precludes attack and penetration testing at scale.

Dynamic analysis is based on system execution (binary code), often using instrumentation.* The advantages of dynamic analysis are that it:

- Has the ability to detect dependencies that are not detectable using static analysis—for example, dynamic dependencies using reflection dependency injection, etc.
- Allows the collection of temporal information
- Allows the possibility of dealing with runtime values
- Allows the identification of vulnerabilities in a runtime environment.
- Allows the use of automated tools to provide flexibility on what to scan for
- Allows the analysis of applications for which you do not have access to the actual code
- Allows identifying vulnerabilities that might be false negatives in the static code analysis
- Permits validating static code analysis findings
- Can be conducted on any application[18]

9.4.2.1 Web Scanning

Vulnerability scanners tend to fall into two categories: those with signatures to test against the runtime that supports execution of applications,

---

* Here, "instrumentation" is the addition of diagnostic messages and stopping points to code for the purposes of analysis.

and scanners that are focused on custom application code. The former are generally applied to infrastructures to assure that appropriate patching and configuration is done on a regular basis, and kept up to date properly. For those applications that will be hosted internally (as discussed in the section on the seven determining questions), runtime vulnerability scanners are essential to keep the infrastructure security posture maintained. Such a scanner might also be run against an appliance type of project to see that its default configuration is without vulnerability.* This type of vulnerability scanner might also be used against the running appliance to guarantee that the appliance presents an appropriate security posture for the intended deployment. However, for many software projects that do not fall into these categories, a runtime vulnerability scanner may be of limited value within the test plan.

As described above, with respect to Web servers, a custom code or application vulnerability scanner is essential. If a Web server has been included in the software, an application vulnerability scanner will help smoke out those sorts of issues that attackers interested in Web application code will likely attack. We believe that every piece of content, whether dynamic or static, that is served through the software's Web server must be tested with an application vulnerability scanner. Considering the level of Web attack today, if that Web server is going to be exposed to the public Internet, we would never allow such an application to go live without such a scan. Attack is certain; it is just a matter of time. Current estimates as of this writing suggest that an attack will come in as few as 30 seconds, and not more than 8 hours after connection. Attackers are very swift to make use of newly found XSS errors and the like. These are precisely the sorts of errors that Web vulnerability scanners focus on.

Effective use of a Web vulnerability scanner, however, is not a trivial operation. Skill with a particular tool is essential. Also, a strong familiarity with how Web applications are structured and built helps the tester refine the test suite in the tool. Further, a good familiarity with typical Web vulnerabilities will help in two ways: First, appropriate test suites

---

* This is because an appliance will likely include a runtime stack, including a supporting operating system and its services. Unless the operating system is entirely proprietary, available tools will probably include appropriate vulnerability signatures against which to test. In the case of an entirely proprietary operating system, a specialized tool may have to be built for this purpose.

can be configured with respect to the application and its intended use; and second, the results of the scan will likely need to be qualified. There are two issues with issue qualification. Depending on the application, the code, and the tool, the results might be "noisy." That is, there may be false positives that have to be removed. We have seen few runs of Web vulnerability scanners that were free of false positives, and some runs that had very high rates of false positives. In addition, most of the Web vulnerability scanners as of this writing attempt multiple variations of each type of issue. Most tools will report every variation as another vulnerability. Despite multiple vulnerabilities reported, all the variations may stem from a single bug in the code. For many tools, there is a many-to-one relationship between vulnerabilities and actual programming errors; a single input validation error may produce many "vulnerabilities." Hence, the tester and/or programming team need to qualify the results in order to find the actual programming errors.

Training and practice need to be available to any testing personnel who will run the Web vulnerability scanning tools. Like static analysis tools, when Web vulnerability scanning tools are simply dropped on project teams, the results are likely to disappoint. Rather, an approach that we've found successful more than once is to start small and limited. Choose projects that are available for experimenting and will derive benefit from Web scanning. Find personnel who are intrigued by security testing, perhaps even hoping to enhance their career possibilities. Then, reduce the tool's vulnerability test suite to only those tests the tool manufacturer believes deliver extremely high confidence—deliver better than 80 percent results, that is, fewer than 20 percent false positives. We have even started with only those test suites that deliver fewer than 10 percent false positives.

In this way, testers will be motivated to learn about the tool, and the tool will produce high-confidence results that can be relied on to find real bugs that need fixing. Everyone's confidence in the process and the tool will be high as a result. Starting from this strong place, testers and development teams will be much more willing to experiment with how many false positives they can tolerate and still get useful results. Different projects will need to find their own balance points.

From these limited, pilot starting points, the team that is rolling out Web vulnerability scanning will gain valuable information about what works, what doesn't work, and what kind of resistance is likely to be encountered. Again, we caution against simply mandating the use of the tool and then tossing it over the wall without any experience and experimentation, without appropriate training and buy-in. We have seen too many programs flounder in exactly this way. Instead, start small, limited, and achieve success and confidence before expanding. A good tipping point for mandating any particular testing method is to achieve 60 percent voluntary participation before making any particular test a requirement.

9.4.2.2 Fuzz Testing

> *Fuzz testing or Fuzzing is a Black Box software testing technique, which basically consists in finding implementation bugs using malformed/semi-malformed data injection in an automated fashion.*[19]

Because of the varied nature of non-Web inputs, finding a single type of tool that is good for each input method is not practical. Development teams may write their own test tool. However, to make that strategy a security strategy, the tool designers and implementers must have considerable knowledge about the sorts of attacks that can be promulgated against the input. The attack scenarios will have to be updated on a regular basis to account for new discoveries, tactic shifts, and changes to existing attacks. This is precisely what tool vendors do. Such a strategy may not be practical for most organizations.

Many attack methodologies are discovered by fuzzing, that is, using a fuzz tool against input attack surfaces. Once an unintended reaction is achieved from the program's input, the attacker (or researcher) can then examine the offending input and the program's behavior to determine what the vulnerability is and how best to exploit it.

Thankfully, software testers don't need to explore this far. If an input produces incorrect behavior, then the program is not defensive enough: A bug has been discovered. That's all that needs to be understood. This is the focus of fuzz testing: incorrect behavior upon processing an input. It can be argued that software, particularly secure software, must handle gracefully any data sequence through any of its inputs. To fail to handle improper or unexpected input gracefully will at the very least cause users concern. Further, the program is likely to expose a vulnerability.

Fuzzing each input of a program is a matter of writing a descriptor of the range of data inputs that will be tested. Most fuzzing tools handle many different kinds of inputs. The tester sets the type and series of inputs. The fuzz tool randomizes inside that range or series, continually sending improper inputs, just as an attacker might who is searching for vulnerabilities.

A fuzz tool automates the process of trying many variations to an input. Configuration files can be fuzzed, command-line interfaces can be fuzzed, APIs can be fuzzed, Web services, network protocols, etc. In fact, any type of input, including Web servers, can be fuzzed. Since there are numerous tools available for scanning Web servers in applications, we have focused on other types of inputs for fuzzing. If an organization develops strong fuzzing capabilities, there's no reason not to apply these capabilities against every input, including Web servers. In our experience, it may make sense to differentiate between Web inputs which can be scanned and other inputs for which there may be no direct scanning tools. It is these other inputs that must be fuzzed in the absence of a more focused tool.

Fuzzing is an undirected type of input validation, while vulnerability scanners are highly focused on known attack methods. A complete security test program will recognize the applicability of each of these techniques and apply them appropriately. There is some overlap; certain bugs will respond to both tool types.

9.4.3 Attack and Penetration Testing

Attack and penetration (A&P) testing involves a skilled human tester who behaves like the most skilled and sophisticated attacker. The tester will reconnoiter the target system, identifying attack surfaces. Then, the same tools as would be applied by a sophisticated attacker are run by the tester to identify not only the more obvious errors, but subtle logic errors and misses in the system. Logic errors are the most difficult to identify. All but the simplest errors in logic generally require a human to identify them.

We have separated out attack and penetration testing because it is usually rather expensive, both in time and effort. There's a reason that penetration testers receive premium salaries. It takes skill and understanding to deliver quality results. Alan Paller once casually suggested to one of the authors that there were not more than 1500 skilled penetration testers extant. We don't know the actual number, but there are not enough highly skilled penetration testers to deliver all the work that is needed. This situation will probably be true for some time. Due to the scarcity, we suggest that attack and penetration testing be reserved for critical components, and major releases that are expected to be under severe attack.

If your organization has sufficient attack and penetration resources, the skilled human element is the strongest testing capability in security. Everything that can be tested probably should be tested. However, we have seen too many findings reports where the tester did not have this kind of skill, did not take time to understand the target of the test, ran the default tests, and reported hundreds of vulnerabilities. These sorts of tests help no one. Development teams may look at the first few vulnerabilities, declare them false positive, and stop looking. This is a classic, typical response to a report filled with possible vulnerabilities rather than real issues. Generally, in these cases, the attack test was not tuned and configured to the target, and perhaps the target was not properly configured as it would be when deployed. In our experience, this is a big waste of everyone's time.

Instead, focus your highly skilled resources or dollars on the most worthy targets. Critical code that must not fail can benefit greatly from an A&P test. And a strong return on investment can be made before major releases or after major revisions. This is where we suggest the most benefit can be gained from skilled attack and penetration testing.

Because an attack and penetration test can take considerable time to complete, the rate of code change must be considered when applying this intensive type of test. If the rate of change (update) is faster than the length of time to test the system, vulnerabilities may be introduced before the test even completes. These two factors must be weighed in order to get the most useful results. Generally, even if updating occurs every day, these will not be major releases, and certainly not major revisions. Hence, testing at the larger code inflections can be a better investment.

What is critical code? We have seen numerous definitions of "critical":

- The highest-revenue system
- The most attacked system
- The largest system

- The system with the biggest investment
- The most strategic system
- The most regulated system
- The highest-risk system
- The system handling the most sensitive data

Each one of these definitions can be blown apart easily with examples of the others. A practical approach is to let business leaders or other organizational leaders decide which systems are critical. Multiple factors may be taken into account. None of the definitions above are mutually exclusive; different factors may add weight to the criticality of a system. We suggest an open approach. A larger net, if the organization can afford it, is probably better in the long run. An organization doesn't want to miss an important system simply because it failed any single factor for criticality.

9.4.4 Independent Testing

There may be situations where it's advantageous to apply third-party security testing. If customers for a product are particularly security-sensitive, they may demand a third-party verification of the security health of the system before purchasing.

In the case of demonstrable customer demand for security verification, one successful approach that we have used is to have third-party testing be accounted for as a direct cost of goods sold. When systems can't be sold to many customers without third-party verification, third-party verification is considered a part of the cost of building the system for those customers. One report can typically be used for many customers.

Indeed, sometimes there are advantages to getting an independent view of the system. As in all human endeavors, if the evaluators are too close to the system, they may miss important factors. Applying some independent analysis will focus fresh eyes on the problems.

"Independent" doesn't necessarily mean outside the organization entirely. We have had success simply bringing in a security architect who hadn't looked at the system yet, who knew nothing about it. If the organization is big enough, there are usually resources tasked with alternative systems who can be brought in to check the work.

It is worth mentioning again that one of the strongest tools security architects have is peer review. It's easy to miss something important. We have instituted a system of peer review within multiple organizations at which we have worked, such that any uncertainty in the analysis requires a consensus of several experienced individuals. In this way, each assessor can get his or her work checked and validated.

If there's any uncertainty about any of the testing methodologies outlined here, getting an independent view may help validate the work or find any holes in the approach.

9.5 Agile: Sprints

We believe that the key to producing secure software with an Agile process is to integrate security into the Agile process from architecture through testing. Rather than forcing Waterfall development on top of an Agile process, security has to become Agile; security practitioners must let go of rigid processes and enter into the dialog and collaboration that is the essence of Agile development. Recognize that we have to trust and work with Agile development teams, and make use of the Agile process rather than fighting the process and its practitioners.

Figure 9.12 demonstrates how the archetypical SDL illustrated in Figure 9.1 changes to reflect an Agile process, in this case, Scrum. Requirements and architecture are a front-end process to Agile cycles, or "Sprints." Architecture feeds into the repeated Sprint cycles. At the end of a series of Sprints, prerelease testing is applied. All the other tasks in the SDL occur during each Sprint.

A Sprint is a cycle of development during which chunks of code—"user stories"—are built. Each Scrum team chooses the periodicity of the team's Sprints. Typically, Sprints last somewhere between 2 and 6 weeks. Each Sprint cycle is precisely the same length; this allows an implementation rhythm to develop. Whatever is not finished in its Sprint is put back into the backlog of items waiting to be built. At the beginning of a Sprint, some design work will take place; at least enough design needs to be in place in order to begin coding. Still, the design may change as a Sprint unfolds. Also, testing begins during the Sprint as soon as there is something to test. In this way, design, coding, and testing may all be occurring in parallel. At the end of the Sprint, the team will examine the results of the cycle in a process of continuous improvement.

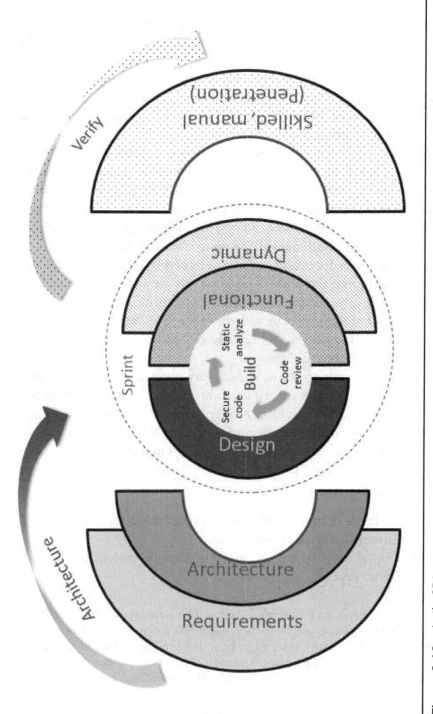

Figure 9.12 Agile SDL.

In Scrum, what is going to be built is considered during user story creation. That's the "early" part. A close relationship with the Product Owner* is critical to get security user stories onto the backlog. This relationship is also important during backlog prioritization. During the Sprint planning meeting, the meeting at which items are pulled into the development process (each "Sprint") for build, a considerable amount of the design is shaped. Make security an integral part of that process, either through direct participation or by proxy.

Security experts need to make themselves available throughout a Sprint to answer questions about implementation details, the correct way to securely build user stories. Let designs emerge. Let them emerge securely. As a respected member of the Scrum team, catching security misses early will be appreciated, not resisted. The design and implementation is improved: The design will be more correct more often.

Part of the priority dialog must be the interplay between what is possible to build given the usual constraints of time and budget, and what must be built in order to meet objectives, security and otherwise. The security expert doesn't enter in with the "One True Way," but rather, with an attitude of "How do we collectively get this all done, and done well enough to satisfy the requirements?"

Finally, since writing secure code is very much a discipline and practice, appropriate testing and vulnerability assurance steps need to be a part of every Sprint. We think that these need to be part of the definition of "done." A proposed definition of "done" might look something like the following, based on the seven determining questions discussed earlier:

Definition of Done

1. All code has been manually reviewed (and defects fixed).
   a. All code has been peer-reviewed.
   b. Critical code has been reviewed by a senior or security subject-matter expert.

---

* The Product Owner is a formal role in Scrum. This is the person who takes the customer's and user's viewpoint. She or he is responsible for creating user stories and for prioritization. A Product Owner might be an independent member of the development team, a senior architect (though not typically) or a product manager, or similar. It should not be someone who has hierarchical organizational power over development team members.

2. All code has been statically analyzed (and defects fixed).
3. All functional tests have been passed.
4. Web server interfaces have been dynamically tested (and defects fixed).
5. All non-Web program input paths have been fuzzed (and defects fixed).

Each of the items designating a security definition of "done" is described in the relevant section.

In an Agile process, everyone is involved in security. Security personnel mustn't toss security "over the wall" and expect secure results. Development teams will likely perceive such a toss as an interjection into the work with which they're already tasked. Rather than collaborative security, the result is likely to be resistance on the part of the Agile team.

More effective is a willingness to enter into the problems at hand. Among those problems and important to the overall objectives of the project, security will be considered. The security experts will do well to remember that there are always trade-off decisions that must be made during development. By working toward the success of all objectives, including security, not only will security be considered in its rightful place, creative and/or innovative solutions are more likely to be found by a collaborating team. Security people will have to get their hands dirty, get some implementation "grease" under their proverbial virtual fingernails in order to earn the trust and buy-in of Scrum teams.

Of course, setting the relative priorities over what will get built is one of the most difficult problems facing any development team. This is especially true with respect to security items. A strong, risk-based approach will help factor real-world impacts into the priority equation.

In our experience, if the Agile team has sufficient risk guidance to understand the implications for prioritizing security items against other tasks, we believe teams will make better decisions. The classic line, "It's a vulnerability that can lead to loss, so fix it now," has long since failed to sway decision makers. Let there be no FUD—fear, uncertainty, doubt.

Instead, consider loss not in terms of information security possibilities, but rather, real-world business impacts for the system under consideration as it will be used within the expected deployment. An approach focused on impacts will go much further in helping to make reasonable decisions. There may be items in the security queue that can be postponed in favor

of other critical features. Team trust is built through everyone participating fully, which includes security expert participation. When a security expert becomes part of the Agile team, everyone wins; security wins.
Indeed, when security is considered carefully and decisions are based on
risk scenarios, there are two great wins for security:

1. Security becomes part of the decision-making fabric, earning its
   rightful place. It's no longer an add-on or an unplanned extra.
   Thinking about security becomes part of the mindset of building
   software rather than an interjection from outside.
2. If risks are considered carefully; the item that has high risk will tend
   to be prioritized as it should. Giving up the idea that every security
   issue is equally important results in the items that truly are dangerous
   (these will be rare) getting the attention they deserve. Items bearing
   less risk can be scheduled according to their relative importance.

For many organizations, there are too few skilled security experts.
There aren't enough security experts that every Scrum team can include
its own, dedicated security guru. Security experts must be matrixed across
multiple teams. These experts will need to develop skills to "time-slice,"
to give a portion of their time to each of multiple projects. Context-
switching time will need to be allotted so that matrixed personnel have
adequate time in which to put down one project's context and remember
another's. Excellent project management skills are required. These can be
performed either by the security expert or through a project management
practice. Project managers can be key to assisting with scheduling and
deliverable tasks that make a matrix assignment strategy effective.

There are dangers, however, to assigning a single security expert to
multiple projects. Foremost, overload is all too common. If a security
expert has too many teams assigned, the expert may begin to "thrash"—
that is, have just enough time to pick up the next project and retrieve
context before having to switch projects again. No real work gets done.
Not only is there no time to provide actual security expertise, security
experts don't thrive without continual technical growth. If the security
expert is overburdened, research time will be curtailed, which can lead to
burn out. More important, without time to research problems properly
and thoroughly, uninformed security decisions may be made.

Avoid overload; watch for the telltale signs, as each person has a different threshold for too many context switches.

With too much overload, projects will be delayed, as teams wait for the security expert to participate. The security expert then becomes a bottleneck to team velocity. Or, worse, designs and implementations proceed without the required security expertise and help. This almost always leads to releases without appropriate security, security logic errors, or expensive rework. These are among the very problems that an Agile process is typically brought in to address.

Indeed, some overloaded security folks may compensate with ivory-tower pronouncements tossed out without appropriate participation. The collaboration and trust that are the hallmark and essence of Agile processes are skipped in favor of what is efficient for the security person. Without sufficient time to build team *esprit de corps*, an overly allocated security person is likely not to have the time to integrate into each Scrum team properly. As noted above, when the security person understands all the issues that must be solved by the whole team, security receives its rightful place and is not an interjection. It is security items as interjections into the functioning and autonomy of the Agile team that including a security expert in the team is attempting to prevent.

Still, it is possible, with just enough security people, to use virtual teams and multiple assignments. We have seen this done successfully multiple times. Just avoid overloading. Indeed, hold in mind that team spirit takes time, exposure, and experience to develop. Mistakes and missteps will occur during forming and learning periods. Build these into the process for success.

9.6 Key Success Factors and Metrics

This chapter is not part of the SDL framework phases laid out earlier in this book. Rather, it is the compendium of applying Chapters 3–8 in real-world situations. Thus, there are no specific success factors/criteria per se which belong to this chapter. Success factors described below are presented from the perspective of applying the SDL in practice.

9.6.1 Secure Coding Training Program

It is imperative that a secure coding program be implemented in an organization. It should cater to multiple stakeholders/groups and not just to development engineers. An effective security coding program will help a product manager to understand these practices, help polish skills of architects-in-training, and provide engineers with specific guidelines for writing correct code. Program modules should also be available for specific languages (e.g., Java, C, C++). Web Services architecture and proper use of cryptography must be part of any effective secure coding training program.

9.6.2 Secure Coding Frameworks (APIs)

In addition to secure coding, developers should be made aware of available secure coding frameworks that exist and any secured APIs that can be used as part of coding. This prevents ad-hoc coding practices to solve well-known security problems (e.g., preventing XSS) and standardizes code—standardization helps to keep code maintainable over time. Different types of security testing will point out defects that result from improper use or failure to use secure coding frameworks (APIs). A secure coding training program should be offered periodically to reinforce best practices and should be updated to cover real defects that have resulted from improper use of APIs.

9.6.3 Manual Code Review

Every line of code that is committed for build should be at least peer-reviewed. No matter how small a module or set of changes is, this is the "hygiene habit" of best practice. Comments from peer review should be taken not as a criticism but as a means to make the code more robust, readable, and secure. Critical code should be reviewed by someone who is well versed in security coding practices and the algorithms being implemented. In our experience, multiple code reviews can be quite beneficial.

9.6.4 Independent Code Review and Testing (by Experts or Third Parties)

Once code is complete, a comprehensive code review by third parties or independent experts should be performed. The idea here is to catch any remaining issues that were not identified during the SDL build and testing activities. Findings from independent review and penetration testing should be shared with the people who've performed the static analysis and code reviews. In the next round of development, many of these issues will then be addressed during peer review, by static analysis, or during the test plan.

9.6.5 Static Analysis

Before code is checked-in for manual review, it should be put through static analysis to find common errors and security best practices violations. This will help to reduce the number of comments during the manual and expert review phases. Performing static analysis on code before check-in should be mandatory and ideally should be tightly integrated into development environments and the developer work flow.

9.6.6 Risk Assessment Methodology

As stated in Chapters 3 and 4, a risk assessment framework (RAF) is essential for the success of a SDL program. Threat modeling and architectural assessment feed into the RAF. The RAF helps to prioritize risks and enable decisions based on risk severity and impact.

9.6.7 Integration of SDL with SDLC

Integration of "determining" questions into the SDLC cycle will allow the SDL, that is, software security, to become easily integrated into project and development practices. The authors strongly emphasize creating an SDL program and mapping it into the SDLC cycle rather than making security requirements a project plan line item. Without proper guidance, pressed project teams are likely to invent their own interpretations of "minimum set of security activities."

9.6.8 Development of Architecture Talent

Security architecture talent is not easy to find, for it sits at the top of a skill set pyramid. Architects need to have background in software development and several different areas in security before they can take on an architect role. This often means a lack of competent candidates who are readily available. It is critical that a program be in place to develop and mentor resources that will eventually take on a security architect role. Hiring architects from outside is often less useful, given the time they will spend trying to understand an organization's software, the environments, and each organization's specific practices in order to apply real-world guidance. An architecture mentoring program will provide a clear return on the investment over time.

9.7 Metrics

As mentioned earlier, this chapter is not part of the SDL phases per se, and so metrics listed below can fit into Chapters 3–8 as well. This list is a compilation of useful metrics from the authors' experience applying SDL in the real world.

- Maturity of security coding program
- Percent of vetted APIs used in the code
- Percent of software code manually reviewed at time of check-in
- Number of lines of code manually reviewed at time of check-in
- Percent of findings missed by manual review but found during expert review
- Percent of findings missed by static analysis but found during manual review
- Number of teams auditing software needed to be tweaked significantly during the SDL
- Percent of developers using integrated static scanning software from their integrated development environment (IDE)
- Number of defects found during manual review, static analysis, and expert review
- Percent of SDL phases "built in" to the SDLC
- Number of "upcoming" architects in the organization
- Percent of software systems assessed to systems produced (Are you reaching every project and every system?)
- Percent of security reviews completed for designs produced
- Maturity of security design review process

- Number of exceptions granted based on recommendations from design review*
- Percent of Web servers covered by Web dynamic analysis
- Number of defects found by input fuzzing
- Number of major releases receiving independent A&P testing
- Number of externally reported security vulnerabilities

9.8 Chapter Summary

As we have seen, there is a menu of security tasks which, taken together, build secure software, the sum total of an applied secure development lifecycle. In order to get these tasks executed well, relationships among development team members and between security people and development teams make the difference between success and failure.

Engagement starts early during requirements gathering and continues throughout the SDL to the delivery of the finished software. Architecture and design-time engagement is meant to build the correct and appropriate security mechanisms into the software, which must be coded correctly and then proved to be functionally correct and free from vulnerability through a testing plan. The test plan includes multiple approaches, as appropriate to the attack surfaces exposed by the software. Security is an end-to-end process whose tasks overlap each other to provide continuity and assurance. No one task solves the security problem; there is no silver bullet.

When security people shift to a developer-centric focus, presenting security not as a deluge of vulnerabilities but rather as attributes that need inclusion for success and errors that developers wish to remove, developers and security people can work together tightly to craft appropriately secure software. Security is not presented as a nonfunctional, top-down command. Instead, security takes its rightful place among the many attributes of complete software that must be considered and prioritized. Appropriate prioritization is achieved through deep and active engagement by security subject-matter experts throughout the entire SDL.

---

* We caution against overreliance on this seemingly innocent metric. Skilled security architects often employ exceptions to shift interactions from "fix or not" to "when to fix and how to fix."

It is also true that each security activity is not appropriate to every project. Projects differ in size, criticality, and scope. A working SDL will scale to account for these differences. We offer seven determining questions as one formula for getting the right security tasks assigned to the appropriate projects.

Stepping back from the specific questions outlined here, instituting a set of project-specific questions that determine the appropriate security activities for each project has proven not only to ensure that the right security is performed for each project, but also to answer typical project management questions:

- "What do we need to do?"
- "What is the minimum set of activities that we must perform?"

Posing your SDL determining questions in a straightforward and easily understandable way will build trust between security and project teams. Ultimately, trust is key to building secure software, just as much as training in secure coding and rigorous security testing. Security must be considered from the beginning of the lifecycle in order to be factored into the design. Code must be written to minimize vulnerabilities and protect attack surfaces. The program's functionality and lack of vulnerabilities must be proven by a thorough series of tests: architect, design, code, test.

Secure software must:

- Be free from errors that can be maliciously manipulated—ergo, be free of vulnerabilities
- Include the security features that customers require for their intended use cases
- Be self-protective—software must resist the types of attacks that will be promulgated against the software
- "Fail well," that is, fail in such a manner as to minimize the consequences of a successful attack
- Install with sensible, "closed" defaults

Failure to meet each of these imperatives is a failure of the software to deliver its functionality, a failure to deliver the safety that should be implicit in a world beset by constant digital attack. There are two important and interlocking paths that must be attended to: building the correct features so the software can protect itself and the software's users, and removing the errors that inevitably creep into software as it's being built. Incorrect implementations (logical errors) must be caught and removed. Any vulnerabilities that are introduced must be discovered and eradicated.

The secure development lifecycle is a relationship-based, real-world process through which teams deliver secure software.

References

1. Perlis, A. (1982). *Epigrams on Programming*. ACM SIGPLAN Notices 17 (9), September, p. 7. Retrieved from http://www.cs.yale.edu/quotes.html.

2. NATO Science Committee (1969). *Software Engineering Techniques*. Report on a conference sponsored by the NATO Science Committee, p. 16, quote from Edsger Dijksta, Rome, Italy, 27th to 31st October 1969. Retrieved from http://homepages.cs.ncl.ac.uk/brian.randell/NATO/nato1969.PDF.

3. U.S. Department of Homeland Security (2013). Software & Supply Chain Assurance: Community Resources and Information Clearinghouse (CRIC), "Mitigating the Most Egregious Exploitable Software Weaknesses: Top 25 CWE Programming Errors." Retrieved from https://buildsecurityin.us-cert.gov/swa/cwe.

4. Mitre Corporation (2013). "Common Weakness Enumeration (CWE)." *CWE-434: Unrestricted Upload of File with Dangerous Type. Phase: Architecture and Design*. Retrieved from http://cwe.mitre.org/data/definitions/434.html

5. Open Web Application Security Project (OWASP) (2013). *Some Proven Application Security Principles*. Retrieved from https://www.owasp.org/index.php/Category:Principle.

6. Open Web Application Security Project (OWASP) (2013). *OWASP Enterprise Security API*. Retrieved from https://www.owasp.org/index.php/Category:OWASP_Enterprise_Security_API.

7. Ibid.

8. Beck, K. (1999). *Extreme Programming Explained: Embrace Change*, p. 18. Addison-Wesley Professional, Reading, MA.

9. Sheridan, F. (2012, June 13). *Deploying Static Analysis I—Dr. Dobbs*. Retrieved from http://article.yeeyan.org/bilingual/334758.

10. Ibid.

11. Golden, B. (2013). *What Is Systems Architecture?* Retrieved from http://www.lix.polytechnique.fr/~golden/systems_architecture.html#principles.

12. The Open Group (2005, November). *Guide to Security Architecture in TOGAF ADM*, p. 5. Retrieved from http://pubs.opengroup.org/onlinepubs/7699949499/toc.pdf.

13. Wahe, S. (2011). The Open Group, *Open Enterprise Security Architecture (O-ESA): A Framework and Template for Policy-Driven Security*, p. 5. Van Haren, Zaltbommel, The Netherlands.

14. McGraw, G. (2013, January 18). Cigital Justice League Blog: *Securing Software Design*

Is Hard. Retrieved from http://www.cigital.com/justice-league-blog/2013/01/18/securing-software-design-is-hard.

15. Saltzer, J. H., and Schroeder, M. D. (1975) *The Protection of Information in Computer Systems*. Retrieved from http://www.acsac.org/secshelf/papers/protection_information.pdf.

16. McGraw, G. (2013, January 18). Cigital Justice League Blog: *Securing Software Design Is Hard*. Retrieved from http://www.cigital.com/justice-league-blog/2013/01/18/securing-software-design-is-hard.

17. Singh, Y. (2011, November 14). *Software Testing*, p. 87. Cambridge University Press, Cambridge, UK.

18. Wolff, B., and Zaidi, F. (2011, December 20). *Testing Software and Systems: 23rd IFIP WG 6.1 International Conference, ICTSS 2011, Paris, France, November 7-10, 2011, Proceedings*, p. 87. Springer-Verlag, Berlin.

19. Open Web Application Security Project (OWASP) (2013). *Fuzzing*. Retrieved from https://www.owasp.org/index.php/Main_Page.

Chapter 10

Pulling It All Together: Using the SDL to Prevent Real-World Threats

Cyber threats result from software flaws, which are weakness that can be exploited by cyber attack or exploitation of a software application or system. In this book, we have covered strategies for implementing specific aspects of software security in the form of SDL best practices to assist software development organizations in avoiding and reducing software flaws as an essential element of effective core software security by providing security at the source.

Although achieving a vulnerability-free product is exceedingly difficult, maybe even impossible, it should always be your goal. By applying the best practices in this book, the software you develop will be as free from security vulnerabilities as possible. The fewer the number of vulnerabilities, the harder it will be for an attacker to exploit a given application. By no means are we going to stop all threats through the use of software security best practices, but maximizing the reduction of the attack surface is our ultimate goal in that it makes our job as software security professionals easier and that of our adversaries more difficult. By implementing the practices outlined in this book, you will be able to a large extent mitigate most threats coming from non-state threat actors.

In this chapter, we will break down the threats into three major categories, specifically, strategic, tactical, and user-specific. We will then provide examples of attacks in each category and how the application of the SDL best practices outlined in this book will assist you in developing software that is resistant to these threats and attack methodologies.

10.1 Strategic, Tactical, and User-Specific Software Attacks

Now that we have described secure software development practices, it is important to finish this book by reminding the reader of the importance of using these practices to protect against today's cyber threats. After a few quotes from industry leaders, we will give a high-level overview of the type of cyber threats that secure software development practices provide a baseline protection against at the core.

> Organizations are implementing policies to address secure software development practices, and beyond using software scanning tools, finding it important to integrate secure software practices into the culture of the organization. Some firms have found that using judicious secure software development processes can reduce vulnerabilities associated with mission critical software by 70%.[1]
>
> —Jeff Snyder, Vice President, Cyber Programs, Raytheon Company, 2012

> Cyber attacks take advantage of software errors, such as not properly validating user input, inconsistencies in the design assumptions among system components, and unanticipated user and operator actions. Software errors can be introduced by disconnects and miscommunications during the planning, development, testing, and maintenance of the components. Although an application development team may be expert

in the required business functionality, that team usually has limited or no applicable security expertise. The likelihood of disconnects and miscommunications increases as more system components have to satisfy security requirements. The necessary communications and linkages among the life-cycle activities, among multiple development teams, and between the system development and eventual usage should be reflected in project management. Project managers should consider the additional communications requirements, linkage among life-cycle activities, and the potential usage environment as these items relate to security needs.[2]

—Robert J. Ellison, "Security and Project Management," 2006

By promoting the best software security practices industry-wide, there is a significant opportunity to improve the overall security of the technology ecosystem.[3]

—Howard Schmidt, Former U.S. Cybersecurity Czar, 2013

The importance of an organization understanding its application security maturity level and the impact it has on their overall IT security profile is critical. **Research has shown that the application layer is responsible for over 90 percent of all security vulnerabilities**, yet more than 80 percent of IT security spending continues to be at the network layer, primarily focused on perimeter security. The findings of this study reveal the need for making greater investment in application security programs to reduce overall organizational exposure to cybercrime.[4]

—The State of Application Security—A Research Study by Ponemon Institute LLC and Security Innovation, 2013

Strategic attacks are typically planned and controlled to target information assets including specifications, technologies, plans, capabilities, procedures, and guidelines to gain strategic advantage. They are typically conducted by state sponsors (or by entities supported by states), organized crime, or competitors. Tactical attacks are typically random and opportunistic; they target information assets for prestige or financial reward through the use of malware, exploits, hackers, surrogates, insider threat, and chat rooms, and they are conducted by professional hackers, script kiddies, and insiders. As you can see, one of the key differentiators between tactical and strategic attacks is motive: Tactical attacks target network assets for prestige or financial reward, whereas a strategic attack is the coordination of multiple tactical attacks (and on a much larger scale) against multiple target networks for strategic advantage or to preempt adversary from getting one. The targets of tactical attacks are random and opportunistic, taking advantage of software vulnerabilities and user ignorance, whereas strategic attacks target a higher-level process and are intelligence driven and carefully planned and orchestrated. For example, strategic attacks may include infiltrating strategic infrastructure, targeting telecommunications infrastructure, and aggregating information in specific technology areas such as stealth technology. The ability to understand strategic attacks requires an understanding of: (1) the business functions and processes supported by individual networks; (2) the business relationships between networks; and (3) sharing of tactical attack data among contractors, suppliers, and target entities. The information gleaned by threats to these business relationships is used to guide and direct strategic attacks.[5]

User-targeted specific software attacks can be strategic, tactical, or opportunistic. They may involve an attack targeting a privilege escalation of a specific user that exploits a vulnerability in software to gain access to resources and information that would normally be unrestricted to the user—including data on the specific user machine or resources that the user can access. Strategic attacks are a super-set that leverage tactical and/or user-specific attacks.

10.1.1 Strategic Attacks

In general, strategic software targets are applications which are essential to critical infrastructure functions of the government, economy, or society at large. Components of the critical infrastructure include highways, airports and aircraft, trains and railways, bus lines, shipping and boat lines, trucking systems, and supply networks for basic goods, electric power plants and lines, along with oil and gas lines and utilities of all kinds, including water and sewer systems, land and cell phone systems, computer networks, television, and radio (not only that which is publicly accessible, but that controlled by private or government entities in special networks or on special frequencies), banks and other financial institutions, and security, fire, hospital, and emergency services. Each element of critical infrastructure is so vital that if it were removed from the equation, even temporarily, the entire nation would experience monumental repercussions. Even when the infrastructure of a particular area is threatened, the results can be disastrous. This can include telecommunications, energy, banking and finance, transportation, water systems, and emergency services.[6] Of course, strategic targets also include critical elements of the government such as defense, intelligence, and other agencies considered of high value to an adversary.

Strategic software attacks are highly repeatable and use general targeting such as against a broad industry (military, finance, energy, etc.) or groups of individuals (politicians, executives), and must have long-term staying power. Strategic attacks are less sophisticated in comparison to tactical threats and typically are lower in cost to develop and maintain. These types of attacks can be categorized in three major areas: espionage, criminal, and socio-political.

10.1.1.1 Espionage

Cyber spying, or cyber espionage, is the act or practice of obtaining secrets without the permission of the holder of the information, from individuals, competitors, rivals, groups, governments and enemies for personal, economic, political or military advantage using methods on the Internet, networks or individual computers through the use of cracking techniques and malicious software including Trojan horses and spyware. It may wholly be perpetrated online from computer desks of professionals on bases in far away countries or may involve infiltration at home by computer trained conventional spies and moles or in other cases may be the criminal handiwork of amateur malicious hackers and software programmers. Cyber spying typically involves the use of such access to secrets and classified information or control of individual computers or whole networks for a strategic advantage and for psychological, political and physical subversion activities and sabotage.[7]

Cyber espionage is highly strategic in nature; key targets include critical infrastructures, industrial attacks, manufacturing, research and development, pharmaceuticals, finance, and government. Government targets may also include the defense industrial base (DIB), which includes defense contractors, research organizations, and political and other high-ranking individuals.

Examples of espionage attacks are Aurora (GhostNet), Shady RAT, Titan Rain, and Night Dragon. Note that some of these attacks can be counted both as espionage and as cyber warfare. They may have multiple utilities depending on how they are deployed. It might be helpful to think of cyber espionage as one part of cyber warfare.

Operation Aurora and GhostNet. The 2012 USCC Annual Report on China contains the following statement:

> China's cyber capabilities provide Beijing with an increasingly potent tool to achieve national objectives. In a strategic framework that leans heavily on cyber espionage, a diverse set of Chinese hackers use pilfered information to advance political, economic, and security objectives. China's pursuit of intellectual property and trade secrets means that much of this espionage targets private enterprises.[8]

The information security community has been aware of cyber espionage activities for some time now. However, the extent and impact of such activities surprised many of us. In 2009, researchers at Information Warfare Monitor gave the name "GhostNet" to large-scale cyber espionage operations conducted by the Chinese government. These operations, associated with advanced persistent threats (APTs), raised awareness of APT attacks in the security community and among the general public. GhostNet enabled infiltration of high-value political, economic, and media targets spread across 90+ countries around the world. Though its command and control centers were based in China, there was plausible deniability for the Chinese government, as there was no way to associate it with actual operations. Note that successful cyber espionage operations will have this trademark, allowing governments to disassociate themselves from the actual groups carrying out these attacks.[9]

The attackers would "social engineer" targets to open a document or a link infected with malware. After that, malware would be installed on the target's system (without raising any red flags for most users). Once this happened, malware would provide almost unrestricted access to the attackers. Code was obfuscated, and multiple Trojans were used to avoid detection by many popular antivirus/antimalware software.

Operation Aurora was a cyber attack conducted from China. Attacks begin in 2009 and continued until the end of the year. The targets for these attacks were multinational companies including Google, Adobe, and Rackspace. Some companies chose to disclose publicly that they had been the targets of attacks, while others remained under suspicion but never came out publicly. According to McAfee, the primary goal of the attack was to get access (and modify) source code of these multinational companies. One should note that many of these companies have development offices in Asia (including China). Thus, protecting their bread and butter—source code—is of paramount importance to them, though it was not considered "severe" enough by some companies before this attack. This trend is changing, but not fast enough. If anything, it has resulted in chaos, especially in China, and suspicion of employees working in off-shore offices. This complicates any SDL activities a security group would like to implement in a global enterprise.[10]

Operation Shady RAT. Dimitri Alperovitch of McAfee reported Operation Shady RAT in 2011. Like Operation Aurora, Operation Shady RAT consists of ongoing cyber attacks and has targeted 70+ countries as well as the United Nations and the International Olympic Committee. RAT is an acronym for Remote Access Tool, and though it is not confirmed who is behind these operations, suspicions point to China in this case a well—especially due to the targeting of Olympic organizations around the time of the Beijing Olympics in 2008.[11] Among other targets were Associated Press offices, the U.S. Energy Department, and U.S defense companies. In this case, as in GhostNet, attackers would "social engineer" users of selected organizations into opening documents, spreadsheets, and other innocent-looking files that actually contained malware. Once the end user complied, malware would be installed and would try to connect to its remote server (hard coded into the malware) and provide attackers with a remote shell.[12]

Night Dragon. In 2011, McAfee reported that well-organized and targeted cyber attacks were taking place on key international oil and energy companies. These attacks seem to have started in 2009 (though, as for many attacks in this class, there is no sure way of knowing this definitively). Based on investigations by McAfee, fingers point again to China (or China-based hackers). Targeted companies were spread across many different countries, including the United States, Greece, and Taiwan. Information that was stolen included specifics on companies and their operations, bidding data, as well as financial information on projects. Attackers exploited vulnerabilities in Windows operating systems, applications (including SQL injection), and active directory infrastructure. Remote Access Tools (RATs) were used to harvest and steal sensitive information. First, the companies' external-facing infrastructure (e.g., Web servers) was compromised through SQL injection attacks. This allowed attacks to execute remote commands to target and compromise internal desktops and servers within the enterprise. Additional information was harvested (e.g., passwords), allowing attackers to access sensitive information inside the infrastructure. Attackers were able to establish direct connections from infected systems to the Internet and infiltrated sensitive information including from senior executives' systems.[13,14]

Titan Rain. APT class attacks were launched against infrastructure in the United States and its allies by hackers believed to be working on behalf of the Chinese government. Attackers were able to get access to many sensitive systems of defense contractors and federal agencies. The purpose of these attacks was to obtain sensitive information, thus putting Titan Rain into the espionage category rather than warfare, although it could be easily used for cyber warfare as well.[15–18]

10.1.1.2 Organized Crime

Along with the evolution of the Internet, cyber crime has evolved from the domain of individuals and small groups to traditional organized crime syndicates and criminally minded technology professionals working together and pooling their resources and expertise. This has been largely due to the speed, convenience, and anonymity that modern technologies offer to those wanting to commit a diverse range of criminal activities. Consequently, just as brick-and-mortar companies moved their enterprises to the World Wide Web seeking new opportunities for profits, criminal enterprises are doing the same thing. The global nature of the Internet has allowed criminals to commit almost any illegal activity anywhere in the world, making it essential for all countries to adapt their domestic offline controls to cover crimes carried out in cyberspace. These activities include attacks against computer data and systems, identity theft, the distribution of child sexual abuse images, Internet auction fraud, money laundering, the penetration of online financial services, online banking theft, illicit access to intellectual property, online extortion, as well as the deployment of viruses, botnets, and various email scams such as phishing. Organized crime groups typically have a home base in a nation that provides safe haven, from which they conduct their transnational operations. In effect, this provides an added degree of protection against law enforcement and allows them to operate with minimal risk. The inherently transnational nature of the Internet fits perfectly into this model of activity and the effort to maximize profits within an acceptable degree of risk. In the virtual world there are no borders, a characteristic that makes it very attractive for criminal activity; yet when it comes to policing this virtual world, borders and national jurisdictions loom large—making large-scale investigation slow and tedious at best, and impossible at worst.[19–21] Some of the more noteworthy groups are the European crime rings, state-sponsored criminal groups and proxies, U.S. domestic crime groups, and Mexican cartels.

As payoff from cyber crime grows, it is no surprise that organized crime groups seek a share in it. Cyber crime allows organized syndicates to finance their other illicit activities in addition to providing hefty profits. Criminal syndicates are involved in everything from theft to extortion, piracy, and enabling online crime in the first place. They are providing a new meaning to the "as-a-service" term. In addition to exploiting cyber infrastructure for monetary gains, they are enabling cyber attacks by providing vulnerabilities, creating tools and offering resources to people who will pay for it. These services include selling vulnerabilities (proactively looking for them in new software products and infrastructure), creating and selling exploits for existing vulnerabilities, spam services, infrastructure (botnets, hosting), as well as malware.[22]

10.1.1.3 Socio-Political Attacks

Socio-political attacks are often intended to elevate awareness of a topic but can also be a component or a means to an end with regard to political action groups, civil disobedience, or part of a larger campaign, and they may be an indicator and warning of bigger things to come.

Evidence is growing that more cyber attacks are associated with social, political, economic, and cultural (SPEC) conflicts. It is also now known that cyber attackers' level of socio-technological sophistication, their backgrounds, and their motivations are essential components to predicting, preventing, and tracing cyber attacks. Thus, SPEC factors have the potential to be early predictors for outbreaks of anomalous activities, hostile attacks, and other security breaches in cyberspace.[23]

Some well-known examples of socio-political attacks have been the result of efforts by Anonymous, WikiLeaks, and Edward Snowden (also an example of an insider threat), and attacks by radical Muslim groups or jihadists (e.g., Al Qaeda).

Anonymous. Anonymous is a group of activists that over the last few years has become well known for its attacks on government and corporate infrastructure. It has a decentralized command structure and can be thought of more as a social movement. This movement has targeted everyone from religious institutions (Church of Scientology) to corporations (Visa, MasterCard, PayPal, Sony) and government institutions (the United States, Israel, Tunisia). Some of the most famous attacks launched by Anonymous are Project Chaology and Operation: Payback Is a Bitch. After a video of Tom Cruise was posted on a blog, the Church of Scientology responded with a cease-and-desist letter for copyright violation. The project users organized a raid against the church, including distributed denial-of-service (DDoS) attacks. In 2010, they targeted the RIAA and MIAA, bringing down their websites.[24] This action was a protest to protect their rights to share information with one another—one of their important principles, in their opinion.

WikiLeaks published classified diplomatic cables in November 2010. Under pressure from the U.S. government, Amazon.com removed WikiLeaks from its servers, and PayPal, Visa, and MasterCard stopped providing financial services for WikiLeaks. This resulted in attacks against PayPal, Visa, and MasterCard, disrupting their websites and services.[25–27]

Anonymous also launched a number of activities in support of the "Arab spring" movement and has targeted websites hosting child pornography. After San Francisco's Bay Area Rapid Transit (BART) blocked cell service to prevent a planned protest, Anonymous targeted the BART website and shut it down.[28]

Jihadists. Threats posed by jihadists are increasing. In one sense, this is part of cyber warfare, though there is a difference from most such activities in that there is a fundamental religious ideology driving these actors. Cyber attacks by terrorists/jihadist organizations started at least as far back as November 2001 (not long after 9/11), though these early attacks were relatively unsophisticated. A terrorist suspect told interrogators that Al Qaeda had launched low-level computer attacks, sabotaging websites by launching denial-of-service (DoS) attacks.[29]

10.1.1.4 Cyber Warfare

The term cyber war gives the impression that the war is happening only in cyberspace, when in fact a more accurate interpretation is cyber weapons are used in the digital theater of war that can be strategically aligned with traditional (physical) warfare activities.[30]

Cyber warfare has been defined by government security expert Richard A. Clarke as "actions by a nation-state to penetrate another nation's computers or networks for the purposes of causing damage or disruption."[31] *The Economist* describes cyber warfare as "the fifth domain of warfare."[32]

William J. Lynn, U.S. Deputy Secretary of Defense, states that "as a doctrinal matter, the Pentagon has formally recognized cyberspace as a new domain in warfare—[which] has become just as critical to military operations as land, sea, air, and space."[33]

From some of the quotes above you can see that there is an acceptance that when we speak of war, cyber and physical are not separate from each other; they are merely different theaters of war. Like other theaters of war, they all have commonalities but typically have different weapons, tactics, and command structure, as well as different rules of engagement, different forms of targets and different methods to identify a target, different expectations of collateral damage, and different expectations of risk. Cyber attacks can have a great impact, but not necessarily focused or highly targeted, such as disrupting communications, affecting processing of information, and disrupting portions of systems that inhibit normal functions.

In contrast to this, when the government or military use the term "cyber war," they are typically thinking of highly targeted and impactful eventualities, such as shutting down power, phones, air traffic control, trains, and emergency services. Cyber attacks are not limited to cyberspace; there is both intended and unintended collateral damage outside the realm of cyber. For example, manipulating a SCADA (supervisory control and data acquisition) system in a chemical plant or a critical infrastructure facility may cause an intended or unintended explosion, possible area contamination, or a toxic chemical spill or floating toxic cloud.

It is no secret that foreign cyberspace operations against U.S. public- and private-sector systems are increasing in number and sophistication. U.S. government networks are probed millions of times every day, and successful penetrations have led to the loss of thousands of sensitive files from U.S. networks and those of U.S. allies and industry partners. Moreover, this threat continues to evolve, as evidence grows of adversaries focusing on the development of increasingly sophisticated and potentially dangerous capabilities.[34]

The potential for small groups to have an asymmetric impact in cyberspace creates very real incentives for malicious activity. Beyond formal governmental activities, cyber criminals can control botnets with millions of infected hosts. The tools and techniques developed by cyber criminals are increasing in sophistication at an incredible rate, and many of these capabilities can be purchased cheaply on the Internet. Whether the goal is monetary, access to intellectual property, or the disruption of critical systems, the rapidly evolving threat landscape presents a complex and vital challenge for national and economic security.

To counter this threat, the U.S. Department of Defense has announced five strategic initiatives it is taking. They are worth reviewing here. First, treat cyberspace as an operational domain of war, just like land, sea, air, and space. Hence, the "fifth domain" of war is recognized as an operational theater. Second, evolve new defense concepts to combat cyber attacks. This entails taking four basic steps, as shown below:

1. Enhance cyber best practices to improve its cyber security.
2. Deter and mitigate insider threats, strengthen workforce communications, workforce accountability, internal monitoring, and information management capabilities.
3. Employ an active cyber defense capability to prevent intrusions onto networks and systems.
4. Develop new defense operating concepts and computing architectures.

The third initiative is to begin to partner with other U.S. government departments and agencies and the private sector to enable a government-wide cyber security strategy. The fourth initiative is to build robust relationships with U.S. allies and international partners to strengthen collective cyber security. Finally, leverage the nation's ingenuity through an exceptional cyber workforce and rapid technological innovation. The most significant thing to note in all of the aforementioned in relation to this book is the first step: recognition of cyber best practices that need to be developed to improve cyber security, which of course includes securing the core by building security into the development process as described in this book.

Examples of cyber warfare threats that strong secure development practices protect against include the cyber attacks on Estonia in 2007 and attacks on assets in Georgia during the Russia–Georgia conflict in 2008.

Cyber Attacks on Estonia. Estonia and Russia have a long (and unstable) relationship. Estonia, one of the Baltic States, was part of the USSR from 1940 to 1991. Estonia became part of NATO in 2004. In 2007, the Estonian government moved the Bronze Soldier—a memorial honoring the Soviet liberation of Estonia from Nazi Germany—to a different location. This resulted in rioting by the Russian-speaking minority community in Estonia, which viewed the move as an effort to further marginalize their ethnic identity. At the same time, DDoS attacks started to target the country's cyber infrastructure. Attacks were able to shut down websites of the government, banks, and political institutions. Estonians accused Russia of waging cyber war and considered invoking Article 5 of the NATO treaty, although it chose not to do so in the end. One should note that cyber war can lead to much wider military conflict in such situations—something we might not have seen so far but which remains a real possibility. Estonia was the first case of a country publicly claiming to be a victim of cyber war.[35-37]

Georgia–Russia Conflict of 2008. In the fall of 2008, hostilities broke out between Russia and Georgia over South Ossetia. At the same time, coordinated cyber attacks against Georgian assets started as well. The Georgian government accused Russia of being behind these attacks (though the Kremlin denied it). Note that this was the first time that cyber warfare actually accompanied a military war. The official website of Georgia

President Mikheil Saakashvili was under the control of attackers before Russian armed intervention started, and so were the websites of other government agencies. Commercial websites were also hijacked. Visits to websites in Georgia were routed through Russia and Turkey, where traffic was blocked, preventing people from accessing them. When Germany intervened and traffic was routed through German servers, attackers again took control to route traffic through servers based in Russia.[38]

10.1.2 Tactical Attacks

Tactical cyber threats are typically surgical by nature, have highly specific targeting, and are technologically sophisticated. Given the specific nature of the attack, the cost of development is typically high. Repeatability is less significant for tactical attacks than for strategic attacks. Tactical attacks can be adjuncts to strategic attacks; in some cases they serve as a force multiplier or augment other activities such as a military campaign or as a supplementary action to a special-interest action group. Given the surgical nature of these attacks, they are also popular for use in subversive operations. Given the cost of these attacks, they are typically financed by well-funded private entities and governments that are often global in nature and popularity—a country, a business, or a special-interest group.

An example of tactical cyber attack (which was leveraged for strategic purposes) is the Stuxnet worm. The U.S. and Israeli governments, aiming to subvert nuclear power plants in Iran, likely designed the Stuxnet worm. However, it ended up infecting more than just the intended target, Iran: It impacted a host of countries, including India, the United States, and Great Britain. By September 2010, more than 100,000+ unique hosts had been infected by this worm.[39] Stuxnet was unique in the way it was designed. It propagated through more than one medium (for example, flash drives and Internet connections). It affected Windows systems and exploited known patched and unknown vulnerabilities in the operating system. However, these Windows systems were not the actual targets of this worm. After infecting a host, it would look for a specific industrial control system, the Programmable Logic Controller made by Siemens. Apparently, this controller was being used by Iran in its nuclear power plants. If it did not detect the particular controller software, it would not do anything but would wait to propagate around to other hosts. If it did find the controller software, it would infect and change it.[40]

10.1.3 User-Specific Attacks

User-specific cyber threats can be strategic, tactical, or personal in nature, and target personal devices that may be either consumer- or enterprise-owned. The use of strategic, tactical, or publically available methods to exploit specific individuals or general populations of users for monetary, political, or personal gain can be specifically targeted to a user as a primary target or as a means to get to another target or random exploitation of a user as a target of opportunity.

In many ways, most strategic and tactical attacks are a form of user attack. The difference between these attacks and user-specific attacks are those of scale. An example of this type of attack is to target a user by installing a key-logger on his system with the intent to use it for immediate financial benefit (e.g., to get passwords to log onto bank accounts), unauthorized access to someone else's e-mail account (for spying on a spouse or celebrities), or to target a quiz with the intention to get around actual results. All these attacks are of benefit to a handful of individuals. Examples of attacks in these categories are ransomware, credit card harvesting, targeting of specific individuals for monetary gains (bank accounts, Social Security numbers, and so on), unauthorized access to social media sites, e-mails, and other online information with intent to blackmail, exploit, or embarrass individuals, identify theft, phishing attacks, and exploitation of "smart home" products. Readers will be familiar with most of these attacks. Ransomware is a kind of malware that tricks users into believing that there is no way out for them except to pay to get rid of a nuisance. An example of such an attack would be locking a user's desktop and asking for a payment to unlock it. Such attacks were initially found in Russia but have spread to other countries over the last couple of years.[41]

10.2 Overcoming Organizational and Business Challenges with a Properly Designed, Managed, and Focused SDL

We have outlined an organizational structure with associated roles and responsibilities specific to the tasks that are outlined in our SDL model that have been field-tested and optimized by the authors of this book. The structure described earlier in the book will serve you well to effectively and efficiently create, deliver, and manage the best practices described in this book. It will also assist in the successful buy-in and management of the tasks through A1–A5 in our SDL model. As an added benefit, by using the organizational structure suggested, you will be able to deliver the tasks described in Chapter 8 for post-release support (PRSA1–5), which are typically conducted by other organizations than your own. By using the metrics described in each section of the SDL model, you be able not only to effectively manage and track your software security programs and SDL success but also provide a dashboard to your corporate management and internal customers as to the current state of your program. This dashboard can also be used to identify gaps, which can be used to justify headcount, funding, and other resources when needed. Most important, by building security in, you will maximize the ability to avoid post-release discoveries of security vulnerabilities in your software and increase your ability to successfully manage these discoveries on the occasions when they do occur.

10.3 Software Security Organizational Realities and Leverage

Although an incremental headcount hire plan based on progressive increase in workload is typically the norm for most organizations, incremental growth isn't the right model for what has been proposed in this book and certainly isn't a reality for those going through austerity realities within their organizations. Doing more with less is a reality we all face, regardless of the risks we are facing. To help solve this conundrum, we have proposed a model for a software security group that doesn't depend on continual growth, linear or otherwise. The virtual team grows against linear growth, allowing a fully staffed, centralized software security group to remain relatively stable. We believe that a centralized group comprised of one seasoned software security architect per main software product group and one for each software product within that group in your software engineering development organization will be sufficient to scale quite nicely as long as the software security champion program is adhered to as proposed in this book. In addition, by sharing the responsibility for a typical product security incident response team (PSIRT) among the key software security champions for each software product in a development organization, a single PSIRT manager should suffice given the shared responsibilities of the task throughout the organization.

As described earlier in the book, excellence is not about increasing numbers; it is about the quality of staff you hire. Each of these seasoned software security architects can coordinate and support the implementation of the SDL within each business unit and software product line and will:

- Provide the associated software security champion with the centralized software security group process and governance.
- Mentor the software security champions in security architecture and reviews.
- Support the associated business unit software security champion in the mentorship of each software product line software security champion.
- Coordinate with product management for early and timely security requirements.
- Help to calculate project security risk.
- Help to ensure that software security champions institute appropriate and full security testing.
- Ensure that appropriate security testing tools are available (static, dynamic, fuzzing) for use in the SDL as appropriate.

While these tasks benefit greatly from senior experience and discretion, there is a significant opportunity cost savings in having these senior technical leaders mentor the software security champions and software security architects, as both a wonderful growth opportunity for the individuals involved and a cost savings to the company and the organization. Someone with the potential to grow into a leader through experience and mentorship is a perfect candidate for the software security champions in our model. We are the sum of everything we have ever done, which is constantly being revised and remembered. The same can be said of software security architects; it is a journey, not a point in time, and requires constant learning, mentoring, and collaboration with those who have been there before.

In our model, there are multiple paths to appropriate "coverage." Unlike a fully centralized function, a virtual team, handled with care, can be coalesced and led by a far smaller central team. The authors have made this model work, sometimes numerous times in a number of disparate organizations, and consider this a proven track record for a model that will constantly evolve with the ever-changing realities we are faced with in software security. Each member of the centralized software security group must be able to inspire, encourage, and lead a virtual team such that the virtual members contribute key subject-matter expert (SME) tasks, but at the same time do not become overloaded with additional or operational tasks. "Just enough" such that the PSIRT function can reap huge benefits through having true SMEs contribute and enable, while at the same time making sure that no one person bears the entire brunt of a set of operational activities that can't be dodged. Since our model for a centralized software security group makes use of an extended virtual team, the need for a large central PSIRT staff, as may be found in other organizations, is not needed. Tasks that can be managed in a decentralized manner are done, such as technical investigations, release planning, and fix development. However, there is a coordination role that must be sophisticated enough to technically comprehend the implications and risks involved in various responses. Peer review is a powerful tool for avoiding missteps. Further, the central role within the engineering software development group itself provides coordination *across* teams, something that is lacking in most organizations. We must not respond individually to a vulnerability that affects many software products in unique and idiosyncratic ways. Further, it is essential to provide an interface between PR (and sometimes marketing) support and the technical teams who are involved in responding. You want your response to vulnerability reporters to be consistent and to avoid putting your company and your brand at risk, externally.

10.4 Overcoming SDL Audit and Regulatory Challenges with Proper Governance Management

In Chapter 2, we gave a brief overview of ISO/IEC 27034. Other than the various software security maturity models mentioned earlier in the book, this will be the first software security standard. It will presumably have a third-party attestation and certification industry built around it in the near future. Given that this standard does not define application security as a specific state of security but rather as a process that an organization can perform for applying controls and measurements to its applications in order to manage the risk of using, we believe our model is applicable to preparing to be in compliance with this standard. The standard provides guidance for organizations in integrating security into the processes used for managing their applications and explicitly takes a process approach in specifying, designing, developing, testing, implementing, and maintaining security functions and controls in application systems. The requirements and processes specified in ISO/IEC 27034 are not intended to be implemented in isolation but rather integrated into an organization's existing process. The combination of ISO/IEC 27034 compliance with the adherence of our SDL practices or any of the maturity models described earlier in the book should serve you well in meeting any audit, regulatory, or governance challenges, since adherence will likely be driven by the guidance driven by the latter.

10.5 Future Predications for Software Security

We have divided this section into to two parts. First, the bad news, which is the things that we see that will likely continue on in industry but that should be changed; and second, the good things we see with regard to software security in the future—the light at the end of the tunnel, if you will.

10.5.1 The Bad News

We'll start with the bad news. For the most part, other than threat modeling and architectural security reviews, which is an art, not a science, software security isn't that difficult, but it is an area that industry has known about for many years and yet has chosen to do almost nothing about. This is evident in the top software vulnerabilities in the Common Vulnerabilities and Exposures (CVE), and the OWASP and SANS top-10 vulnerability lists, which have remained essentially the same over 10 years. Although industry has started to take leadership in this area over the last few years, and ISO ISO/IEC 27034, 29147, and 30111 have been announced, we see software security as an ongoing problem for the foreseeable future. Although the future looks bright in this area, it will take time to finally steer industry in the right direction. As discussed throughout the book, building security into the software development process is more about an attitude change, management acceptance, and business/operational process changes than about blazing new trails in new scientific or technical disciplines.

The price to fix vulnerabilities later in the cycle is very high. The level of effort that is required to tune and maintain current product security tools can be more expensive than buying the tool. Although much of the burden of making this change is on the vendor, we have some thoughts that may help change this paradigm. We propose a paradigm shift away from vulnerabilities in software security. Not every vulnerability gets exploited, or is even exploitable. Often, mitigations that are not obvious to vanilla vulnerability scanners make even garden-variety vulnerabilities unattractive to attackers. We are not suggesting that we stop fixing bugs in code. Quite the opposite, as should be clear from the contents of this book. Still, delivering reports with thousands of vulnerabilities have not made software secure. However, as a collective whole, the security industry continues to focus on vulnerability: every new type of attack, every new variation, and every conceivable attack methodology. Instead, a focus on correct program behavior aligns well with how developers approach designing and creating code. Correctness goes to the heart of the software process. In our experience, developers are rewarded for correctness. And it should be obvious that vulnerabilities are errors, plain and simple. Focusing on correctness would, unfortunately, be a sea change in software security. Tools today often don't report the one, single bug that will respond to multiple variations of a particular type of attack. Instead, too often, tools report each variation as a "vulnerability" that needs to be addressed by the developer. This is the way security people think about the situation. It's an attacker's view: Which attack methods will work on this particular system? That is the question that most vulnerability scanners address today (as of this writing). However, people who write code simply want to know what the coding error is, where it is in the code, and what is the correct behavior that must be programmed. Often, if the tool contains any programming hints, these tend to be buried in the tool's user interface. Instead, we propose that a tool should be no more difficult to use than a compiler. The results could be a list of code errors, coupled to line numbers in the code, with a code snippet pointing out where the error lies. Of course, this is an oversimplification. Some kinds of security vulnerabilities lie across code snippets, or even across a whole system. Still, focus could be on what is the coding error and what is its solution. Logical errors could be described in terms of the design solution: things like randomizing session IDs properly, or including nonpredictable session identifiers with each Web input (to prevent cross-site request forgery, for instance). In a world where tens of millions of people are writing Web code, and a great deal of that code contains exploitable vulnerabilities, we need an approach that simplifies the finding of the actual coding errors. Massive counts of the millions of vulnerabilities have not reduced the attack surface. We like to suggest calling this new approach "developer-centric software security." "Developer-centric" means that security people should understand developers' focus, and developers' problems. The security industry must begin to address these in order to get security considered in its rightful place, right next to maintainability, correctness of algorithm, correctness of calculation, and all the other problems that a skilled programmer must face.

10.5.2 The Good News

As discussed throughout the book and in the previous section, industry knows what to do, that they should do it, and how to do it, but they don't do it. Knowing what to do is a significant portion of the battle that needs to be won, and we believe that pressure resulting from new ISO standards (27034, 29147, and 30111) and the recent increase in business and government community awareness and oversight for software security that is built into the software development process pressure industry to finally make software security a priority and business enabler. Other good news is that the tools and training for software security continue to improve. We also see more and more mentoring of the next generation of software security architects, which will serve our industry well over time. Most important, new organizational and management SDL models based on real-life experiences and successes, like the one described in this book, are being developed.

10.6 Conclusion

The criticality of software security as we move quickly toward this new age of tasks previously relegated to the human mind and now being replaced by software-driven machines cannot be underestimated. It is for this reason we have written this book. In contrast and for the foreseeable future, humans will continue to write software programs. This also means that new software will keep building on legacy code or software that was written prior to security being taken seriously or before sophisticated attacks became prevalent. As long as humans write the programs, the key to successful software security is to make the software development program process more efficient and effective. Although the approach of this book includes people, process, and technology approaches to software security, the authors believe the people element of software security is still the most important part to manage. This will remain true as long as software is developed, managed, and exploited by humans. This book has outlined a step-by-step process for software security that is relevant to today's technical, operational, business, and development environments. We have focused on what humans can do to control and manage a secure software development process in the form of best practices and metrics. Although security is not a natural component of the way industry has been building software in recent years, the authors believe that security improvements to development processes are possible, practical, and essential. We believe that the software security best practices and model presented in this book will make this clear to all who read the book, including executives, managers, and practitioners.

When it comes to cyber security, we believe it is all about the software and whether it is secure or not, hence the title of our book: *Core Software Security: Security at the Source*. You can have the world's best client, host, and network security, including encrypted transmission and storage of data, but if software application vulnerabilities exist and can be exploited, your defense-in-depth security approach has just become a speed bump to the inevitable. As the old adage goes, you are only as good as your weakest link, and in today's world, that is still the software; and software permeates everything we do, from defense to medicine, industry, banking, agricultural, transportation, and how we manage and live our lives. This is very serious and daunting vulnerability. You only have to look at how many years the same software vulnerabilities have remained on the CVE Top 25 or OWASP and SANS Top 10 to realize that organizations are still not taking software security seriously. Even worse, experienced and professional adversaries will target vulnerable software and don't necessarily need it to be Internet-enabled to be at risk—that just makes the exploitation easier, but software is still the primary target because if you can own the software you can own the data and processes that it controls. In today's world, this can result in life-threatening and serious local, regional, and global consequences. Throughout this book, we have described the SDL best practices and metrics to optimize the development, management, and growth of a secure software development lifecycle and program to maximize the mitigation of this type of risk. Managing software security is an area that the authors live in on a daily basis, and this book is based on our real-world experiences. We have worked with Fortune 500 companies and have often seen examples of breakdown of security development lifecycle (SDL) practices. In this book, we have taken an experiences-based approach to applying components of the best available SDL models in dealing with the problems described above in the form of a SDL software security best practices model and framework. Most important, our SDL best practices model has been mapped to the standard model for software development lifecycle, explaining how you can use this to build and manage a mature SDL program. Although security issues will always exist, the purpose of this book has been to teach you how to maximize an organization's ability to minimize vulnerabilities in your software products before they are released or deployed, by building security into the development process. We hope you enjoyed reading this book as much as we have writing it, as we are passionate about our efforts to help alleviate the risk of vulnerable software in the world at large and specifically our readers' organizations.

References

1. Snyder, J. (2012). "Growing Cyber Threats Demand Advanced Mitigation Methodologies." Retrieved from http://www.raytheon.com/capabilities/rtnwcm/groups/iis/documents/content/rtn_iis_cyber_whitepaper_wcs.pdf.
2. Ellison, R. (2006). "Security and Project Management." Retrieved from https://buildsecurityin.us-cert.gov/articles/best-practices/project-management/security-and-project-management.
3. Acohido, B. (2013, February 27). "Former Cybersecurity Czar Pursues Safer Software." Retrieved from http://www.usatoday.com/story/tech/2013/02/27/howard-schmidt-executive-director-safecode/1952359.
4. Ponemon Institute and Security Innovation (2013, August 27). *The State of Application Security—A Research Study by Ponemon Institute LLC and Security Innovation*, p. 21). Retrieved from https://www.securityinnovation.com/uploads/ponemon-state-of-application-security-maturity.pdf.

5. Gilbert, L., Morgan, R., and Keen, A. (2009, May 5). "Tactical and Strategic Attack Detection and Prediction," U.S. Patent 7530105. Retrieved from http://www.freepatentsonline.com/7530105.html.

6. Encyclopedia of Espionage, Intelligence, and Security (2013). *Espionage Encyclopedia: Critical Infrastructure.* Retrieved from http://www.faqs.org/espionage/Cou-De/Critical-Infrastructure.html.

7. Linktv.org (2013). *Cyber Espionage.* Retrieved from http://news.linktv.org/topics/cyber-espionage.

8. U.S.–China Economic and Security Review (2012). *2012 Report to Congress of the U.S.–China Economic and Security Review Commission*—One Hundred Twelfth Congress—Second Session. Retrieved from http://origin.www.uscc.gov/sites/default/files/annual_reports/2012-Report-to-Congress.pdf.

9. Information Warfare Monitor (2009). *Tracking GhostNet: Investigating a Cyber Espionage Network.* Retrieved from http://www.scribd.com/doc/13731776/Tracking-GhostNetInvestigating-a-Cyber-Espionage-Network.

10. McAfee Labs and McAfee Foundstone Professional Services (2010). *Protecting Your Critical Assets—Lessons Learned from "Operation Aurora."* Retrieved from http://www.mcafee.com/us/resources/white-papers/wp-protecting-critical-assets.pdf.

11. Nakashima, E. (2011, August 02). "Report on 'Operation Shady RAT' Identifies Widespread Cyber-Spying." *The Washington Post.* Retrieved from http://articles.washingtonpost.com/2011-08-02/national/35269748_1_intrusions-mcafee-china-issues.

12. Symantec (2011, August 4). "The Truth Behind the Shady Rat." *Symantec Official Blog.* Retrieved from http://www.symantec.com/connect/blogs/truth-behind-shady-rat.

13. Hsu, T. (2011, February 10). "China-Based Hackers Targeted Oil, Energy Companies in 'Night Dragon' Cyber Attacks, McAfee Says." *Los Angeles Times.* Retrieved from http://latimesblogs.latimes.com/technology/2011/02/chinese-hackers-targeted-oil-companies-in-cyberattack-mcafee-says.html#sthash.d7PrG6Iy.dpuf.

14. McAfee Foundstone Professional Services and McAfee Labs (2011, February 10). *Global Energy Cyberattacks: "Night Dragon."* Retrieved from http://www.mcafee.com/us/resources/white-papers/wp-global-energy-cyberattacks-night-dragon.pdf.

15. Graham, B. (2005, August 25). "Hackers Attack via Chinese Web Sites." *The Washington Post.* Retrieved from http://www.washingtonpost.com/wp-dyn/content/article/2005/08/24/AR2005082402318.html.

16. Thornburgh, N. (2005, August 25). "Inside the Chinese Hack Attack." *Time Magazine.* Retrieved from http://content.time.com/time/nation/article/0,8599,1098371,00.html.

17. Onley, D. and Wait, P. (2006, August 17). "Red Storm Rising." *GCN.* Retrieved from http://gcn.com/Articles/2006/08/17/Red-storm-rising.aspx?Page=2&p=1.

18. Sandlin, S. (2007, October 14). "Analyst, Sandia Settle Suit." *Albuquerque Journal.* Retrieved from http://www.abqjournal.com/news/metro/602547metro10-14-07.htm.

19. Interpol (2013). *Cybercrime*. Retrieved from http://www.interpol.int/Crime-areas/ Cybercrime/Cybercrime.

20. Williams, P. (2013). *Organized Crime and Cyber-Crime: Implications for Business*. CERT Coordination Center (CERT/CC). Retrieved from www.cert.org/archive/ pdf/cybercrime-business.pdf.

21. Williams, P. (2013). *Organized Crime and Cybercrime: Synergies, Trends, and Responses*. Retrieved from http://www.crime-research.org/library/Cybercrime.htm.

22. Samani, R., and Paget, F. (2011). *Cybercrime Exposed—Cybercrime-as-a-Service*, McAfee—An Intel Company White Paper. Retrieved from http://www.mcafee. com/us/resources/white-papers/wp-cybercrime-exposed.pdf.

23. Gandhi, R., Sharma, A., Mahoney, W., Sousan, W., Zhu, Q., and Laplante, P. (2011, February). *Dimensions of Cyber-Attacks: Cultural, Social, Economic, and Political*. ResearchGate.net, Source: IEEE Xplore. Retrieved from http://www. researchgate.net/publication/224223630_Dimensions_of_Cyber-Attacks_ Cultural_Social_Economic_and_Political.

24. Vaughan-Nichols, S. (2012, January 20). "How Anonymous Took Down the DoJ, RIAA, MPAA and Universal Music Websites." *ZDNet*. Retrieved from http:// www.zdnet.com/blog/networking/how-anonymous-took-down-the-doj-riaa- mpaa-and-universal-music-websites/1932.

25. Tucker, N. (2008, January18). "Tom Cruise's Scary Movie; In Church Promo, the Scientologist Is Hard to Suppress." *The Washington Post*. Retrieved from http:// www.highbeam.com/doc/1P2-15129123.html.

26. *The Economist* (2008, February 2). "Fair Game; Scientology. (Cyberwarfare Against a Cult) (Anonymous)." Retrieved from http://www.highbeam.com/ doc/1G1-174076065.html.

27. BBC (2010, December 9). "Anonymous Hacktivists Say Wikileaks War to Continue." Retrieved from http://www.bbc.co.uk/news/technology-11935539.

28. Swallow, E. (2011, August 14). "Anonymous Hackers Attack BART Website." *Mashable*. Retrieved from http://mashable.com/2011/08/15/ bart-anonymous-attack.

29. Kingsbury, A. (2010, April 14). "Documents Reveal Al Qaeda Cyberattacks— The Attacks Were Relatively Minor but Show the Group's Interest in Cyberwar." *U.S. News & World Report*. Retrieved from http://www.usnews.com/news/ articles/2010/04/14/documents-reveal-al-qaeda-cyberattacks.

30. Tiller, J. (2010, June 10). "Cyberwarfare: It's a New Theater of War, Not Just a New Form of War." *Real Security*. Retrieved from http://www.realsecurity.us/ weblog/?e=104.

31. Clarke, R. A. (2010). *Cyber War*. HarperCollins, New York.

32. The Economist, (2010, July 1). "Cyberwar: War in the Fifth Domain." *The Economist*.

33. Lynn, W. J., III. (2010, Sept./Oct.) "Defending a New Domain: The Pentagon's Cyberstrategy." *Foreign Affairs*, pp. 97–108.

34. *U.S. Department of Defense Strategy for Operating in Cyberspace*, July 2011, p. 3.

35. Herzog, S. (2011, Summer). "Revisiting the Estonian Cyber Attacks: Digital Threats and Multinational Responses." *Journal of Strategic Security*, Vol. 4,

No. 2, Strategic Security in the Cyber Age, Article 4. Retrieved from http://scholarcommons.usf.edu/cgi/viewcontent.cgi?article=1105&context=jss.

36. RIANOVOSTI (2007, September 6). "Estonia Has No Evidence of Kremlin Involvement in Cyber Attacks." Retrieved from http://en.rian.ru/world/20070906/76959190.html.

37. Rehman, S. (2013, January 14). "Estonia's Lessons in Cyberwarfare." *U.S. News Weekly.* Retrieved from http://www.usnews.com/opinion/blogs/world-report/2013/01/14/estonia-shows-how-to-build-a-defense-against-cyberwarfare.

38. Swaine, J. (2008, August 11). "Georgia: Russia 'Conducting Cyber War.'" *The Telegraph.* Retrieved from http://www.telegraph.co.uk/news/worldnews/europe/georgia/2539157/Georgia-Russia-conducting-cyber-war.html.

39. Falliere, N., Murchu, L., and Chien, E. (2011, February). *W32.Stuxnet Dossier, Version 1.4—Symantec Security Response.* Retrieved from http://www.symantec.com/content/en/us/enterprise/media/security_response/whitepapers/w32_stuxnet_dossier.pdf.

40. Schneier, B. (2010, October 7). "Stuxnet." *Schneier on Security—A Blog Covering Security and Security Technology.* Retrieved from https://www.schneier.com/blog/archives/2010/10/stuxnet.html.

41. Dunn, J. (2012, March 9). "Ransom Trojans Spreading Beyond Russian Heartland: Security Companies Starting to See More Infections." *Techworld.* Retrieved from http://news.techworld.com/security/3343528/ransom-trojans-spreading-beyond-russian-heartland.

Appendix

Key Success Factors, Deliverables, and Metrics for Each Phase of Our SDL Model

In Chapters 3 through 7, we have outlined key success factors, deliverables, and metrics that should be captured as part of our Security Development Lifecycle (SDL) model. In Chapter 8, the SDL post-release phase, we outline the key deliverables and metrics. The key success factors, deliverables, and metrics are not set in stone and may need to be tweaked as you map the SDL to your own Software Development Lifecycle (SDLC). In this Appendix, we have summarized (in tabular form for your quick reference) the key success factors, deliverables, and metrics that we have outlined in Chapters 3 through 8.

Table A.1 Key Success Factors for Each Phase of the SDL

Phase	Key Success Factor	Description
Security Assessment (A1): SDL Activities and Best Practices	1. Accuracy of planned SDL activities	All SDL activities are accurately identified.
	2. Product risk profile	Management understands the true cost of developing the product.
	3. Accuracy of threat profile	Mitigating steps and countermeasures are in place for the product to be successful in its environment.
	4. Coverage of relevant regulations, certifications, and compliance frameworks	All applicable legal and compliance aspects are covered.
	5. Coverage of security objectives needed for software	"Must have" security objectives are met.
Architecture (A2): SDL Activities and Best Practices	1. Identification of business requirements and risks	Mapping of business requirements and risks defined in terms of CIA
	2. Effective threat modeling	Identifying threats for the software
	3. Effective architectural threat analysis	Analysis of threats to the software and probability of threat materializing
	4. Effective risk mitigation strategy	Risk acceptance, tolerance, and mitigation plan per business requirements
	5. Accuracy of DFDs	Data flow diagrams used during threat modeling
Design and Development (A3): SDL Activities and Best Practices	1. Comprehensive security test plan	Mapping types of security testing required at different stages of SDLC
	2. Effective threat modeling	Identifying threats to the software
	3. Design security analysis	Analysis of threats to various software components
	4. Privacy implementation assessment	Effort required for implementation of privacy-related controls based on assessment
	5. Policy compliance review (updates)	Updates for policy compliance as related to Phase 3

Design and Development (A4): SDL Activities and Best Practices	1. Security test case execution	Coverage of all relevant test cases
	2. Security testing	Completion of all types of security testing and remediation of problems found
	3. Privacy validation and remediation	Effectiveness of privacy-related controls and remediation of any issues found
	4. Policy compliance review	Updates for policy compliance as related to Phase 4
Ship (A5): SDL Activities and Best Practices	1. Policy compliance analysis	Final review of security and compliance requirements during development process
	2. Vulnerability scanning	Scanning software stack for identifying security issues
	3. Penetration testing	Exploiting any/all security issues on software stack
	4. Open-source licensing review	Final review of open-source software used in the stack
	5. Final security review	Final review of compliance against all security requirements identified during SDL cycle
	6. Final privacy review	Final review of compliance against all privacy requirements identified during SDL cycle
	7. Customer engagement framework	Framework that defines process for sharing security related information with customers

Table A.2 Deliverables for Each Phase of the SDL

Phase	Deliverable	Goal
Security Assessment (A1): SDL Activities and Best Practices	Product risk profile	Estimate actual cost of the product.
	SDL project outline	Map SDL to development schedule.
	Applicable laws and regulations	Obtain formal sign-off from stakeholders on applicable laws.
	Threat profile	Guide SDL activities to mitigate threats.
	Certification requirements	List requirements for product and operations certifications.
	List of third-party software	Identify dependence on third-party software.
	Metrics template	Establish cadence for regular reporting to executives.
	Business requirements	Software requirements, including CIA
	Threat modeling artifacts	Data flow diagrams, elements, threat listing
	Architecture threat analysis	Prioritization of threats and risks based on threat analysis
	Risk mitigation plan	Plan to mitigate, accept, or tolerate risk
	Policy compliance analysis	Analysis of adherence to company policies
Design and Development (A3): SDL Activities and Best Practices	Updated threat modeling artifacts	Data flow diagrams, elements, threat listing
	Design security review	Modifications to design of software components based on security assessments
	Security test plans	Plan to mitigate, accept, or tolerate risk
	Updated policy compliance analysis	Analysis of adherence to company policies
	Privacy implementation assessment results	Recommendations from privacy assessment

Phase	Deliverable	Description
Design and Development (A4): SDL Activities and Best Practices	Security test execution report	Review progress against identified security test cases
	Updated policy compliance analysis	Analysis of adherence to company policies
	Privacy compliance report	Validation that recommendations from privacy assessment have been implemented
	Security testing reports	Findings from different types of security testing
	Remediation report	Provide status on security posture of product
Ship (A5): SDL Activities and Best Practices	Updated policy compliance analysis	Analysis of adherence to company policies
	Security testing reports	Findings from different types of security testing in this phase of SDL
	Remediation report	Provide status on security posture of product
	Open-source licensing review report	Review of compliance with licensing requirements if open-source software is used
	Final security and privacy review reports	Review of compliance with security and privacy requirements
	Customer engagement framework	Detailed framework to engage customers during different stages of product life cycle
Post-Release Support (PRSA1–5)	External vulnerability disclosure response process	Process to define evaluation and communication of security vulnerabilities
	Post-release certifications	Certifications from external parties to demonstrate security posture of products/services
	Third-party security reviews	Security assessments performed by groups other than internal testing teams
	Security strategy and process for legacy code, M&A, and EOL plans	Strategy to mitigate security risk from legacy code and M&As

Table A.3 Metrics for Each Phase of the SDL

Phase	Metric
Security Assessment (A1): SDL Activities and Best Practices	Time in weeks when software security team was looped in
	Percent of stakeholders participating in SDL
	Percent of SDL activities mapped to development activities
	Percent of security objectives met
Architecture (A2): SDL Activities and Best Practices	List of business threats, technical threats (mapped to business threats), and threat actors
	Number of security objectives unmet after this phase
	Percent compliance with company policies (existing)
	Number of entry points for software (using DFDs)
	Percent of risk (and threats) accepted, mitigated, and tolerated
	Percent of initial software requirements redefined
	Number of planned software architectural changes (major and minor) in a product
	Number of software architectural changes needed based on security requirements
Design and Development (A3): SDL Activities and Best Practices	Threats, probability, and severity
	Percent compliance with company policies (updated)
	Percent of compliance in Phase 2 versus Phase 3
	Entry points for software (using DFDs)
	Percent of risk accepted versus mitigated
	Percent of initial software requirements redefined
	Percent of software architecture changes
	Percent of SDLC phases without corresponding software security testing
	Percent of software components with implementations related to privacy controls
	Number of lines of code
	Number of security defects found using static analysis tools
	Number of high-risk defects found using static analysis tools
	Defect density (security issues per 1000 lines of code)

Design and Development (A4): SDL Activities and Best Practices	Percent compliance with company policies (updated)
	- Percent of compliance in Phase 3 versus Phase 4
	Number of lines of code tested effectively with static analysis tools
	Number of security defects found through static analysis tools
	Number of high-risk defects found through static analysis tools
	Defect density (security issues per 1000 lines of code)
	Number and types of security issues found through static analysis, dynamic analysis, manual code review, penetration testing, and fuzzing
	- Overlap of security issues found through different types of testing
	- Comparison of severity of findings from different types of testing
	- Mapping of findings to threats/risks identified earlier
	Number of security findings remediated
	- Severity of findings
	- Time spent (approximate) in hours to remediate findings
	Number, types, and severity of findings outstanding
	Percentage compliance with security test plan
	Number of security test cases executed
	- Number of findings from security test case execution
	- Number of re-tests executed

(continued on following page)

Table A.3 Metrics for Each Phase of the SDL (*continued*)

Phase	Metric
Ship (A5): SDL Activities and Best Practices	Percent compliance with company policies (updated)
	- Percent of compliance in Phase 5 versus Phase 4
	Number, type, and severity of security issues found through vulnerability scanning and penetration testing
	- Overlap of security issues found through different types of testing
	- Comparison of severity of findings from different types of testing
	- Mapping of findings to threats/risks identified earlier
	Number of security findings remediated (updated)
	- Severity of findings
	- Time spent (approximate) in hours to remediate findings
	Number, types, and severity of findings outstanding (updated)
	Percentage compliance with security and privacy requirements
Post-Release Support (PRSA1–5)	Time in hours to respond to externally disclosed security vulnerabilities
	Monthly FTE (full-time employee) hours required for external dis- closure process
	Number of security findings (ranked by severity) after product has been released
	Number of customer-reported security issues per month
	Number of customer-reported security issues not identified during any SDL activities

Index

Printed in the United States
by Baker & Taylor Publisher Services